Managerial
Decision Making

Managerial Decision Making

K. J. Radford

Department of Management Sciences
University of Waterloo
Waterloo, Ontario

Reston Publishing Company, Inc., A Prentice-Hall Company
Reston, Virginia 22090

Library of Congress Cataloging in Publication Data

Radford, K   J
     Managerial decision making.

     Includes bibliographical references.
     1. Decision-making.   2. Management.   I. Title.
HD69.D4R27   658.4'03   74-31316
ISBN 0-87909-473-7

Managerial Decision Making

K. J. Radford

658.403
R128m

© 1975 by
RESTON PUBLISHING COMPANY, INC.
A Prentice-Hall Company
Box 547
Reston, Virginia 22090

10   9   8   7   6   5   4   3   2   1

Printed in the United States of America

Contents

Preface   **xi**

1   The Nature of the Decision Process   **1**

Introduction, 1
Some Preliminary Systems Concepts, 5
The Background to a Decision, 6
   Organizational Objectives
   Multiple Objectives
   The Need for Review of Objectives
   Objectives of Components of an Organization
   Objectives in Relation to Management
Steps in the Decision Process, 12
   Perception and Formulation of the Problem
   Construction of a Model
   Determination of Quantitative Parameters Involved
   Specification of Available Options

v

Evaluation of Outcomes of Options
Criteria of Choice Between Options
Resolution
Rationality and Personalistic Involvement in Decision Making,
        19
Types of Decision Process, 21
    Completely Specified Decision Processes
    Partially Specified Decision Processes
    Personalistic or Non-completely Specified Decision
        Processes
Organizational Decision Processes, 24
Summary, 25
Discussion Topics, 26

2 Quantitative Parameters in Decision Problems   29

Introduction, 29
Easily Defined Quantitative Parameters, 30
    Efficiency and Effectiveness
Less Easily Identified Quantitative Parameters, 32
Ordinal Ranking, 35
Utility, 36
Utility of Money (or Some Other Commodity), 37
Scales of Measurement, 44
von Neumann-Morgenstern Interval Scale Utility, 47
Assumptions Underlying the von Neumann-Morgenstern
        Interval Scale Utility Measurement, 49
Some Extensions of Utility Theory, 52
Summary, 53
Discussion Topics, 55

3 Factors Affecting the Choice Between Options   57

Conditions Under Which Decisions Are Made, 58
    Decisions Under Conditions of Certainty
    Decisions Under Risk
    Decisions Under Uncertainty
    Decisions Under Competition or Conflict
Decision Criterion Under Conditions of Certainty, 62
Decision Criteria Under Conditions of Risk, 62
    Arguments Against Choice by Maximum Expected Value
    Subjective Probability

Subjective Expected Utility (SEU)
The Acceptability of the Expected Value Criterion
An Interesting Historical Diversion
Decision Criteria Under Uncertainty, 71
    The Criterion of Pessimism
    The Criterion of Optimism—and Variations
    The Criterion of Regret
    The Laplace Criterion
Decision Criteria Under Conditions of Competition or Conflict,
    76
The Principle of Bounded Rationality, 77
The Minimization of Uncertainty, 78
Summary, 79
Discussion Topics, 80

**4   Decisions Involving Well-defined
        Quantitative Parameters   83**

Introduction, 83
Routine Administrative and Operational Decisions, 84
Completely Specified Decisions Based on Mathematical
        Models, 84
    Linear Programming
    Variations of the Linear Programming Model
    Dynamic Programming
    The Application of Mathematical Models
Decisions Under Certainty with Multiple Objectives, 92
A First Introduction of Uncertainty—Sensitivity Analysis, 96
Models Involving Parameters Represented by Probability
        Distributions, 98
Gathering of Data for Use in Probabilistic Models, 100
Simulation, 101
The Use of Subjective Probabilities, 102
    The Value of Information
    The Effect of Increasing the Available Options
    The Value of Partial Information
    Advantages of the Bayesian Method
Decisions Under Conditions of Conflict, 114
    Two-Person, Zero-Sum Decision Situations
    N-Person Games and Coalitions
Summary, 121
Discussion Topics, 122
Problem, 124

5 More Complex Decision Processes   **127**

Introduction, 127
Strictly Competitive Decision Situations, 129
   *Do Strictly Competitive Situations Occur in Managerial
      Decision Making?*
   Procedures in a "Single Play" Strictly Competitive Situation
   Objective and Subjective Rationality
Decision Situations that Are Not Strictly Competitive, 134
   The Prisoners' Dilemma Situation
   An Approach to Non-zero-sum Decision Situations
The Nature and Theory of Metagames, 141
Application of Metagame Theory, 145
The Analysis of Options, 148
Examples of the Application of Analysis of Options, 149
A More Complex Example of the Analysis of Options, 158
A Critique of the Analysis of Options, 166
Applications of the Analysis of Options to Decisions Under
      Uncertainty, 168
More on Conflict Situations, 172
   Inducement
   The Game of Chicken
Summary, 177
Discussion Topics, 178

6 Joint Decisions by Two or More Parties   **181**

Introduction, 181
Risk Sharing, 182
Jointly Preferred Solutions and Pareto-optimality, 186
Group Decision Making, 190
The Basis of Group Choice, 191
   The Arrow Social Welfare Function
The Characteristics of Decision Making Groups, 197
   Types of Groups Found in Organizations
   Decision Making Behavior in Groups
   The Risky Shift Phenomenon
   Dominance Within a Group
   Experimental Evidence from Within Organizations
Decision Making in a Committee, 204
Summary, 208
Discussion Topics, 209

7 Decision Making in Organizations   **211**

Introduction, 211
Completely Specified Decision Processes, 212
Decisions That Are Not Completely Specified, 214
Managerial and Organizational Behavior in Decision Making, 216
  Satisficing versus Optimizing
  The Minimization of Uncertainty
The Relationship of Decision Making to Organizational Structure, 220
The Systems Group and the Special Project Team, 221
The Information System in Support of Decision Making, 223
  The Operation of the Information System
  The Information System in Support of Non-Completely Specified Decision Processes
Summary, 230
Discussion Topics, 231

Index   **233**

Preface

There have been many approaches to managerial decision making in recent years. These have ranged from the strictly quantitative—as typified by the methods of operations research—to those based on human and organizational behavior, of which the works of Herbert A. Simon, Richard M. Cyert, and James G. March are classic examples. It is only recently that those working in the field have begun to combine approaches in the study of the decision making problems that arise in modern organizations. This book is an attempt to assist those concerned with managerial decision making in this combination of approaches.

One of the difficulties in preparing this book has been to know where to start. Managerial decisions can be classified in a number of ways, each of which has some attraction in terms of the desire to present a logical and unfolding development of the subject. For example, the subject can be approached in terms of any one of the following characteristics of the decision process:

- it may be routine, well understood, and documented in all of its aspects, or it may be such as to require human involvement and judgment at one or more stages of the process;

- it may involve well-defined quantitative parameters, such as money, or it may refer to matters for which numerical values of outcomes are difficult to define (such as health and welfare);

- it may be undertaken against a background of certainty in terms of the outcome of any course of action chosen or in the face of uncertainty with regard to future events or the actions of others;

- it may be such that well-developed mathematical techniques can be applied or it may be that no well-defined structure has yet been developed for a problem of its type;

- it may be a problem existing and requiring a solution at one point in time or it may consist of a sequence of interrelated decisions;

- it may be such that it can be resolved by an individual acting alone or it may be the responsibility of a group of individuals, who may not have identical views and approaches with regard to the problem;

- it may arise in a small community of individuals or in a large organization consisting of a number of subgroups with divergent interests.

As an additional complication, the above classifications are not necessarily mutually exclusive. Any particular decision process may present characteristics drawn from all or some of the above classes. Most of the existing texts present detailed treatments of one or of a few of these characteristics of decision processes. This book attempts to present a discussion of them all.

The diffuse approach is not without its hazards. Because of the interrelation between the various classifications of decision processes, some repetition of ideas is inevitable. Because of the breadth of the subject, it has not been possible to provide a detailed treatment of every aspect of decision making. Fortunately, such detailed treatment is not necessary here because of the excellence of many of the existing texts in dealing with particular facets of the subject. These works have been referenced extensively. Most of the references give the page or pages of the text where detailed material can be found; the reader requiring more depth in any portion of the subject is urged to seek out this material. On the other hand, in areas where little has been published to date (as in the applications of metagame theory) considerable detail is provided in this book.

The book begins with a broad discussion of the nature of managerial decision processes, ranging from the background to such decisions and the steps involved in the process, to the degree of human involvement in decision processes arising in modern organizations. Since the question of what quantitative parameters are involved is vital to most decision processes, this is the subject of Chapter 2. The discussion then proceeds to a treatment of the conditions under which decisions are made, ranging from certainty through uncertainty to conflict. The effects of these conditions on the approach to managerial decision processes are considered in Chapter 3.

Once the preliminaries have been considered, Chapter 4 reviews decision processes involving well-defined quantitative parameters, ranging from the well-documented techniques of operations research to the more recently developed methods for introduction of managerial judgment into such decision processes by way of subjective probability estimates. The chapter closes with a brief review of the elementary conflict situations to which quantitative analysis can be applied.

Chapter 5 is a detailed treatment of more complex decision situations for which well-defined analytical techniques are not available and which cannot be considered entirely in terms of well-defined quantitative parameters. In such situations, it may not be clear whether the "opposition" to the decision maker arises from natural uncertainty or from the actions of others with directly or indirectly opposed interests. The recent approach to such decision processes in terms of conflict analysis derived from the theory of games and metagames is covered in detail. In a later section of Chapter 5 the techniques that have been derived for treatment of conflict situations are seen to be equally applicable to decision processes in the face of natural uncertainty. The non-quantitative methods discussed in Chapter 5 are thus linked to the quantitative techniques covered in the earlier parts of the book.

In Chapter 6, the discussion turns to decision processes that are the responsibility of groups of individuals rather than of a single manager acting alone. The manner in which such groups are formed is treated first in a section devoted to risk sharing. Having considered how groups are formed, the discussion proceeds to the subject of how groups of individuals with dissimilar preferences and objectives should make a decision on behalf of the group. This leads naturally to the subject of decision making in committees.

Finally, the nature of organizational decision making is considered in Chapter 7. The subject of managerial and organizational behavior in such decision processes is discussed, leading to consideration of the role of the systems group in an organization. The chapter ends with a short introduction to the subject of the information system that is necessary in support of managerial decision making. This is the subject of my earlier text, *Information Systems in Management*, published in 1973.

Considerable care has been taken to maintain the material presented in as readable form as possible, considering the complexity of the subject. Although the whole work is mathematically based, a minimum of mathematics is included in the text. Where necessary, mathematical derivations have been referenced or included in exhibits accompanying the description of the decision process to which they refer.

The book has been designed to be suitable for senior undergraduate and graduate courses in business, commerce, and management science, as well as for similar courses in technical and community colleges. The extensive referencing makes it possible to use the book as reading for courses of greater or lesser depth as required. Managers engaged in day-to-day decision making will also find the material useful to them in their work.

ACKNOWLEDGEMENTS

I am indebted to all those authors whose work is referenced in the text and especially to Dr. Harvey M. Wagner, Professor Nigel Howard, and Professor Sang M. Lee for permission to quote verbatim portions of their work. I am indebted also to the Sloan Management Review for permission to include material that originally appeared in that publication.

My special thanks are due to Professor Nigel Howard, whose work in metagame theory forms the basis of a substantial chapter of this book. I have had the advantage of numerous detailed discussions with him, during which much of the tenor of Chapter 5 of this book was determined. The support and encouragement of my colleagues in the Department of Management Sciences, University of Waterloo, and of Derek M. Jamieson of the University of Guelph is also much appreciated. The final product would not have been possible without the perseverance and dedication of Lynne Ferguson-Tan, who did much of the literature research on which the book is based. Pam Umbach, Lyn Mills, and Marj Geiger made major contributions in the preparation and modification of the numerous drafts and, once again, the book could not have been produced without their contribution.

Some of the research done in the Department of Management Sciences, University of Waterloo, that forms the basis of several sections of the book was supported by research grants to the author from the National Research Council of Canada and the Canada Council. This support is most deeply appreciated.

K. J. Radford

1

The Nature of the Decision Process

Introduction

Decision making is an essential part of modern management. Many decisions are relatively minor and can be taken almost subconsciously, following rules and patterns of behavior established over many previous encounters with the problem. The choice of an answer to the question "what is two times three plus four?" is an example of such an elementary decision. Although this problem is relatively simple, it can nonetheless be regarded as a decision process for which a structure and an established procedure for resolution exists. A large number of such simple decision processes arise in modern organizations and can now be delegated to the computer once the pattern and logic of the decision process has been established and agreed.

The other end of the spectrum of decision processes is represented by the work of managers in modern organizations who may be faced with very complex problems such as where to locate a new plant or a hospital. The manner in which such decisions should be approached may not be well established because similar problems have not arisen in the past. It may be difficult in the time available to assemble all the necessary considerations and information bearing on the decision. What is more, it may not be possible to determine when all the relevant information has been gathered. Such decisions usually involve the application of considerable human judgment and experience before a solution is obtained. Despite the difficulties that surround them, however, managers *do* make such decisions successfully and continuously in their day-to-day work.

Sometimes a combination of the capabilities of the computer and the human decision maker is necessary for the solution of a decision problem. In such cases the computer contributes the ability to undertake a large number of simple calculations very quickly and to fit these operations into a logical sequence designed by a skilled analyst. In this way the combination of a large number of simple decisions can result in the solution of a much more complex problem. The contribution of the human decision maker in these situations is in the design or choice of the routines delegated to the computer, in the selection and verification of the data to be used with these routines and in the assessment of the results of the computer analysis relative to the questions at hand. In many cases the manager may make the final decision on the basis of the summarized results of the work done on the computer. In this way he brings into play his own judgment and experience in the area concerned.

Some of the decisions encountered in an organization are repeated many times. In such cases a manager has the opportunity to correct his methodology and approach in later situations should this be found to be necessary in the light of earlier experience. However, many of the more important decisions arise only once or, at best, infrequently. Even if a decision of a certain type occurs more than once, the conditions surrounding the problem may be so different in the individual cases as to make each decision essentially unique.

Many decisions can be broken down into a series of component parts that can be taken in sequence. Resolution of the later aspects of the decision process are then delayed until the effects of earlier stages of the decision are known or until more information is available on the various factors surrounding the decision process.

In any case, in approaching a decision it is usually best to assemble as much information as can be gathered within the time available before a choice between options must be made. However, delay in taking the decision may or may not be advantageous. The effect of any delay caused by the gathering of information must be assessed relative to any likely expected improvement in the quality of the decision making. Similarly, the cost of information gathering may be significant. It is clearly not desirable to spend more on this aspect of the decision making than is justified by the expected improvement in the outcome.

In the simplest terms, decision making consists of a choice between two or more available options after an evaluation of these options and in the light of progress toward fulfilling an objective or objectives. In some more routine situations the outcome of each option is known with certainty and the decision process consists of comparing the available outcomes and choosing that which is preferred. In many other cases the decision involves uncertainty in terms of future events or the actions of competitors. In these circumstances the outcomes cannot be calculated with certainty. Combinations of events or unforeseen conditions and actions of others may result in a decision that has been made on a considered and logical basis having a less desirable outcome than had been forecast. In all cases the lessening of uncertainty about the future is a major objective of the decision maker.

In some important decision processes, the outcome can be expressed in terms of an easily appreciated quantitative parameter. An example of this is the profit, measured in dollars, arising from the choice of a particular product. The choice between the options in such cases reduces to selecting that which produces the desired profit in the given period. However, many decisions involve considerations that cannot be easily measured; for example, the welfare of a section of the population or personal health and happiness. Perhaps some attempt can be made to attach a quantitative parameter to these factors, but this is difficult. There is a danger that an oversimplified quantitative approach to such problems may result in neglect of important considerations that are not represented in the simple quantitative parameter chosen to evaluate outcomes. In other cases no quantitative parameter is immediately apparent as a measure of outcomes and only the preferences of the various parties concerned for the available options are known to the decision maker. In complex decision situations those preferences for options may vary from day to day or according to the manner in which the problem is viewed. Many of the most important decisions facing managers today fall into this latter class.

In many decision processes the responsibility for choice between options lies with one particular individual who can decide on the basis of the information he has gathered and can act alone in the final resolution of the decision. In other cases a group of individuals can form a team to represent an organization. Part of the decision process in such circumstances consists of preliminary discussion and negotiation between the individuals in order to arrive at a set of "opinions" for the organizational entity. These opinions are then used in decision making as if the organizational entity were an individual decision maker.

A much more complex situation arises when the members of a group faced with a decision cannot arrive at an agreed set of opinions representing the views of the group. This may occur when the individuals are each pursuing a different set of objectives. Small subgroups may arise within such a group, consisting of individuals who have entered into some form of coalition with respect to their approach to the particular decision process. Decision making on behalf of the group may be very difficult under such circumstances.

Good decision making has always been seen as the path to success and there have been many treatments of the subject by eminent authors such as H.A. Simon,[1-3] C. West Churchman,[4] Samuel Eilon,[5] Armen A. Alchian,[6] Richard M. Cyert,[7] James G.

[1]Herbert A. Simon, "Theories of Decision Making in Economics and Behavioral Science," *American Economic Review,* 1959.

[2]Herbert A. Simon, *Administrative Behavior* (New York: Free Press, 1965).

[3]Herbert A. Simon and Allen Newell, "Human Problem Solving: the State of the Theory in 1970," *American Psychologist* 26 (1971):145–59.

[4]C. West Churchman, *Prediction and Optimal Decision* (Englewood Cliffs, N.J.: Prentice-Hall, 1961).

[5]Samuel Eilon, "What Is a Decision," *Management Science* 16 (December, 1969): B172–89.

[6]Armen A. Alchian, "Uncertainty, Evolution and Economic Theory," *The Journal of Political Economy* 58 (1950).

[7]Richard M. Cyert and James G. March, *A Behavioral Theory of the Firm* (Englewood Cliffs, N.J.: Prentice-Hall, 1963).

March[7,8] and Howard Raiffa.[9] Their work will be referenced extensively in this text.

Some Preliminary Systems Concepts

Decision making is a characteristic of systems that strive toward ideals, objectives, or goals. Such systems have been called *purposeful.*[10,11] The amount and degree of decision making undertaken is related to the purposefulness of the system. Simpler systems, such as a thermostat, are concerned with simpler decisions, such as whether the temperature of the water has exceeded 160°F. More purposeful systems are concerned with more complex decisions, although not necessarily to the exclusion of the simpler decision processes.

A system can be considered as a set of elements that are interrelated. Generally speaking, therefore, a human being can be considered to be a system since the various components of the body operate in a manner that is coordinated by the brain and the central nervous system. Organizations in which human beings work can similarly be regarded as systems since each individual plays his part and coordination is provided by management. By the same line of argument, the communities in which we live constitute systems, although the coordination between components in such cases may be looser. Other systems do not involve humans, but nonetheless are sets of coordinated elements; for example, the flight control system of a lunar space vehicle, the automatic pilot of an airplane or, at a simpler level, the governor that regulates the speed of a motor.

Systems of greatest interest in the study of decision making are called *open systems* because they operate in an environment and react to stimuli that impinge on them in that environment. By

[8]James G. March and Herbert A. Simon, *Organizations* (New York: John Wiley & Sons, 1958).

[9]Howard Raiffa, *Decision Analysis: Introductory Lectures on Choices Under Uncertainty* (Reading, Mass.: Addison-Wesley, 1968).

[10]Russell L. Ackoff, "Towards a System of System Concepts," *Management Science* 17 (July, 1971):661–71.

[11]Russell L. Ackoff and Fred E. Emery, *On Purposeful Systems* (Chicago: Aldine-Atherton, 1972).

contrast, *closed systems* do not react with an environment and are seldom, if ever, found in management. The simplest of open systems as far as decision making is concerned are *state-maintaining* insomuch as they react to internal or external events to maintain a given state. The more complex purposeful systems not only can react to internal or external events in pursuit of their goals, but also can change their goals and their chosen means of obtaining these goals as a result of internal or external stimuli.

The Background to a Decision

Ideals, objectives, and goals form the background against which decisions are made. Organizations have ideals, objectives, and goals that are related to their *functions*, as expressed, for example, in their terms of reference or their charters under law. Individuals who work in organizations also have ideals, objectives, and goals that may or may not coincide completely with those of the organization. The relationship among the ideals, objectives, and goals of the individual members of an organization (or a decision-making group) and those of the organization itself is a most important factor in many decision processes.

It is helpful at this stage to differentiate between ideals, objectives, and goals by means of the following definitions. These definitions are not unique, but they can serve as a basis for the discussion of decision making in this text. For our purposes, therefore, an *ideal* can be regarded as something that is ultimately desirable but not necessarily ever attainable; an *objective* as a situation that it is desired to attain, but not necessarily in a given time period; and a *goal* as an outcome to be obtained within a particular time period. For simplicity in what follows, the word "objective" will be used to cover the meaning of the three terms, which will be used individually only when it is necessary to emphasize the time period over which the desired condition is to be attained. Furthermore, objectives will be considered in terms of an organization such as a business, corporation, or government department. The discussion applies, however, with minor modifications to individuals and to communities of individuals.

Organizational Objectives

A statement of objectives is the foundation of the whole work of an organization and should therefore be formulated with care. As a general guide, the objectives should be:

- well thought out and explicitly stated;
- directly related to the function of the organization;
- stated in a form easily communicable to members of the organization;
- defined such that methods of measuring performance in achieving the objectives can be readily devised;
- defined with sufficient precision that the activities supporting one objective can be identified from those supporting another;
- stated so as to permit and encourage the postulation of alternative methods of achieving the objectives.

It is important that the objectives not be so general as to be almost meaningless when the time comes to relate programs of activity to them. For example, "fostering the well-being of the population" is a good-sounding objective sometimes put forward by governments. However, without specification of the areas in which this should be done it is almost impossible to translate into action.

Statements of objectives prepared for organizations sometimes contain only those items that management is prepared to see published. It is natural that a business organization should not wish to reveal objectives that might alert a possible competitor to future activities. Under these circumstances statements are published consisting of what may be termed *overt* objectives, while there remains in company confidential files a supplementary list of *covert* objectives. In some cases, the overt and covert objectives may be mildly contradictory, or even in direct conflict. Both types of objectives are important because management policies and decision-making will necessarily be related to *all* objectives of the organization.

Multiple Objectives

The objectives of an organization can seldom be described in a single, simply stated pursuit, although this may appear to be the case in a first approach. It is sometimes assumed, for example, that the sole objective of many businesses is to maximize the return on investment. Even if this were the case (as has been pointed out by Christenson[12]), does this mean maximization in the short term or in the long term and how are these terms defined? Even if maximization of return on investment were the major objective (and even though the terms in which this return is to be obtained were defined) a number of contributing, or supplementary, objectives might need to be stated. These supplementary objectives are usually necessary to the achievement of the main objective, but may in fact conflict with it in the short or long term. For example, an objective of maintaining the public image of the company may well detract from short-term profits, but be essential to the maintenance of return on investment in the long term. Substantial sums spent on the reduction of pollution from manufacturing plants and on informing the public of this investment provide an example of this phenomenon.

Most organizations, therefore, have multiple objectives. Some members of the set of multiple objectives may have more importance (or may be given more priority) than others at any one time, but nonetheless, all objectives necessary to the purpose of the organization must be taken into account by management. In some cases, one objective of a multiple set may act as a constraint on the others. This is particularly the case when resources are limited and allocation of some amount of resources toward the achievement of one objective reduces the amount of resources that can be used toward the achievement of the others. A major role of management is to decide the priorities to be assigned to individual objectives of a multiple set, taking into account conflicts that may arise and the action of certain objectives as constraints on the achievement of the others.

[12]Charles Christenson, "Some Lessons in Business from PPBS," included in *Analysis for Planning Programming Budgeting* (Washington, D.C.: Washington Operations Research Council, 1968), p. 59.

The Need for Review of Objectives

The objectives of an organization (or the area of application of these objectives) may change with time and as conditions change. It is another function of management to ensure that the objectives of the organization are continually reviewed in order that it may be kept purposeful under changing conditions. For example, the objectives of the Emergency Measures Organization, which was set up initially to protect the population from the after-effects of a nuclear attack, have now been modified to give greater emphasis to protection against the effects of natural catastrophes. If objectives are not kept continually under review, the organization may become less purposeful and less appropriate under changed conditions. This may ultimately result in it being disbanded. However, one usual (and sometimes implicit) objective of an organization is to ensure its own survival. Management may take steps to achieve this, in many cases instinctively, even though a conscious process of formulating objectives has not taken place.

Continual review of objectives is especially important where they form the background of decisions involved with state-maintaining or homeostatic processes.[13] External conditions, such as a change in the market, may require a change in objectives or goals for production of a product. The need for review of objectives may tend to be forgotten under the pressure of day-to-day business with resulting loss of effectiveness of the overall operation.

Objectives of Components of an Organization

The foregoing discussion has referred entirely to the objectives of the organization-as-a-whole. In addition, each subgroup in the organization, from a major division down to the individual staff member, has objectives that may be explicitly stated or may exist in implicit form. Ideally, the objectives of each component of an organization should be a subset of those of the whole so that all parts work toward a common end. In practice, however, this is sometimes not the case.

Unless management conducts continual and meaningful re-

[13]K.J. Radford, *Information Systems in Management* (Reston, Va.: Reston Publishing Co., 1973), pp. 8–9.

views of objectives at all levels it is not uncommon that some components diverge from the purpose of the organization-as-a-whole. This may occur from a sense of frustration felt by members of the staff arising from the lack of discussion of objectives. It may also be due to a feeling in middle- and lower-level personnel that they are "nearer the problem" than senior management and can therefore more clearly see the path that should be taken. Unless management takes the lead by establishing communication and discussing objectives, the diverging goals of components may cause the overall effort of the organization to become diffuse or self-defeating.

In particular, it is important that the personal objectives of staff members at all levels be considered. People work in organizations to make a living and, to some extent, personal objectives are subordinated to those of the organization. This subordination is tolerated in the short-run if it is felt that progress toward longer term personal objectives will be enhanced by the success of the organization, or of the component of the organization in which the staff member works. Satisfaction of personal objectives and their matching with those of the organization are the keys to successful personnel management.

The relationship of the objectives of the overall organization with those of its component parts depends to some extent on the stage of development of the organization. In the early stages of the life of an organization, or after a reorganization, the sense of purpose is usually strong. Direction of the enterprise is in the hands of a group of men who work together singlemindedly and who delegate tasks to subordinates who are similarly inspired by the objectives of the organization. The personal objectives of staff members are closely linked to those of the organization by the feeling that success will bring high personal rewards. Competent management seeks to maintain this situation in the face of the diffusing effects of growth of the organization, frustration by external conditions and conflicts between personalities. However, frequently the tendency over a period of time is for the objectives of components and of individuals to diverge from those of the organization, so that the organization disintegrates slowly and falls short of the standards of effectiveness and competence that were set in the early days. This phenomenon has been called *organizational entropy.*[14] The decrease of effectiveness is related to the decrease in purposefulness and to an increase in the disorder existing in the management of the organization. The counter to this tendency lies in a continued and meaningful review of objectives of the organization as a whole, of the component parts and of the staff members involved. A concurrent evaluation of progress obtained toward achievement of goals and objectives is also necessary.

The preceding discussion of organizational objectives has assumed that the practice of setting these objectives is desirable and practicable. From many points of view this is so, but many counter examples can be found of organizations that have operated successfully for long periods without an explicit process of setting objectives. It can be argued that such organizations worked with implicit objectives and that these were used as the basis for decision making. Nevertheless, it is important to consider whether the somewhat idealistic and formal process of conscious setting of organizational objectives is possible as a general practice. Cyert and March have approached this question in their work describing a behavioral theory of the firm.[15]

Starting from the premise that individuals have goals and objectives, Cyert and March propose that the organization be viewed as a coalition of individuals, some of whom form subcoalitions. They then propose a theory under which the objectives of the organization and of its component parts are arrived at by a bargaining process. In the course of this process a series of "side-payments" are arranged as a means of overcoming conflicts. These side payments, which may be in salaries or other benefits, are such as to satisfy (at least partially) the desires of the coalition members for progress toward achieving their own objectives. This concept of the organization as a coalition is important in discussion of group and organizational decision making (Chapters 6 and 7).

---

[14]Chris Argyris, *Intervention Theory and Method* (Reading, Mass.: Addison-Wesley, 1970), pp. 56–88.

[15]Richard M. Cyert and James G. March, *A Behavioral Theory of the Firm* (Englewood Cliffs, N.J.: Prentice-Hall, 1963).

Objectives in Relation to Management

The setting of objectives, either by an explicit and conscious process or by the implicit exercise of managerial intuition, is an important part of planning. Other aspects of management, as described by Fayol in his classical analysis,[16] are organizing, commanding, coordinating and controlling. For simplicity these may be condensed into three as follows:

- *planning and budgeting,* in which goals and objectives are set in advance of the operations under consideration, activities are conceived that can lead to the fulfillment of the goals and objectives, and available resources are allocated to the activities judged most likely to be successful in achieving the goals and objectives;

- *directing of on-going operations,* in which the resources are expended on the chosen activities, implying "management by objectives"[17];

- *evaluation,* in which the results of expenditure of resources are reviewed in the light of the previously determined goals and objectives.

This management process is necessarily continuous and usually iterative. New plans and resource allocations may be necessary at any time during the period as a result of changes in the external environment in which the organization is operating or to take account of internal changes and events. Decision making is a vital part of all these aspects of management and we must now turn to a consideration of what constitutes a decision in this context.

Steps in the Decision Process

The question of what constitutes a decision process has been discussed by a number of authors, notably by Robert Tan-

[16]Henri Fayol, *General and Industrial Management* (New York: Pitman, 1949).

[17]J.D. Wickens, "Management by Objectives: An Appraisal," *Journal of Management Studies* 5 (1968):365–79.

nenbaum,[18] Samuel Eilon,[19] R.M. Cyert and J.G. March,[20] and Peter F. Drucker.[21] These authors each approach the problem from a slightly different point of view. However, all agree that the decision process can be viewed as consisting of a number of steps that are taken by the decision maker in arriving at a solution. What follows is a description of these steps in the decision process, which the present author has found useful in many presentations on the subject. It provides a structure for the study of managerial decision processes later in the text.

Against the background of a goal, objective, or policy, the decision process may be envisaged as consisting of the following steps:

- Perception and formulation of the problem

- Construction of a model of the decision process

- Determination (as possible) of quantitative parameters involved in the process

- Specification of available options, strategies, or alternatives open to the decision maker

- Evaluation of the outcomes of each of the available options

- Selection of criteria of choice between available options

- Resolution of the decision process

Following the last step of resolution, *action* can be taken to implement the decision. The result of this action in the circumstances surrounding the decision process is the *outcome* of the decision.

It must immediately be said that the above description of the decision process is not unique nor necessarily better than any other. The steps are not meant to be taken as being rigidly in sequence, although certain of them must necessarily precede

---

[18]Robert Tannenbaum, "Managerial Decision Making," *Journal of Business* 23–24 (1950–51):22–39.

[19]Eilon, "What Is a Decision?"

[20]Cyert and March, *A Behavioral Theory of the Firm*, pp. 84–86.

[21]Peter F. Drucker, "The Effective Decision," *Harvard Business Review* (January–February 1967): pp. 92–98.

others; for example, perception and formulation of the problem is desirable before specification of options available to the decision maker. Furthermore, the majority of decision processes involve a number of iterations through all or part of the above steps before a final decision is made.

Many of the more complex decision processes cannot be immediately broken down into steps in this manner. The exact way in which managers approach these problems and arrive at solutions may not be fully understood. What is more, any attempt to observe these processes directly may result in disturbance of what may be a very efficient decision-making operation, with consequent loss of time and some irritation on the part of the managers involved. However, many of the simpler decision processes can be seen to follow a sequence like that described above; for example, the decision on whether to fuel a factory with oil or coal. This problem can be perceived and formulated relatively easily. The need is to provide a certain amount of energy and models are available to determine the energy equivalent of quantities of oil and coal. The parameters involved are units of heat and cost; we have assumed for simplicity that only the two options are available and we can no doubt calculate the outcome of each option. Given a simple criterion of choice, such as minimum cost, it is easy to proceed to resolution of the problem.

Many assumptions have been made to keep the above example simple and many factors that might influence a real-life manager have been neglected. For example, any constraints on the availability of either of the two fuels were neglected, as were possible costs of necessary pollution control measures. Study of the structure of simpler decision processes does, however, offer some insight into the more complex problems facing modern management.

Perception and Formulation of the Problem

Decision problems may arise and be perceived by managers in a number of ways, most of which are concerned with monitoring of operations and of external events. Drucker lists four different types of situations with which the manager may be faced.[22]

---

[22] Drucker, "The Effective Decision."

- the true "generic" event of which a single occurrence is only a symptom;

- an event that is unique in the particular department or organization in which the manager is working, but in fact is generic in terms of many organizations operating in the field;

- an event that appears to be unique, but, in reality, is the first manifestation of a new generic problem;

- a truly exceptional event unlikely to occur again in the foreseeable future.

The task of management is to structure a decision process for each of the above types of problem. Most important, it must distinguish between them so that the necessary decision making can be done most efficiently and with a minimum of re-investigation of repeated problems. It is, however, as much a mistake to treat a routine situation as if it were a new and unique problem as it is to classify a unique problem as one of a number of routine situations already faced in the organization.

The symptoms of the problem that are observed may be misleading. They may lead the manager to suspect one part of the system or operation when, in fact, another defective component (which is perhaps less visible) is producing conditions in which the suspected component was not designed to operate. Omond Solandt provides some interesting examples of this phenomenon,[23] including one in which anti-tank gunners complained of the accuracy of a gun sight when in fact defective traverse gears on the gun mount made it impossible to lay the gun accurately.

There is no complete prescription for accurate diagnosis other than persistence and dogged determination to explain the observed phenomena. This involves repeated inquiry as to whether the perception and formulation of the problem explains all the observed events. It is important to establish whether some event has been ignored or forgotten that is not compatible with the

[23]Omond Solandt, "Observation, Experiment and Measurement in Operations Research," *Journal of the Operations Research Society of America* 3 (February, 1955).

proposed formulation. If that is the case, a modification of the problem definition may be necessary.

Construction of a Model

Perception and formulation of the problem leads to the construction of a model, giving full details of the factors that are involved and the relationships between them. With some of the more routine problems it may be appropriate to describe these relationships in mathematical formulations. These provide a shorthand method of description in a format for which rules of manipulation of the parameters involved have already been established. The attractiveness of mathematical models, however, should not tempt the manager into their application without considerable thought. Mathematical models have been established for many routine decision problems, but hurried application of these models to situations they do not completely describe can lead to serious error. In particular, many such models involve assumptions that are clearly stated in their formulation. The applicability of the assumptions included to the decision situation at hand must be checked thoroughly before any such model is adopted.

John D.C. Little states in a recent article that the model adopted should be ". . . simple, robust, easy to control, adaptive, as complete as possible and easy to communicate with."[24] In addition it should contain a complete statement of the constraints or boundary conditions existing in the problem. A solution to a decision problem that does not satisfy the existing constraints is, in fact, a solution to the wrong problem. Tannenbaum has listed five types of constraints that may occur:[25]

- *authoritative constraints*, which result from policies or directives within the organization;

- *biological constraints*, which arise from the limitations of individuals who may be affected by the decision;

- *physical constraints*, including such factors as geography,

[24]John D.C. Little, "Models and Managers: the Concept of a Decision Calculus," *Management Science* 16 (April, 1970).
[25]Tannenbaum, "Managerial Decision Making," 22–39.

climate, physical resources and the characteristics of man-made objects;

- *technological constraints,* involved with the state of the art in relevant technological development;
- *economic constraints,* concerned with the money or resources available to implement the decision.

A constraint of any one of the above types, or a combination of them, may limit the options available to the decision maker and, therefore, are a necessary part of the model of the decision problem. It is particularly important in a situation covering a long period of time (rather than a short, instantaneous decision problem) that the estimated future behavior of the constraints and boundary conditions of the problem be included in the model.

Determination of Quantitative Parameters Involved

An important type of decision for a manager is one in which the outcomes of his available options can be expressed in quantitative terms. Decision making is easier when the outcome of each of the options can be expressed in the *same* quantitative parameter. As mentioned previously, there would probably be little difficulty in choosing between two options, one of which was estimated to produce more profit (measured in dollars) than the other. Unfortunately, many of the more important decision problems cannot be resolved in such a simple manner because progress toward the objectives with which the decisions are concerned is not measurable in an easily appreciated quantitative parameter such as dollars.

Harry P. Hatry has considered the problem of determining quantitative measures of progress in achieving objectives in areas where an easily appreciated measure of such progress cannot be used.[26] He contends that there are three approaches to the selection of quantitative parameters in decision problems that are *not* adequate in such situations:

- the assumption that effectiveness in terms of progress toward objectives is measurable in terms of cost of the activities;

[26]Harry P. Hatry, "Measuring the Effectiveness of Non-Defense Public Programs," *Operations Research* (September–October, 1970):772–84.

- the assumption that immediately observable parameters
  such as workload measures are necessarily adequate measures of effectiveness;
- the assumption that the outcomes of all options and activities can be expressed in the same units.

He concludes that quantitative parameters should be sought that
are appropriate to the assessment of progress toward the objectives underlying the decision process. This is seldom simple. In
many cases it may not be possible to establish satisfactory quantitative parameters in which the outcomes of options can be expressed. It may be that only the *preferences* of managers for
options are available expressed in *qualitative* rather than
quantitative terms. This whole question is of great importance in
the theory and practice of decision making and it is addressed in
the later chapters of this book.

Specification of Available Options

Faced with a decision problem, the manager must list the options that are available to him within the constraints or boundary conditions of the problem as he sees it. It is important that he
list all the available options and possible courses of action, basing
this primarily on his experience and judgment. The listing can be
checked and modified as a result of discussion with others, as far
as available time allows.

It is important that *all* available courses of action be considered
including those not immediately coming to mind. For this reason
it is sometimes useful to seek the opinions of one or more persons
with substantially different backgrounds or experience before
being satisfied that the list of options is complete. Furthermore, in
cases where it is not clear whether a particular option is available
within the constraints of the problem, that option should be
included pending evidence that it is not available.

Evaluation of Outcomes of Options

Given a set of available courses of action and a model of the decision problem, it is possible (at least in theory) to evaluate the
outcomes to be expected from any option in terms of the chosen
parameters representing progress toward the objective. In simple

cases this is relatively straightforward. In more complex situations the evaluation is more difficult. It is with such cases that the majority of the content of this book is concerned.

Criteria of Choice Between Options

Criteria for selection of an option or course of action, such as maximization of profit or minimization of cost, are simple examples of rules that can be applied in decision situations with a single objective. In situations involving multiple objectives each member of the objective set may give rise to a different criterion of choice. Resolution of the decision problem in such cases may involve the assignment of priorities to the individual members of the multiple objective set. Different managers may assign different priorities. Furthermore, the criterion chosen by any one manager may reflect his attitude to risk. One individual may feel that he can gamble and may therefore select a criterion of choice that involves a higher degree of risk under conditions of uncertainty while another may wish to be more conservative. This is one of the major areas in which human behavior and attitudes influence the process of decision making.

Resolution

Once all the above steps have been taken, resolution is the final aspect of the decision process and is the prelude to implementation of the action necessary to the particular situation.

Rationality and Personalistic Involvement in Decision Making

Rationality is a much-used word in the context of decision making. Starting from the somewhat flippant "That man is rational—he agrees with me," a number of definitions of rationality have been included in the literature. For the purposes of this text, the definition will be used (at least as a starting point) that a manager is rational if he chooses the option he prefers or sees as best. If he carries out all the steps in the decision process outlined above and arrives at the resolution stage with an evaluation of options and a criterion of choice between these options, he is regarded as rational if he chooses the option that is selected as best by this process.

Many types of decisions encountered in the day-to-day work of an organization cannot be approached according to a predetermined standard procedure. Individual managers may be involved in any or all of the steps and each may bring his personal judgment, experience, beliefs and, perhaps, prejudices to bear on the decision process. In a major study of human problem solving conducted by Herbert A. Simon and Allen Newell, the first proposition of a proposed theory states that "a few, and only a few, gross characteristics of the human information processing system are invariant over task and problem solver."[27]

The individual and personal characteristics of the decision makers, therefore, may lead to a decision problem being treated differently according to which individual is engaged in the problem. This is less likely to happen in situations in which the symptoms and events surrounding the problem have been encountered many times before and by many individuals who are in communication. New problems and those that have not yet been classified as generic, however, may be interpreted differently by different managers. They may be perceived differently, formulated differently and a different model of the decision process may be constructed by each individual manager. This in itself is a compelling reason for continuous communication and passage of information between those managers in an organization who may be faced with new decision problems.

The personalistic input of the individual decision maker can influence the decision process at any one or more of the steps outlined above. For example, in organizations with multiple objectives it is common for these objectives to be discussed and for some agreement to be reached on the relative priorities to be afforded to each objective in certain situations. If this process is not maintained as events unfold or if the agreements reached are not fully accepted or are imperfectly understood, individual managers may place different priorities on members of the set of multiple objectives. One may be concerned more with long-range profits while another may give more priority to short-range results. Again, with decision problems involving profit there would

[27]Allen Newell and Herbert A. Simon, *Human Problem Solving* (Englewood Cliffs, N.J.: Prentice-Hall, 1972):chap. 14.

probably be no disagreement between individual decision makers on the choice of dollars as a parameter for measuring outcomes. However, the *value* that individual managers place on a particular amount of dollars may vary. Their individual *preferences* for different amounts of profit may be different; in an organizational setting their appreciation of the preferences of the organizational entity for different amounts of profit may not be exactly the same.

Individual judgment enters also into the selection of a criterion of choice between available options. This judgment may be a function of certain behavioral characteristics of the decision maker at the time when he makes his decision. He may, for example, be feeling optimistic and willing to take a risk or he may be in a pessimistic mood at that time. As an additional factor, his mood may change from day to day or even from hour to hour, according to the manner in which he is affected by events and circumstances.

Types of Decision Process

On the basis of the preceding discussion, organizational decision processes can be classified by reference to two characteristics:[28]

1/ whether there is managerial involvement in the decision process at the time of each resolution of the particular decision; and

2/ whether the resolution is rational.

Completely Specified Decision Processes

Those decision processes in which there is no managerial involvement at the time of each resolution *and* where the resolution is rational are those that were called *programmed* by Simon in his early work.[29] More recently, the term *completely specified* has been adopted to describe these decision processes.[30]

[28]K.J. Radford, "An Approach to Managerial Decision Making," paper presented to the Annual Meeting of the Operational Research Society (UK), November, 1973.

[29]Herbert A. Simon, "The New Science of Decision Making," reprinted in *Management Decision Making*, eds. Lawrence A. Welsch and Richard M. Cyert, (Baltimore: Penguin Books, 1970).

[30]Radford, *Information Systems in Management*, p. 39.

In such decision processes the background to the decision, the model of the decision process, the quantitative parameters involved and the criteria for selection between available options are explicitly known and agreed among the managers concerned. Therefore, a set of specifications describing the decision process in detail can be agreed among all those who are concerned with them. That is not to say that these specifications should not be changed in the event of a change in the circumstances surrounding the decision process. In fact, good management practice requires that the specifications of such decision processes be kept continually under review.

It is important to note that the personal input of the individuals involved goes into the writing of the specifications and into the discussions leading to agreement on these specifications. Once this agreement has been achieved the decision process can be run repeatedly without further personal involvement until a change in the specifications becomes necessary. Assuming that the resolution is made rationally at all times (that is, assuming that specifications are followed) repeated resolutions of the same decision process with the same data will always result in the same answer. Examples of such processes are those governing the preparation of a payroll, an accounts payable or receivable routine or an industrial process controlled by a mathematical model. These decision processes can be safely delegated to a computer.

Another category of decision process is that in which there is no managerial involvement at the time of each resolution, but in which the resolution is irrational. This class represents a malfunction of a completely specified process (such as when a cheque is issued for one million dollars by mistake) and is of little interest in this discussion.

Partially Specified Decision Processes

A third class of decision process is that in which only a portion of the process can be completely specified. These decisions are called *partially specified*. Typically they consist of decision processes in which a great deal of the pertinent data can be processed and arranged according to a specification, but the final judgment (including possibly the choice of a criterion for selection) is left to the individual decision maker. This individual then brings his personal judgment and experience to bear on the problem of arriving at a solution. A typical example of a partially specified process is the choice of a man to fill an important position in an organization. The manager who is to make the choice would probably agree to writing some broad specifications describing the type of staff member he requires, including such characteristics as age, education, experience and so forth. These specifications can then be used to select from the personnel files all those who meet the general requirements for the job. The manager is thus relieved from the routine work of scanning all the personnel files. He can then concentrate on interviewing those individuals that the completely specified portion of the process has selected as a short list of candidates.

Personalistic or Non-completely Specified Decision Processes

The final category is that in which there is managerial involvement in each specific solving of the decision problem. This involvement may occur at any stage of the decision process. Since each manager may bring his own personal beliefs, attitudes and value judgments to bear on such a decision process, it cannot be completely specified in advance of resolution. This type of decision has been called *personalistic*[31] or *non-completely specified.*[32]

Many of the decision processes encountered in the management of modern organizations are such that they cannot be completely specified. This is due to the fact that the structure of these decision processes has not been precisely determined or that the managers involved with the decision have not agreed on an approach or on an exact structure for the process. In such cases the behavior of an individual in decision making may be different from that of his colleagues, just as one person's experience, judgment and beliefs may be different from those of others. Closeness of experience such as usually exists between partners who have worked together for some time tends to bring about a similar approach to decision making. However, the possibility exists that two managers faced with a decision process that had not been completely specified would reach distinctly different solutions, even assuming that each was acting logically and rationally. This

[31]Samuel Eilon, "What Is a Decision?"
[32]K.J. Radford, "An Approach to Managerial Decision Making."

can happen particularly if the two individuals involved have different attitudes toward risk. One may be inclined to take a gamble and the other to play safe. In such cases the criteria for choice between available options selected by the two managers involved may be different, with the result that different solutions might be obtained by the two persons involved.

Ideally, of course, two managers engaged in such a problem would consult each other before reaching a final decision. During the course of this consultation one might persuade the other, opinions could change and they might eventually reach a common position. In a large organization, however, each individual's appreciation of the objectives applicable to the decision may be different from those of his colleagues. Personal objectives may be defended and a degree of conflict among the managers involved may prevent a truly cooperative approach to the decision problem.

Organizational Decision Processes

All organizational decision processes are of one or other of the types just described and illustrated in Fig. 1-1:

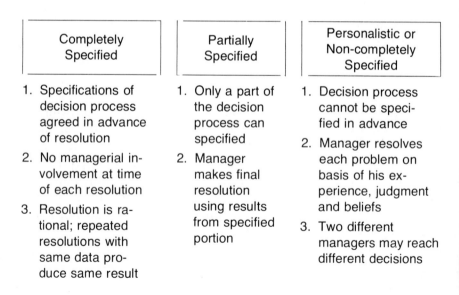

Completely Specified	Partially Specified	Personalistic or Non-completely Specified
1. Specifications of decision process agreed in advance of resolution	1. Only a part of the decision process can specified	1. Decision process cannot be specified in advance
2. No managerial involvement at time of each resolution	2. Manager makes final resolution using results from specified portion	2. Manager resolves each problem on basis of his experience, judgment and beliefs
3. Resolution is rational; repeated resolutions with same data produce same result		3. Two different managers may reach different decisions

Figure 1-1   Types of Organizational Decision Process

Sisson and Canning have estimated that 80 to 90 percent (by number) of the decisions made in a business organization can be completely specified (they call this "computable").[33] They go on to say, however, that 60 to 80 percent of the decisions in such an organization (by *type* of decision) are of a sort that are not directly computable and that involve human judgment at one stage or another. However, there is a tendency in modern organizations for more and more decision processes to be completely or partially specified and delegated to the computer for complete or partial resolution.

Summary

Decision processes range from the simple and routine to the very complex. Many of the routine decision processes in modern business can be delegated to the computer, thus freeing managers to concentrate on the more complex problems. Some decision problems are repeated many times so that experience in handling them may be built up. Others occur only infrequently. Some decisions can be broken down into components that can be handled in sequence, thus allowing time for gathering information applicable to the later stages of the process.

Decision making consists of making a choice between two or more available options after an evaluation of the outcome to be expected from each option. In some cases the outcomes are known with certainty. In many cases, however, the decision process involves uncertainty about future events or the actions of others. Some of the simplest decisions involve well-understood quantitative parameters, such as money. In other decision processes it is not easy to find a simple quantitative parameter with which to measure progress toward fulfillment of objectives.

Decision making is a characteristic of systems that strive toward ideals, objectives or goals. Most people and organizations have multiple objectives, some of which may be openly discussed and others that may be held confidential. Some of the items in the multiple objective set may be in conflict with others and setting of priorities may be necessary. Objectives should be reviewed continually to ensure that the organization remains purposeful.

[33]R.L. Sisson and R.G. Canning, *A Manager's Guide to Computer Processing* (New York: John Wiley & Sons, 1967), p. 9.

The various components of an organization have sets of objectives also and it is important that a close relationship be maintained between these objectives and those of the organization as a whole. One way of viewing an organization is as a coalition of its members and its subgroups.

Decision processes can be thought of as comprising a number of steps. The actual decision may involve a number of iterations through all or part of these steps. Many of the more complex decisions cannot be broken down immediately into these steps, but a study of the approach to simpler decision processes may be helpful in understanding the more complex ones.

Two important factors in managerial decision making are the concepts of rationality and personalistic involvement in the process. Decision processes in which there is no personalistic involvement at the time of resolution and where the resolution is rational are called "completely specified." Most of the more routine decision processes in an organization can be completely specified; or, at least, a portion of them can be completely specified. The non-specified decision processes are those in which the manager is involved at the time of each resolution. His approach to those processes is colored by his experience, judgment and beliefs. It is possible for two managers to reach different solutions to the same problem, each declaring that he is acting rationally.

Discussion Topics

1/ Herbert A. Simon has said that management is synonymous with decision making. Do you agree with that? Give your reasons.

2/ Organizations can be thought of as purposeful systems. How is the nature and the quality of decision making in an organization related to its purposefulness?

3/ Can you think of an organization that has only a single objective? If not, are there organizations with multiple objectives for which one objective is far more important than all the others?

4/ How would you go about discovering whether an organization has any covert objectives?

5/ What are the more important state-maintaining or homeostatic processes in an organization?

6/ How can the tendency for the objectives of an organization and those of its staff members to diverge be corrected?

7/ Is the concept of an organization as a coalition useful? If so, what are the important factors concerned with the formation and maintenance of the coalition? If not, what other models of organizational behavior provide a suitable background for the study of decision making?

8/ Do you agree that all or most decision processes can be thought of in terms of the explicit steps that we can outline for the simpler processes?

9/ How would you ensure that decision making problems that are truly "generic" are not treated each on an individual basis in your organization? What is the relationship of policies and standard operating procedures to these generic decisions and to completely specified decision processes?

10/ What steps would you take to ensure that a model constructed to describe a decision process is in fact applicable to the situation as you see it?

11/ What proportion of the decision processes (by *type*) in your organization are completely specified? What steps would you take to ensure that all decision processes in your organization that are eligible are in fact completely specified? Would you encounter any opposition in this work?

12/ Why do you think cost is so readily appreciated by individuals? What can be done to express such matters as health, service or convenience in quantitative terms?

13/ Different managers may take a different approach to a decision problem that cannot be completely specified. What can be done to reduce the occurrence of this phenomenon? Under what circumstances is such a reduction desirable?

2

Quantitative Parameters in Decision Problems

Introduction

Many of the simpler decision problems (and most of those that can be completely specified) involve quantitative parameters that are relatively easily defined, measured, and understood. The most familiar of these is money, which is a measure of such factors as profit, cost, salary, and indebtedness. The unit in which money is expressed is dollars or some other currency. A number of other parameters may be involved in the decision problems faced in an organization, such as manpower, working space, and use of specialized facilities. These may be expressed in units such as man days, square feet, and hours of use, all of which may be convertible into the unit of money at the appropriate rate. In some cases, however, scarcity of these items may be a constraint in a decision process. Additional amounts of certain commodities may not be immediately available. In such cases it is not appropriate to convert units of these items into the unit of money and the decision problem may need to be considered in terms of the

29

commodities concerned. Definition of the quantitative units involved is part of the process of specifying a decision process. It is a necessary step before a decision can be classified as completely specified and possibly delegated to a computer.

Some of the more complex problems facing managers are those for which an easily defined quantitative parameter cannot be found or where the choice of such a parameter cannot be agreed upon by all concerned with the decision process. For example, it may be very difficult to agree on units in which to measure the benefits of an urban transportation scheme or a company diversification program. Some of the effects of such programs may not be directly convertible into units of a widely understood parameter, such as money. Quantitative measures of these effects must be related to the objectives of the activities. Furthermore, in measuring the benefits of an activity such as an improvement in one aspect of the standard of life of a section of the population, it is important to measure any disbenefits associated with the program, particularly if they cause some major disadvantages to another segment of the population.

In considering this aspect of decision making, we will start with situations in which quantitative parameters are easily identified and move progressively to areas where this is more difficult. Finally, we shall consider situations where only qualitative preferences are available.

Easily Defined Quantitative Parameters

In problems involving profit or cost it is common practice to specify a means of calculating the outcome of selecting an option in terms of the amount of money involved. This means of calculating profit or cost is called an *objective function*. For example, in a situation where the options involve production of different numbers of units of various products, each unit of which brings a particular amount of profit or cost, the objective function is simply the sum of the numbers of each item produced times the individual unit profits or costs. The resolution of the decision problem in such cases involves only the calculation of the value of the objective function for each of the available options and the choice of the option considered most advantageous. This is a relatively simple procedure and one that can be readily applied to decision problems involving quantitative parameters such as profit. For this reason, there is a temptation to treat more complex problems by an analysis of this type, even if the quantitative parameters considered are not fully representative of the particular decision problem. When using simple quantitative techniques, therefore, it is necessary to be certain that the factors measured and the units in which they are included in the objective function are, in fact, those that are appropriate to the problem at hand.

Efficiency and Effectiveness

There are two particular types of measurement that may be found in some decision processes, namely *efficiency* and *effectiveness*.[1] Efficiency usually relates to the optimum use of resources toward a given end. For example, it might be concerned with the best method of arranging the shared use of a given facility, such as an oil pipeline or the complement of rooms in a hotel. Effectiveness, on the other hand, is a measure of fulfillment of an objective, such as a required return on investment or the reduction of air pollution. It is possible to be effective while not operating at the optimum efficiency, and it is possible to work with optimum efficiency, but not be effective.

This may seem to be a play on words. As a further explanation, let us consider that we are engaged in manufacturing a product from certain ingredients and that our objective is simply to make a profit. Let us assume further that we have a very good market for the product. At this stage we are both efficient and effective in our operations. Now let us suppose that our market disappears and we cannot sell the product. The *efficiency* of the manufacturing process is unchanged by this development. However, the *effectiveness* of the operation in terms of the objective of making a profit is now zero. By a similar argument, if the efficiency of the process is reduced the effectiveness may also be reduced, but not necessarily below that required to meet the objective. Measures of efficiency are important in many decision processes and are generally easier to define in quantitative terms than are measures of effectiveness.

A problem may arise with the use of measures of effectiveness

[1]Harry P. Hatry, "Measuring the Effectiveness of Non-Defense Public Programs," *Operations Research* 18 (September–October, 1970):772–84.

in a situation involving multiple objectives. Let us suppose, for the sake of simplicity at the start, that there are two objectives concerning profit in the short term and in the long term. Progress toward these objectives can be expressed in terms of the same quantity—money—measured in the unit dollars. The question may be raised as to which option to select to produce a certain level of achievement of each of the objectives of the multiple set. This is the equivalent of assigning a priority or degree of importance to each objective. In some simple cases this can be approached by defining weighting factors for profit in each category. Suppose it was required, for example, that for every amount of profit made in the short term another amount is to be made in the long term. This can be achieved by a simple combination of the objective functions related to short- and long-term profits. If these are denoted by z_1 and z_2 respectively, a new objective function can be set up in the form:

$$z = k_1 z_1 + k_2 z_2$$

where k_1 and k_2 are the weighting factors to be applied to the two categories of profit. This is a useful procedure in situations where progress toward different objectives can be measured in the same unit. There is a danger, however, that the ease of application of this method of evaluation may result in the representation of different effects by a common measure in situations where this is not justified. They may be a temptation, also, to assign arbitrary weighting factors to simplify solution procedures. This is, of course, undesirable and can lead to bad decision making.

Less Easily Identified Quantitative Parameters

In many situations, the measure of benefit in which the outcome of an option can be expressed is not immediately apparent. This is the case in many government-sponsored activities[2] such as the control of nonmedical use of drugs or of communicable diseases. Measures of efficiency, such as the number of patients treated by a particular unit, come readily to mind. Measures of

[2]Robert Dorfman, ed., *Measuring the Benefits of Government Investments* (Washington, D.C.: The Brookings Institution, 1965).

benefits of such programs are less easy to identify. The benefits or drawbacks of such programs may go far beyond the effect on those directly involved.

One approach to this problem is the establishment of *proxy measures* of effects. These are not necessarily measures of the direct effects of a program but of effects that are directly related to benefits that need to be measured. For example, a proxy measure of the effect of a drug control program might be the price of the drug on the illegal market. In one practical case[3] the effectiveness of different variants of ambulance service was assessed in terms of the response time. This was measured as the elapsed time between the alarm and the time when the patient was delivered to the hospital.

The use of proxy measures is most often necessary in public service activities where profit is not a primary objective relating to specific programs. Such measures arise, however, in profit-making concerns, especially in those with important secondary objectives, such as the maintenance of a public image. How is the benefit of a public service sponsored by a major company to be assessed? How should the benefits of the re-equipment of the rooms in a hotel be measured? Future return on investment may be the proxy measure in such cases.

There is a danger that the selected proxy measure may not be appropriate to all aspects of the activity. Considerable attention should be given to this problem. In the ambulance service case mentioned above, for example, was it established that speed of response was directly related to the benefit to a victim of an accident? Might there be cases where a slower response would be more appropriate, so that qualified people or better equipment could be available for treatment on the scene? Furthermore, if the ambulance drivers got the notion that their efficiency was being measured by reference to the response times would they be tempted to concentrate on reducing that time rather on other aspects of aid to the patient?

The most common types of proxy measures are those that can be expressed in terms of an easily appreciated quantity such as money. Hatry has given examples of the use of "future estimated

[3]Office of Administration, Office of The Mayor, New York City, "Emergency Ambulance Service," May 8, 1968.

earnings" as a measure in decisions concerning health care programs.[4] He points out that calculation of future earnings discriminates against the elderly, who have less time left to work, and women, who may be paid less for their work (although, hopefully, this will be less common in the future). Use of future earnings tends to give priority to those just entering the more highly paid occupations. This may be the intention of those charged with the direction of such programs. On the other hand, it may not be, and the use of the proxy measure "future earnings" may be misleading in their decision making.

There may also be a temptation to assign a dollar value to such effects as increased leisure time or reduced travel time. This may be suggested by the demonstrated willingness to pay for some improvement, such as a new bridge, on the part of a section of the population. At best, willingness to pay is subjective and variable over the many groups of people that a program may affect. The addition of dollar values assigned to a variety of program effects may result in the neglect of important intangibles that are not well represented in those terms.

Hatry has summarized the problems that may arise with the use of proxy measures as follows. First, the use of proxy measures implies that some key value judgments have been made. There is a danger that, in the pressure of a decision making situation, these judgments may be given insufficient attention and that some major concerns may be neglected completely. Moreover, there may be a tendency for analysts concerned with assembling data to make these judgments implicitly by their choice of quantitative measures. Under pressure of time, they may not report these matters to the decision maker who will have final responsibility for the option selected.

Second, the measures selected may not have equal applicability to different sections of the population or to the different groups of people affected by the program of activities. Third, in the desire to work with a measure that is easily understood and manipulated, dollar values may be assigned to effects that cannot be properly described in this way.

This is not to say that no attempt should be made to establish measures in decision situations where quantitative parameters

[4]Hatry, "Measuring Effectiveness."

are not immediately apparent. In fact, it can be argued that when decisions are taken without explicit establishment of parameters in terms of which options are evaluated, the act of decision making *implies* evaluation of the benefits of the various options. If time allows it is surely better to investigate the possibility of a more explicit evaluation. On the other hand, such an evaluation should not be in terms of a single parameter if this causes neglect of important factors.

Ordinal Ranking

If no quantitative parameter can be found with which to evaluate the available options, the decision maker may be able only to rank the options in terms of their usefulness in his opinion. This process is qualitative rather than quantitative. The decision maker may place outcomes in the order 1, 2, 3, 4 . . . n, but the numbers assigned have no significance other than to show the order of preference. Such a procedure is called *ordinal ranking*.

Ordinal ranking is subjective. It refers to the preferences of a decision maker either personally or as he sees the preferences of the organization that he is representing. In the latter case he may be guided by the policies of the organization as he understands them. Although managers of like mind or similar appreciation of policies may produce identical rankings of available options, this cannot be assumed to be true in all cases.

Consistent ranking can usually be achieved as long as there is only one factor or objective in mind. This is not to say that in any one case two persons would necessarily agree on the actual order of preference. It is theoretically possible, however, to rank outcomes unequivocally with respect to a single factor. Immediately upon more than one factor becoming involved (as may be the case in an organization with a multiple objective set) ranking may become equivocal.[5,6]

Another important concern in ordinal ranking is with *transitivity* of preferences. Transitivity requires that if an indi-

[5]D.W. Miller and M.K. Starr, *The Structure of Human Decisions* (Englewood Cliffs, N.J.: Prentice-Hall, 1967), pp. 54–55.

[6]Samuel Eilon, "What Is a Decision?" *Management Science* 16 (December, 1969): B172–89.

vidual prefers A to B and B to C, then he must, if transitivity is to be preserved, prefer A to C. This is also seen to be *consistent*. Whereas transitivity may hold as long as only one factor is involved, it may break down if there are two considerations or objectives. A manager may say with perfect consistency that on the basis of one objective he prefers A to B and B to C, but on another consideration he prefers C to A. In such cases consistency is preserved but transitivity is not.

Herein lies a major problem in the application of mathematical logic to managerial decision making. Much logical development is dependent on an assumption of the preservation of transitivity. However, a great deal of managerial decision making is done in a situation that involves more than one objective. The method of analysis chosen in any particular decision problem should not be such as to prevent the manager from using as input his preferences in the light of all the objectives that he sees as important. To do otherwise would be to constrain managerial decision makers unnaturally for the sake of the requirements of a theory.

A compromise is possible in many situations. Let us suppose that the decision problem involves multiple objectives. It is possible to ask the manager to assign priorities to the individual objectives and to rank available options in terms of the objective with highest priority. This provides some information. Following this, we can ask for a ranking of options treating the second priority objective as if it were the most important and so on through all the objectives of the set. If the ranking obtained is the same for each of the objectives, then consistency and transitivity have been preserved. Even if this occurs for only the first two or three objectives in the priority listing, something has been gained. Some of the most difficult decision problems are those in which the order of ranking varies considerably between each of the objectives. Such cases are treated, as best we can, in Chapter 4.

Utility

In cases where the outcome of an option is expressed in terms of an agreed quantitative parameter the usefulness of that outcome may vary according to the circumstances under which the individual or organization is operating at the time of the decision. Furthermore, the estimates of usefulness of an outcome may be *subjective* and may vary according to the judgment of the indi-

vidual decision makers. As a simple example of this phenomenon, the value of a profit of $50,000 may be less to a large firm than
to a small one: each firm's appreciation of the usefulness of
$50,000 may be different. A similar statement might be made with
regard to some other commodity such as manpower or a manufac-
tured product.

In certain transactions between individuals and organizations
these effects are ignored, at least in the short term. In the calculation of a paycheck, for example, neither employee nor employer
usually considers the value of the money involved at the time of
the calculation, although this may ultimately be an important
consideration in bargaining for revised salary scales. In certain
completely specified decision processes, therefore, the subjective
view of the value of an outcome is either omitted or included in
the agreed specifications of the process.

The question of the perceived usefulness of outcomes has been
treated in the literature under the heading *utility*.[7-10] The word
"utility" has been used to describe a number of related but somewhat different concepts. These will now be described in a sequence that is appropriate to our study of managerial decision
making.

Utility of Money (or Some Other Commodity)

The question of the utility of money was considered in the early
eighteenth century by the Swiss mathematicians Cramer and Bernoulli. Their basic philosophy was that the utility of an additional
amount of money decreases with the amount of money possessed;
that is to say, the value of an additional dollar if one has one
thousand dollars is less than if one has only ten dollars. This
concept has come to be known as *Bernoullian utility*.[11]

In line with the philosophy of his day Bernoulli assumed that

[7]John von Neumann and Oskar Morgenstern, *Theory of Games and Economic Behavior*, 2d
ed. (Princeton, N.J.: Princeton University Press, 1947).

[8]Wayne Lee, *Decision Theory and Human Behavior* (New York: John Wiley & Sons, 1971),
pp. 70–108.

[9]R.D. Luce and Howard Raiffa, *Games and Decisions* (New York: John Wiley & Sons, 1957),
pp. 12–38.

[10]Miller and Starr, *Structure of Human Decisions*, pp. 81–98.

[11]For an historical account of this work see L.J. Savage, *The Foundations of Statistics* (New
York: John Wiley & Sons, 1954), pp. 91–104: reprinted in Ward Edwards and Amos
Tversky, eds., *Decision Making* (Baltimore: Penguin Books, 1967), pp. 96–110.

all men, being rational, would behave in the same way. He therefore proposed what he regarded as a fundamental law that he
maintained governed such behavior. This law stated that the
utility of money could be measured in terms of the logarithm (to
any base) of the amount of money. Both Cramer and a French
scientist named Buffon argued in favor of different laws (Cramer
for the square root and Buffon for the reciprocal of the amount of
money) as a measure of utility, but the hypotheses all had the
effect that the curve of utility for money plotted against money
had the general shape shown in Figure 2-1. With such a curve
incremental amounts of money contribute less utility as the level
of money involved increases.

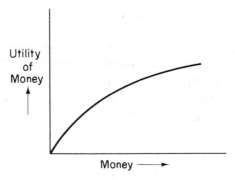

Figure 2-1   Bernoullian Utility of Money

Much more recently, Friedman and Savage made some proposals regarding the shape of the curve representing the utility
function.[12] They noted that two common aspects of human
behavior—gambling and buying insurance—were apparently inconsistent. In gambling one gives up a sure thing (the stake) to
accept a risk, while a buyer of insurance gives up a risk (for
example, that his house burns down) in favor of a sure thing (the
relatively minor loss represented by the premium). It has previously been pointed out that the shape of the utility curve suggested by Bernoulli and his contemporaries did not explain
gambling behavior since it supposed that people had less and less

[12]M. Friedman and L.J. Savage, "The Utility Analysis of Choices Involving Risk," *Journal of Political Economy* 56 (1948):279–304.

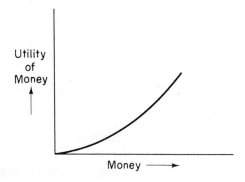

Figure 2-2   Concave Upward Utility Function

utility for money as the amount increased.[13] Some types of gamblers clearly have more and more utility for money as the amounts get larger, at least up to a point. This type of behavior can be described by a utility function of the type (concave upward) shown in Figure 2-2.

It was suggested further that behavior in buying insurance could be explained by a curve in the negative quadrant similar to that shown in Figure 2-3. With this curve additional amounts of loss contribute greater amounts of disutility as the loss increases.

Friedman and Savage combined these ideas and proposed a utility curve of the shape shown in Figure 2-4. The part of this curve in the negative quadrant was said to explain behavior in

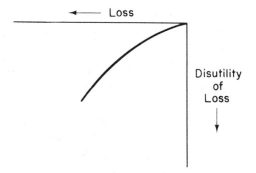

Figure 2-3   Function Representing Disutility of Loss

[13]W. Vickrey, "Measuring Marginal Utility by Reactions to Risk," *Econometrica* 13 (1945): 319–33.

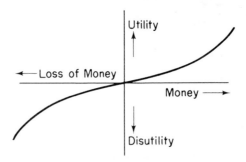

Figure 2-4   Friedman-Savage Utility Function

buying insurance and the part in the upper, positive quadrant to explain gambling behavior. Note that the portions of the curve near the intersection of the two axes are close to straight lines, although the straight line parts in the two quadrants do not necessarily have the same slope. It must be pointed out at this stage that both the Bernoulli curve and the Friedman-Savage function were proposed with a major assumption in mind—that an individual's preferences for outcomes in risk situations where money is involved are based on a rational assessment of the *expected* outcome of the risk. The assumption that individuals make decisions on evaluation of the expected value of an outcome will be discussed (and questioned) in Chapter 3.

The utility function proposed by Friedman and Savage was modified some years later by Markowitz.[14] He suggested that individuals with different amounts of wealth would not act in accordance with the shape of the utility function corresponding to their present holdings of money. He said, rather, that the changes of behavior implied by the changes in slope of the utility function would take place at different points on the money scale. This is the equivalent of saying that the intersection of the axes on the diagram in Figure 2-4 would be at a different point on the absolute money scale for each individual: the exact point at which this intersection is placed should be determined by what Markowitz called the *customary wealth* of the individual.

Markowitz proposed further that there should be a modification of the shape of the Friedman-Savage function at each end of

[14]H. Markowitz, "The Utility of Wealth," in *Mathematical Models of Human Behavior* (Stamford, Conn.: Dunlap, 1955), pp. 54–62.

the curve. He said that there must surely be a point at which an individual (or organization) becomes satiated with gain and that the right-hand end of the curve should therefore turn downward. Similarly, at very large losses there is presumably a leveling off of disutility and, therefore, the left-hand end of the curve should reflect this.

These arguments lead to a proposed curve for the utility of money of a form shown in Figure 2-5. The intersection of the axes is at the customary wealth of the individual or organization.

Care should be taken not to interpret these suggested utility functions too literally. Only the general shape is important and only then as an interpretation of the observed behavior of individuals in risk situations involving money. Note that no units of utility or money have been shown on the axes and that the exact meaning of "customary wealth" is not well defined. Nevertheless, the curves do provide some insight into the "value" of money as seen by individuals; particularly that it cannot necessarily be assumed that this value increases or decreases linearly with the amount of money involved. The same can be said of any other commodity, the amount of which can be measured in an easily defined unit.

There has been some discussion in the literature over the years on the interpretation of utility curves. This is summarized by Ralph Swalm in an article in which he discusses whether utility theory is *descriptive*, that is, useful in describing the behavior of

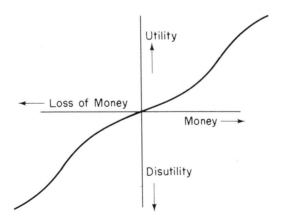

Figure 2-5   Markowitz Utility Function

managers, or *prescriptive*, that is indicating how mangers *should* behave rather than how they *do* behave.[15] Without entering into this discussion, from which little agreement has so far emerged, the position taken here is that utility theory should be regarded as *descriptive* and that its study can lead to a useful understanding of the behavior of managers in decision making. Furthermore, as more and more evidence of *past* behavior is obtained, this may be indicative of *future* behavior under similar circumstances.

One very important factor arises in the consideration of decisions taken by managers on behalf of organizations. The utility function to be considered in such situations should be that of the organization, or, at least, the individual manager's appreciation of the organizational utility function. The utility function of the manager taking the decision in relation to his personal affairs is not usually appropriate to the organization's decision. It might be that the decision maker is so much a part of the organization that the two utility functions are essentially the same. This can happen, for example, in small owner-operated firms. In other cases a manager can be expected to have a utility function and a customary wealth that are different from those of the organization or the component that he represents. Use of a personal utility function in an organizational decision situation may then result in considerable error.

Swalm reports the results of a study of the utility functions of executives of corporations when engaged in decision making on behalf of their firms.[16] One of the first steps in the study was to establish a "planning horizon" for each man. This was defined as twice the maximum single amount he might recommend be spent in any one year. The utility function obtained later in the study for each individual was then plotted in terms of the appropriate planning horizon rather than actual dollar amounts. This enabled those conducting the experiments to examine the executives' utility functions on a scale related to corporate planning horizons.

Swalm found some widely differing examples of decision making behavior even among executives from the same company. These ranged from extremely conservative to gambling, as illustrated in Figure 2-6.

[15]Ralph O. Swalm, "Utility Theory-Insights into Risk Taking," *Harvard Business Review*, (November–December, 1966).

[16]*Ibid.*

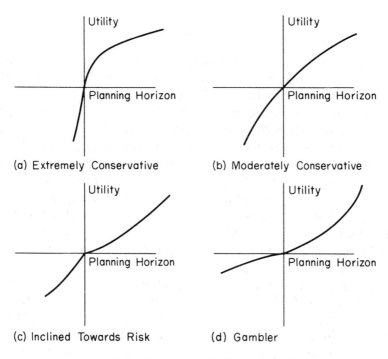

(a) Extremely Conservative   (b) Moderately Conservative

(c) Inclined Towards Risk   (d) Gambler

Figure 2-6   Executives' Utility Functions

These utility functions are strikingly different. However, many of the curves determined in the study were very similar. The most common similarity was in the sharp slopes found in the negative quadrant, denoting conservatism in situations involving loss to the organization. This attitude to risk, where loss is a possible outcome, may not be to the advantage of the company. It may be that it inhibits the selection of options where the possibility of gain justifies the assumption of a risk of loss. It indicates, perhaps, that in organizational decision making the penalty for being wrong is considered by some managers to be much greater than the reward for being right.

The above remarks refer to studies of the utility of money or of a commodity that can be measured in well-defined units. We must now move on to consider utility in the broader context of preferences, where outcomes cannot necessarily be evaluated in terms of well-defined parameters. First, however, it is necessary to discuss briefly the types of scale on which measurements of parameters are made.

Scales of Measurement

All quantities used in decision making must be measured at some time in the process. Measurements are made when it is desired to create information that can be shared with others.[17] By this process, it is possible to talk about things in terms of the measurement rather than by the more detailed qualities to which the measurement relates. For example, if there is a group of men and their heights have been measured, it is possible to discuss the characteristic of the individuals involved in terms of feet and inches. However, this measurement would not be useful in describing other characteristics of the individuals to which height is not closely related, such as eyesight. Measurements must therefore be appropriate to the characteristic under review.

Measurements are made according to a scale. There are four types of interest in this discussion. These are the absolute, ratio, interval and ordinal scales. An *absolute* scale is one that is completely defined. A *number* of items is measured on an absolute scale and there is no arbitrariness or equivocation concerned with such a measurement. A *ratio* scale is one in which some degree of arbitrariness exists. The height of an individual can be measured in inches or in centimeters for example. The choice of unit is left to the one making the measurement although it is understood that a direct multiplication factor exists between this and other units in which the measurement could be made.

A further increase in arbitrariness leads us to an *interval* scale of measurement in which there is no absolute zero point and the relation between units that can be chosen is governed by a positive linear transformation of the form $y = ax + b$. Temperature is usually measured on such a scale. In the Fahrenheit and centigrade scales the zero point is set arbitrarily. To convert from the centigrade to the Fahrenheit scale, the linear transformation $x = 9/5\ y + 32$ is used, where x and y are the Fahrenheit and centigrade measurements respectively.

An *ordinal* scale is one in which the items considered are placed in rank only. Numbers used to indicate rankings have no significance other than to show the rank order.

These four scale types can be compared in terms of the follow-

[17]C. West Churchman, *Prediction and Optimal Decision* (Englewood Cliffs, N.J.: Prentice-Hall, 1961), pp. 99–100.

ing characteristics: degree of arbitrariness (as above); the type of transformation between one type of measurement on the scale and another (such as the direct multiplication between units on a ratio scale) and what remains unchanged when such transformation is applied. This comparison is shown in Table 2-1. Note that, whereas we may count in different systems (such as decimal and binary) this does not affect the character of the absolute measurement.

These characteristics of scales of measurement are reflected in our intuitive use of the measurements involved. If we prefer one car to another, it matters little to us whether we assign ranks numbered 1 and 2 to these cars or 1 and 200. The *ordering* is understood in either case, as long as the convention "high number most preferred" is stated. If some significance is given to the numbers, that is if a greater preference is indicated by (1, 200) than by (1, 2), then we have moved toward an interval scale. In terms of temperature, we do not say that 80°F is necessarily twice as hot as 40°F. This would be true by definition if temperature, like the weight of an object, were measured on a ratio scale.

In practice, an ordinal scale is used to express preferences where no quantitative measurement has been or can be made. An interval scale is used when no absolute zero can be specified but when differences of measurement are important. An important property of an interval scale over the ordinal is that it allows averages to be calculated over a number of measurements of a parameter. Ratio scales are used when an absolute zero is conceivable (for example, zero money) and when the choice in measurement is limited to the selection of a unit such as dollars or pounds sterling. A direct multiplier in terms of the exchange rate is available for conversion between units on a ratio scale. An absolute scale is used for counting.

The above discussion has been necessary in order to consider the type of scale on which the quantitative parameters and utilities involved in decision making can be measured. The degree of quantification possible and its significance increase from the ordinal scale through to the absolute. For easily quantified commodities such as money, little difficulty arises and a ratio scale can be used. However, there is a major question regarding the type of scale on which utility can be measured.[18]

---

[18]Tapas Majumdar, *The Measurement of Utility* (New York: St. Martins Press, 1958).

Table 2-1 Scales of Measurement

Type of Scale	Degree of Arbitrariness	Type of Transformation Between Units in Two Scales of this Type	Unchanged when Transformation Applied	Example
Absolute	none	none	not applicable	Number of people in a room.
Ratio	low	Multiplication by a positive constant	1. rank order 2. ratio of distances between items on scale 3. ratio of measured values of items	1. Weight, height 2. Temperature in °K
Interval	medium	Positive linear of the form $y=ax+b$	1. rank order 2. ratio of distances between items on scale	Temperature in °F and °C
Ordinal	high	Positive monotonic (i.e., for measurements in any two scales, $x_1 x_2$ and $y_1 y_2$, if $x_2-x_1>0$ then $y_2-y_1>0$)	Rank order of items measured	I prefer that car to this.

If a single objective exists or if one objective of a multiple set is dominant, it is generally agreed that ordinal ranking of the utility of options is possible. This is essentially the same thing as saying that managers can express preferences between available options. There is no general agreement, however, as to whether utility can be measured on an interval scale, although many authorities hold that it can be under specified circumstances. No one has seriously suggested that utility can be measured on a ratio or on an absolute scale. If a quantitative measure of utility is to be introduced, therefore, the question is under what circumstances, if at all, utility can be measured on an interval scale. This is the question that von Neumann and Morgenstern addressed in their classical work published originally in 1945.[19]

von Neumann-Morgenstern Interval Scale Utility

The basic contribution of von Neumann and Morgenstern was to prove that under certain conditions utility could be represented on an interval scale. The most basic of these conditions was that preferences could be expressed for options in a risk situation (that is, for gambles) and that transitivity is preserved. Before discussing the conditions and their implications in detail, however, let us consider the procedure that was developed for setting up the interval scale measurement. Von Neumann and Morgenstern called this the *standard gamble* method. It must be said immediately that this method is not generally applicable to (or recommended for) the day-to-day practice of managerial decision making. Most busy decision makers would rightly regard it as impractical for such purposes. It is described here primarily for its value in understanding interval scale utility measurements.

Suppose that a decision maker has three options, A, B and C, and that he prefers A to B and B to C. The maintenance of transitivity requires that he prefers A to C. Having obtained his preferences on an ordinal scale, we wish to investigate whether a more quantitative expression of the decision maker's preferences can be obtained. The method of von Neumann and Morgenstern suggests that we set up the following question and investigate the decision maker's reaction to it.

[19]Von Neumann and Morgenstern, *Theory of Games.*

The decision maker is to be asked which of the following alternatives he prefers:

B for sure	OR	a risk situation involving: A with probability p and C with probability (1 − p)

Remembering that the decision maker prefers A to B and B to C and that transitivity requires that he prefers A to C (i.e., $A>B$, $B>C$, $A>C$), the above question is the equivalent of asking whether the decision maker would choose the intermediately-preferred option for sure over the gamble giving him a chance (p) of his *most* preferred option and the complementary chance $(1-p)$ of his *least* preferred option. The method consists of investigating the decision maker's behavior as p is varied from 0 to 1.

When $p=1$, this is the equivalent of asking the decision maker to choose between B for sure and A with probability 1, that is, for sure. He must, according to his assumed preferences, choose A in this case, which is the right-hand side of the above alternatives. If $p=0$, the choice is between B for sure and C with probability 1 and he must choose B, the left-hand side. It can now be argued that because the decision maker has changed his choice from the right-hand to the left-hand alternative as p has varied from 1 to 0, there must be a value of p between 1 and 0 at which he is indifferent between the two sides. This value is denoted by p^*.

Suppose now that we set up an interval scale with the zero arbitrarily set at the utility for the least preferred option C and the value 1 set as the utility for the most preferred option A. Von Neumann and Morgenstern proved that the utility for the intermediate option B could be represented on this interval scale by the value of the probability p^*. If there are initially more than three options the procedure can be repeated in groups of three. In each case the indifference probability is obtained for a choice between an intermediately preferred option and a gamble between the most and least preferred. In the case of five options say, A, B, C, D and E, the interval scale might look like that in Figure 2-7. Note that:

Option	$\rightarrow$ E	D	C		B	A
Interval Scale	0	p^*_D	p^*_C		p^*_B	1

Figure 2-7   Interval Scale Utility for 5 Options

whereas this scale has a zero, it is an *arbitrarily set* zero. Any scale derived from that shown by a linear transformation of the type $y = ax + b$ would be equally representative of the measured utility.

Assumptions Underlying the von Neumann-Morgenstern Interval-Scale Utility Measurement

The von Neumann-Morgenstern interval scale utility measurement is based on several assumptions. These have been called axioms in some treatments. Their effect is to limit the area in which such a measurement of utility is valid. The major assumptions involving managerial behavior are as follows:

1/ Preferences are assumed to exist for the available options. For any two options the manager must express preference for one or the other, or indifference between them.

2/ Transitivity must be preserved. If $A > B$ and $B > C$ then A must be preferred to C. Since preferences are to be represented by numbers that obey transitivity, the preferences themselves must obey transitivity.

3/ If a manager prefers A to B, then he must prefer a certainty of· obtaining A to a gamble that provides him with only a probability of obtaining A and the complementary probability of obtaining the less preferred option.

Certain other assumptions, which are less concerned with managerial behavior, are necessary to the analysis. If O_i, O_j and O_k are any three options and p is the probability of obtaining an option in a gamble, then the following must hold:

1/ If $O_i > O_j > O_k$ then there exists a value p such that $(pO_i, (1-p)O_k) < O_j$: and similarly, there exists a p such that $(pO_i, (1-p)O_k) > O_j$. This states that in a choice between a sure thing (O_j) and a gamble involving options more and less preferred than O_j, then a value of p exists such that the sure thing is preferred and another value of p exists such that the gamble is preferred. This is essential to the procedure of varying p from 0 to 1 in the standard gamble.

2/ The order in which the constituents of a gamble are stated does not affect preferences; i.e., there is indifference between $(pO_i, (1-p)O_j)$ and $((1-p)O_j, pO_i)$.

3/ The consequence of a gamble may itself be a gamble and the form of the gamble has no effect on preference.

Given that the above assumptions are observed, the von Neumann-Morgenstern analysis proves that the quantities p^* obtained in the standard gamble procedure represent interval scale utility measurements. In fact, the utility functions obtained for executives by Swalm[20] were derived from a procedure based on the standard gamble. In this case, the available options had outcomes that could be represented completely by sums of money. It was not unreasonable to assume that the executives involved could express preferences for different sums of money, that their preferences would obey transitivity and that they would prefer the certainty of a larger sum of money to a gamble involving only a probability of a lesser amount. Further, the assumption made implicitly that the executives were working toward a single objective (that is, maximum profit) is reasonable under the terms of the experiments reported.

The question remains of whether the assumptions necessary to the derivation of interval scale utility are met in day-to-day managerial decision making. Some attempts have been made to investigate this experimentally, notably by Mosteller and Nogee.[21] However, laboratory experiments involving persons with less immediate responsibility than executives and sums of money far smaller than are involved in real life are probably not a satisfactory representation of the conditions under which managers must make decisions.[22] On the other hand, experimentation and investigation in real life situations are very difficult.

It is probably not unrealistic to assume that a manager has preferences for the available options, given that he is asked to

[20]Swalm, "Utility Theory-Insights."

[21]F. Mosteller and P. Nogee, "An Experimental Measurement of Utility," *Journal of Political Economy*, 59 (1951):371–404; reprinted in W. Edwards and A. Tversky, eds., *Decision Making* (Baltimore: Penguin Books, 1967), pp. 124–69.

[22]Jacob Marschak, Actual and Consistent Decision Behavior," *Behavioral Science* (April, 1964):104.

express these preferences in terms of a single objective. The problem most likely to arise is that he is faced with a situation involving multiple objectives. He may then be able to express preferences in terms of each member of the multiple set, but these preferences may be different for each objective. This may be consistent managerial behavior, but it produces a situation where transitivity is not maintained. A further difficulty may arise if a manager is asked to assign priorities to the achievement of the individual objectives in the multiple set to determine which has highest priority. This may be very difficult and managers may be unwilling or unable to be specific about their priorities. Even if the priorities are expressed, they are a result of individual opinion. Two different managers may express very different opinions on this subject.

One further assumption in the von Neumann-Morgenstern analysis may affect results in practical applications. The standard gamble technique requires a decision maker to choose between a sure thing and a gamble to obtain the interval scale measurement. This procedure could give rise to error if the decision maker has an aversion to, or a liking for, gambling, which would influence his choice. This choice must be made strictly on the basis of his preferences for the options involved. Any influence on the choice introduced by the standard gamble method itself would necessarily cause errors in the interval scale measurement.

These are major considerations in any attempt to apply the von Neumann-Morgenstern technique in decision situations arising in day-to-day business. However, if the assumptions can be observed, obtaining an interval scale measurement of utility does allow a new approach to certain of these decision problems. In situations in which only ordinal scale (nonquantitative) preferences previously were available, a quantitative utility measurement can be obtained. The mathematical operations that can be performed using this measure of utility are limited to those appropriate to the interval scale. In practice, however, this allows the calculation of average utilities and, more generally, of expected values, given the utilities of outcomes and the corresponding probabilities of their occurrence. The use to which expected values can be put in practical decision making is considered in detail in Chapter 3.

Some Extensions of Utility Theory

A number of authors have tried to build on the von Neumann-Morgenstern treatment of utility to overcome some of the problems in applying it to practical decision making. This is an area in which a great deal of research and investigation is still needed. There has been little progress so far.

Some researchers have attempted to develop a theory that would incorporate the observed fact that individuals often appear to be inconsistent in their preferences for options.[23] The assumption is made that one option is preferred to another according to a probability distribution, rather than consistently. Such approaches are known as *stochastic utility theory*. Although there has been a great deal of development of such theory from a mathematical point of view it has yet to be applied widely in practical decision making.

Other research has been directed toward the situation where an option may embrace several attributes; for example, May carried out a study of preference for marriage partners in which the prospects differed in intelligence, wealth and looks.[24] If utilities can be assigned to each of the attributes, the question arises as to whether a compound utility can be assigned to a combination of attributes. Work in this area has centered around proposals for simple relationships between the component utilities and the compound utility. For example, a model has been proposed in which the compound utility is equal to the sum of the component utilities[25] and a series of assumptions has been derived under which this model can be shown to hold. The model has been tested under experimental conditions. Once again, although a great deal of ingenious and original work has been done in this area, the application of the results in practical decision making is still limited.

Much the same can be said of work to date on what has been

[23]D. Davidson and J. Marschak, "Experimental Tests of a Stochastic Decision Theory," in C.W. Churchman and P. Ratoosh, eds., *Measurement: Definition and Theories* (New York: John Wiley & Sons, 1959), pp. 223–69.

[24]K.O. May, "Intransitivity, Utility and the Aggregation of Preference Patterns," *Econometrica* 22 (1954):1–13.

[25]R.D. Luce and J.W. Tukey, "Simultaneous Conjoint Measurement: A New Type of Fundamental Measurement," *Journal of Mathematical Psychology* 1 (1964):1–27.

called (perhaps misleadingly) the social welfare problem. This problem concerns a group or community of members in a situation in which application of an amount of resources can result in the availability to the members of a set of benefits, services or goods. Each member is assumed to be able to assign interval scale utility measurements to his preferences for particular mixes of these benefits, services and goods. The problem posed is to seek the mix of benefits, services and goods that results in the greatest possible aggregate of the individual member's utilities. This might be supposed to be the allocation of resources that would provide the greatest good for the group or community as a whole. As can be seen immediately, this is a problem that has many applications in the modern world. A summary of recent approaches to this problem has been given by Wayne Lee.[26]

Unfortunately, no general method has yet been found of treating the preferences of the individual members that does not eventually lead to contradictions and inconsistencies in the eventual choice of allocation. Much of this is due to the fact that the interval scale utility measurements for the members of the group are somewhat arbitrary. It is possible, for example, to transform the individuals' utilities in such a way as to bring about a change in "optimum" allocation. This may make the whole procedure meaningless. There have been attempts to avoid this difficulty by retreating from interval scale utility measurements and measuring the preferences of the individual members on a basis of ranking (ordinal scale) only. However, no consistent method has been yet found of deriving an overall social preference ranking from the individuals' preference rankings[27-28] except when the preferences of the individuals are not too dissimilar. This problem is considered in more detail in the context of a group decision making in Chapter 6.

Summary

Many decision problems involve quantitative parameters that are easily defined, measured and understood. The most common of these are expressed in absolute numbers of units associated

[26]Lee, *Decision Theory*, pp. 101–103.

[27]K.J. Arrow, *Social Choice and Individual Values* (New York: John Wiley & Sons, 1951).

[28]Luce and Raiffa, *Games and Decisions*, pp. 327–70.

with the parameter, as dollars are associated with cost. Most completely specified decision processes are concerned with such well-defined parameters. Others may involve measures of efficiency or effectiveness. Efficiency usually relates to the optimum use of resources, whereas effectiveness is measured in terms of the degree of fulfillment of a goal or objective. Some problems may arise in measuring effectiveness when multiple objectives exist. In particular, there may be a temptation to translate different effects into a common measure for analytical convenience.

In many situations the measure of benefit (or pay-off) is not easily identified and defined. In such cases proxy measures may be proposed, but care should be taken that such a proxy measure is directly related to the benefit in question. It is important that value judgments implicit in the selection of a proxy measure be recognized and also that the measures have equal applicability over the various groups of people affected.

In some cases no quantitative measures can be identified and the decision maker is left to work with ordinal ranking of preferences for options. The question of whether these rankings are transitive and consistent is important. Managers engaged in day-to-day decision making may not preserve transitivity, particularly over a period of time in changing conditions. Consistency may be preserved, but not transitivity. This problem arises particularly in situations involving multiple objectives. Under such circumstances, a solution may lie in the assignment of priorities to members of the multiple objective set.

Estimates of the *usefulness* of the outcome of an option, expressed in an agreed quantitative parameter may vary according to the judgment of individual decision makers. Different people have different utilities of money, for example. Many transactions do not take this into account. In other cases, varying utility of money may affect the choice between available options. A great deal of work has been done to describe utility of money. This work seeks to explain behavior in such activities as gambling and buying insurance. Utility for money is said to be different for individuals (or organizations) of different "customary wealth." In taking decisions on behalf of an organization, it is important that an organizational utility function be considered rather than that of any individual involved.

Utility can be measured on an interval scale as long as certain necessary assumptions are met. The most important of these are consistency and transitivity. A method exists of deriving interval scale utility measurements from expressed preferences, but there is considerable doubt as to whether this can be applied in practical decision-making situations. If conditions exist such that interval scale utilities can be obtained, the major advantage is that average (or expected) utilities can be calculated.

Some attempts have been made to develop extensions of the von Neumann-Morgenstern utility theory, notably in the areas of (a) stochastic utility theory to allow for inconsistency in preferences; (b) compound utility functions for use where an option may embrace many attributes and (c) when it is desirable to use resources for the maximum benefit of members of a group. None of these theories has yet been developed to the point where it can be widely applied to practical decision making.

Discussion Topics

1/ Why is money measured in dollars, or some other unit, a most readily understood parameter? Are there any other such commodities?

2/ Do you think that it is usually possible to obtain agreement in an organization on the relative priorities to attach to members of a multiple objective set?

3/ What are the advantages and disadvantages of using proxy measures?

4/ What is the difference between transitivity and consistency? Which is the more important to preserve?

5/ Has your utility for money changed over the years (neglecting the effect of inflation)? If so, why do you think this has happened?

6/ How does the concept of utility of money enter into the activities of a corporation?

7/ It is generally conceded that preferences exist and that utility is a means of describing these preferences. Do you agree?

8/ Can utility functions be used to predict behavior? Or is a utility function merely a description of behavior?

9/ Is it possible and desirable for an individual to determine the utility function of that part of an organization for which he has decision making responsibility?

10/ Can you envisage any circumstance in your organization in which you could use the standard gamble technique to obtain interval scale utility measurements?

11/ Do managers operate in a manner that would allow the assumptions necessary to von Neumann-Morgenstern interval scale measurement of utility to be applied? If not, what are the major characteristics of managers that would cause a breakdown in the analysis?

12/ Do you think that experiments can be carried out to test the validity of von Neumann-Morgenstern interval scale utility measurements? If so, how would you set them up?

13/ Use the standard gamble technique to establish a utility function describing your own approach to monetary gain and loss. Try to do the same for the part of your company or organization for which you have decision making responsibility. Note any differences. (See Ralph O. Swalm, Utility Theory: Insights into Risk Taking, *Harvard Business Review*, Nov.–Dec., 1966).

3

Factors Affecting the Choice Between Options

In the classical treatments of decision making, decisions are said to be encountered under four conditions: certainty, risk, uncertainty and competition (or conflict).[1-3] The decision maker's choice between options is described as being influenced by his appreciation of which of these conditions applies to the problem at hand. It is necessary, therefore, to consider this approach in some detail as a preliminary to the more comprehensive treatment of decision making in the following chapters. It will be convenient at first to think of these conditions as discrete categories of decisions. However, as we proceed it will become apparent that

[1]R.D. Luce and Howard Raiffa, Games and Decisions (New York: John Wiley & Sons, 1957), p. 13.

[2]Wayne Lee, Decision Theory and Human Behavior (New York: John Wiley & Sons, 1971), pp. 23–25.

[3]David W. Miller and Martin K. Starr, The Structure of Human Decisions (Englewood Cliffs, N.J.: Prentice-Hall, 1967), pp. 108–11.

they may be thought of as points in a range of conditions between which no clear boundaries exist. Furthermore, a problem may appear to be in one category at one time and near another at some other time.

Conditions Under Which Decisions Are Made

Decisions Under Conditions of Certainty

Decisions are regarded as being made under conditions of *certainty* when there is seen to be only one consequence or outcome of each of the options available to the decision maker. This is the equivalent of saying that the effect of choosing any option is known in advance with certainty. This may be regarded as an unlikely condition in an uncertain world, but nevertheless, in situations in which considerable past experience exists, many decisions fall in or close to this category.

Consider, for example, a factory capable of producing a number of different products from the same basic ingredients. Each product requires a different mix of ingredients and, therefore, production of one unit of each product involves a different cost for the basic ingredients. Production costs and selling price may vary among products. Assuming for the moment that a market exists for any and all products that are produced, it is necessary to know what mix of products can be made from given amounts of input ingredients to give the maximum profit.

If, for the moment, it is assumed that all the quantities are known exactly, the profit from a given product mix can be determined with certainty. Such a problem is said to be *deterministic*. For given conditions a product mix can be determined to provide maximum profit. The results of such an analysis can be represented in a table showing individual options (i.e., product mixes) against the profit to be expected from selecting that option (Table 3-1). This profit can be considered as the *payoff* as a result of the decision to choose a particular option.

Students of operations research will recognize the above problem as one to which the mathematical technique of linear programming can be applied under certain circumstances. Whereas in Table 3-1, a series of *discrete* options have been listed, the method of linear programming allows consideration of

Table 3-1   Decision Under Certainty

Option	Payoff (profit)
O_1	\$ x_1
O_2	x_2
O_3	x_3
O_4	x_4
etc.	etc.

continuous variation of the input ingredients. Therefore, it is possible to consider a much wider range of options using the mathematical model. However, the nature of the problem may be such that use of a simple analytical model such as linear programming is not possible. We may be reduced in such circumstances to analysis of a number of discrete options, as in the above table. The number of options to be considered may become very large in real-life problems. The output of the calculations in each case is a payoff representing the profit from the products. Assuming that it is desired to maximize profits, the appropriate product mix can be determined.

Decisions Under Risk

Decisions are said to be taken under *risk* when there is more than one possible payoff resulting from the selection of an option and the decision maker is assumed to know the probability of occurrence of each of these payoffs. The variation of payoffs can be considered to be the result of factors occurring outside the control of the decision maker. Assuming that a number of these factors can occur and that the probabilities of occurrence are known, the chance of various combinations of these factors (sometimes called *states of nature*) can be calculated. The decision maker is then faced with a payoff table (or matrix) like that shown in Table 3-2.

A simple example of a decision under risk is one dependent on the roll of two dice. The possible "states of nature" in this case are the various combinations of the values of the upturned faces of the dice, ranging from 2 to 12. The probability of occurrence of each combination can be calculated in advance, assuming the dice are fair and not biased in any way. Note also, in this case, that the number of possible states of nature is known as well.

This type of decision may seem to be rather artificial when

Table 3-2   Pay-off Matrix for a Decision Under Risk

Options	States of Nature N_1 N_2 N_3 . . . etc. Probability of State of Nature		
	p_1	p_2	p_3 . . . etc.
O_1	x_{11}	x_{12}	x_{13}
O_2	x_{21}	x_{22}	x_{23}
O_3	x_{31}	x_{32}	x_{33}
O_4	x_{41}	x_{42}	x_{43}
. . .		. . .	
etc.		etc.	

compared to real life conditions and there are many who argue that it is. On the other hand, many problems occur in areas where considerable experience has been gained in the past. In such cases, reasonably accurate estimates of the number of possible states of nature and their probabilities of occurrence can be estimated. The manner in which these estimates are made may be dependent on human behavior and judgment. The use of personal estimates of probabilities in these circumstances is discussed later in this chapter.

Decisions of this type can be viewed as a sort of game against nature, with the following steps:

1/ the decision maker chooses an option from a set of available options, having calculated the outcome or payoff for each of the set of options under each of a set of future states of nature, the probabilities of occurrence of which are known;

2/ the decision maker having made his choice, "nature" chooses a state that actually occurs;

3/ the decision maker receives the payoff corresponding to the actual state occurring.

It can be seen, therefore, that even though the decision maker chooses the option that provides him with the most preferred payoff under the state of nature that is considered to have the highest probability of occurring, that state may not in fact occur in a single play of the game. Therein lies the risk and it is in the face of that risk that methods to be described in the next chapter have been devised to guide decision makers in such conditions.

Decisions Under Uncertainty

Decisions are said to be made under uncertainty when neither the number of possible future states of nature nor their probabilities of occurrence are known to the decision maker. He is assumed to be uncertain of whether he has listed all possible states of nature in his payoff matrix and also of the relative likelihood of each occurring. This is the condition that many hold is the most likely to be that facing the decision maker in practical situations.

The decision maker's ignorance under the condition called uncertainty may be only partial. Also, it may be possible for him to obtain further information at a cost in time and money. This suggests that it may be advantageous to postpone the decision, or at least part of it, until more information can be gathered. Decisions under uncertainty may therefore be developed into sequential decision processes, which cannot be represented conveniently by the table or matrix form suitable to one-stage decisions. The information gathered may be used as the basis for defining more comprehensively the possible future states of nature and their probabilities of occurrence, as well as the options available to the decision maker. Thus, information gathering may cause the condition under which the decision is considered to move from what has been described as uncertainty nearer to the state defined as risk. Methods by which this can be accomplished and the attendant conditions and assumptions are dealt with in detail in the next chapter.

Decisions Under Competition or Conflict

In consideration of decisions under risk and uncertainty, it has been assumed that the "opposition" (or other player in the game) is the result of a set of circumstances that determines the future state of the world, independently of the desires and hopes of the decision maker. We have called this "player" nature, or chance, and assumed that its part in the game is played without competitive opposition to the decision maker. A further class of decisions concerns those in which an identified opponent exists, whose actions may be in direct conflict with those of the decision maker. Examples of this occur in economic competition in the market-place and in certain games, such as poker, that closely parallel some aspects of competition in business.

Cases of direct man-to-man or organization-to-organization conflict are rare in modern society. In most cases, government is a party in such conflicts in one form or another and many other players may be more or less involved. In some conflict situations, it may in fact be difficult to identify exactly where the opposition is coming from although its effects can be readily observed. It may not be possible to be sure whether the future states are brought about by the conscious actions of real opponents of the decision maker or whether they are the result of a combination of the actions of a large number of parties, each acting in his own interest in a competitive world. Many events that we classify as natural may in fact be influenced by other individuals or organi-zations, particularly in areas where there is competition for re-sources and other necessary amenities of modern life. In some such cases the situation may approach that described under un-certainty.

Decision Criterion Under Conditions of Certainty

The choice of a criterion for selection between options presents little difficulty in dealing with decisions under conditions of certainty. Each option has only one payoff that represents the degree of achievement of the objective against which the decision is to be made. All that the decision maker needs to do is to select the option that provides the greatest degree of achievement of the objective in question. This may be less simple in situations where more than one objective is involved. Special methods for dealing with these situations are discussed in Chapter 4.

Decision Criteria Under Conditions of Risk

In some of the earliest studies of risk situations, the principle was advanced that the correct choice of option should be that which provides the *maximum expected value* of the payoff. Daniel Bernoulli (1700–1782) was aware of this principle and was one of the first to examine it critically. As a simple example of its application, suppose that a game is proposed in which prizes are awarded as a result of the toss of a fair coin. The stipulation that the coin is "fair" denotes that the probabilities of the two outcomes "head" and "tail" are each one-half. Suppose that the game provides a payoff of +$200 if the result of the toss is heads and a payoff (loss) of −$100 if the result is tails. The expected value of the game is then:

$$\tfrac{1}{2} \times (+\$200) + \tfrac{1}{2} (-\$100) = +\$50.$$

If the sole criterion for decision is maximization of the expected value of the game, the decision must be to play, since the expected value is positive and the value of not playing is zero.

As another example, let us consider the following situation. A manager is faced with a decision as to whether to remain with his present manufacturing plant, to build a small extension or to build a large extension. His decision is influenced by the possible future states of the world; in this simple case, the possible future markets for his product. We may assume for simplicity, at this stage, that the future market will be either low, medium or high. Let us further assume that the manager is able to calculate the net profits that each of his options would bring under each possible future market condition and that he can arrive at quantitative values that express his preferences, or utilities for those profits. Suppose that the probabilities of a low, medium and high market are ¼, ¼ and ½ respectively. The manager can then express his problem in a matrix of the form shown in Table 3-3.

Table 3-3   A Plant Expansion Problem—An Example of Expected Values

	Future States of the Market			Expected Values
Assumed Probabilities	Low ¼	Medium ¼	High ½	
Manager's Options				
1. Stay with present plant	0	0	0	0
2. Build small extension	50	300	200	187.5
3. Build large extension	−500	100	600	200

The expected value appropriate to each option is shown in the Table, calculated from the payoffs for each of the options and the probabilities of the future states of the market. If the criterion of choice were the maximum expected value, the option to be selected would be to build the large extension.

Arguments Against Choice by Maximum Expected Value

The main argument that can be advanced against maximum expected value as a criterion of choice between available options is that it is appropriate only to decisions that are repeated many times. This argument is based on the fact that the outcome in a single decision is that resulting from choice of one of the options and an unknown future state of nature. It is only in many repeated decisions of the same type that the *average* outcome approaches the expected value. For example, in the coin tossing example just considered, the outcome in a single play is either a gain of $200 or a loss of $100. The fact that the expected value is positive may be very little consolation to the man who loses $100 in a single play. In a multiplay game (and assuming each toss of the coin is an independent event),the *average* of the payoffs can be expected to be positive as the number of plays increases. With a large number of plays, this average approaches the expected value of +$50.

In the plant expansion problem in Table 3-3 the option with the maximum expected value is to build the large extension. However, a prudent manager might not wish to risk an outcome of −500 that would occur with the large extension if the market turned out to be low. He might be tempted to build the small extension and so avoid the possibility of a loss in the single decision situation confronting him.

A number of authors have pointed out that in many practical situations, decision makers choose the option with the *lower* expected value. In their personal lives people continually pay for tickets in lotteries where the chance of winning a prize is very low and the expected value of the option of entering the lottery is less than that of not participating. Similar situations arise in day-to-day business. Suppose, for example, that a letter containing a $100 bill is to be mailed and that the chance that it will be lost is one in five thousand. The *expected* loss if the letter is mailed without registration (insurance) is $100/5000, or two cents. The expected loss in registering the letter is the registration fee, say fifty cents. Nevertheless, people consistently register letters under such circumstances and in doing so choose the option with the lower expected value. Perhaps this is because the registration fee is small (with an insignificant disutility) and the real criterion used in the decision process is the minimization of uncertainty.

The amounts of money involved in the above example are probably very small compared with the customary wealth of the decision maker. If however, a company with a net worth of say five million dollars was considering insurance on an item representing 20 percent of that net worth, the situation might be different. Suppose that the chance of loss of the item were one in a hundred. The expected loss without insurance would be $1,000,000/100 = \$10,000$. The insurance premium would be greater than that to allow for the expenses and profit of the insurance company. Let us suppose that the premium is \$15,000. The problems associated with loss of 20 percent of the net worth of the company no doubt would be much greater than those associated with payment of the premium. Once again, it is likely that the company would choose the option with the lower expected value. This might be explained by pointing out that the disutility associated with a very large loss is proportionately much greater than that associated with the premium.

The situation is different if the decision is to be repeated many times. For example, if a thousand letters were to be mailed and no letter had a significance other than the \$100 value, the \$500 cost of registration is much greater than the expected loss (\$20) and the principle of maximization of expected value would suggest that the letters not be registered.

Protagonists of the criterion of maximum expected value counter the arguments against it by making the following points:

1/ The argument with regard to the inapplicability of the criterion in a single resolution of a decision problem loses its force if the payoff considered is the *utility* of the decision maker for the outcome rather than monetary value. In the coin tossing example (they point out), if the disutility for loss of the decision maker is very great it will make the *expected utility* of playing the game negative. Application of the criterion of maximum expected utility would then lead the decision maker to the option of refusing to play. To illustrate this, suppose that the utility of the decision maker for $200 gain is +200 units and the disutility for a $100 loss is −1,000 units. The expected value of the game is then:

$$\tfrac{1}{2} \times 200 + \tfrac{1}{2} \, (-1,000) = -400 \text{ units}$$

and the option of not playing has the maximum expected utility.

2/ In practical decision situations, decision makers often consciously or unconsciously make use of *personal* or *subjective* probability estimates. These are based on their personal experience and judgment and sometimes on considerations of skill and luck. The factors that should be considered under conditions of risk, therefore, are not only the decision maker's utility for options, but, in addition, his subjective probability estimates. This leads us to a decision criterion under risk of maximization of *subjective expected utility.*

Before proceeding further with this argument it is necessary to consider the nature of subjective probability.

Subjective Probability

Subjective probability may be discussed in comparison with *objective* probability, which is often linked with the concept of frequency of occurrence. An adherent to the "frequency school" of probability theory would say that the objective probability of an event is based on the percentage of occurrences of that event in an infinite series of trials. Suppose that a fair coin is tossed a very large number of times and that the number of heads in the trials is equal to the number of tails. The objective probability of a head in any toss with that coin is then said to be ½, based on the frequency of occurrence in the trials.

By contrast, subjective probability is seen as a degree of belief about an event.[4] Such probability values are generally different for different persons and are based on an individual's knowledge, beliefs and opinions about the event. Subjective probabilities depend on the amount of information that an individual has about the event in question. Therefore, probabilities can be expected to change as more information is obtained. For example, if one is in the habit of catching the 5:40 P.M. plane from a certain city, it is possible to express a subjective probability that the plane will be

---

[4]L.J. Savage, *The Foundations of Statistics* (New York: John Wiley & Sons, 1954).

on time tomorrow. This can be called a *prior* probability, inasmuch that it is arrived at on the basis of prior information. Suppose now that information is received that there is likelihood of fog. Depending on an individual's evaluation of that information and its relation to prior information, a new probability estimate can be made (called the *posterior* probability).

Information obtained during processes of management and decision making is almost always imperfect. Life would be simpler if somehow one alone could buy a copy of next week's newspaper. Without such an opportunity, a great part of managerial judgment consists of weighing what information is available and arriving (implicitly or explicitly) at subjective probabilities of future events.

A number of empirical studies have been undertaken in recent years to investigate the nature of subjective probability estimates in situations where the "true" probability is known, such as in the toss of a coin.[5] The general conclusion of these studies is that individuals are not consistent in their formulation of subjective probabilities. For example, mathematical probability theory requires that the sum of the probabilities of members of a set of mutually exclusive and exhaustive events (such as a plane early, late or on time) must be equal to 1. Experiments have shown that this is not always so when individuals estimate subjective probabilities. Again, in experiments with groups of individuals, the average subjective probabilities for the lower probability events have been shown to be larger than the "objective" probabilities, whereas the average subjective probabilities for the higher probability events are smaller than the corresponding "objective" probabilities.

Two other considerations—skill and luck—may affect subjective probabilities. Each of us has a perception of skill and luck based on our own experiences and observation of those of others. These are highly subjective and may not be based on all the available information. We may refer to a successful man as being lucky in order to explain the success that might have been ours under a different set of circumstances. A sequence of successes in what is taken to be a game of chance may be the result of a systematic effect that has not been appreciated in the analysis of

[5]Wayne Lee, *Decision Theory*, pp. 56–65.

the game. The application of skill may in fact change the situation to the advantage of one of those involved.

All these factors may be present in a decision situation confronting a manager. Considerable care must be taken, therefore, in the conversion of opinions to subjective probabilities. If this can be done with confidence it provides a means by which decision situations, which previously could be treated only under the condition defined as uncertainty, can be treated more quantitatively under risk.

Subjective Expected Utility (SEU)

Once subjective probabilities enter into a decision problem under conditions of risk, the subjective expected utility can be calculated for each of the available options. For example, in the plant expansion problem shown in Table 3-3, the column headed "expected value" would be replaced by one headed "subjective expected utility" when (a) the payoffs corresponding to an option and a state of the market had been replaced by a quantitative expression of utility to the decision maker or his organization and (b) when the probabilities of occurrence of each state of the market were the subjective estimates of the decision maker. The quantitative factors involved in the decision, therefore, are particular to the individual decision maker in two senses.

For the payoff matrix shown in Table 3-3 and assuming for the moment that the payoffs shown are in terms of utilities to the decision maker, the following table can now be taken to show the subjective expected utilities for the three options:

Table 3-4   Subjective Expected Utility in the Plant Expansion Problem

	Future States of the Market			Subjective
Subjective Probability	Low $\frac{1}{4}$	Medium $\frac{1}{4}$	High $\frac{1}{2}$	Expected Utility (SEU)
Manager's Options				
1. Stay with present plan	0	0	0	0
2. Build small extension	50	300	200	187.5
3. Build large extension	−500	100	600	200

The option to be chosen using the criterion of maximum SEU would be to build a large extension. If in coming to that decision (the argument goes) there is any thought of the dire effects of a low state of the market, then the disutility of this event has not been set low enough. If the utilities in the payoff matrix truly reflect the manager's utilities, then such fears would be automatically taken care of by the utility values and the maximization of SEU is the only logical criterion. A similar argument applies to the case where it is "felt" that the market is going to be low. Such feelings should be reflected entirely in the subjective probabilities.

The Acceptability of the Expected Value Criterion

The question remains as to whether the maximization of subjective expected utility is the appropriate decision criterion under conditions of risk. Leaving aside, for the moment, consideration of whether subjective expected utilities can be determined in practical situation, many authorities hold that maximization of SEU is the *only* criterion that can be defended in these circumstances.[6-9] Their arguments, quoted earlier, are that if the maximization of SEU appears to be the wrong decision criterion, then either (a) the preferences of the decision maker have been incorrectly represented by the utilities in the payoff matrix; and/or (b) the subjective probabilities used in the analysis are not in accordance with the opinions of the decision maker.

These arguments may not convince a busy manager engaged in the day-to-day direction of his office. Faced with an important decision situation he is unlikely to agree to an assessment of his utilities using the standard gamble technique unless ample time is available for the decision. Even if he does take part in such an analysis he is unlikely to place absolute reliance on it and discard completely the qualitative preferences that he feels. Furthermore, he is unlikely to be consistent in his estimates of subjective probability. At best, then, the manager may allow the calculation of subjective expected utilities as one avenue of exploration of the problem. He will no doubt wish to retain his intuitive judgment and seek a solution based on that and consensus from a number of different approaches.

[6]Howard Raiffa, *Decision Analysis—Introductory Lectures on Choices Under Uncertainty* (Reading, Mass.: Addison-Wesley, 1968), pp. 86–89.

[7]Luce and Raiffa, *Games and Decisions*, pp. 19–37.

[8]Miller and Starr, *Structure of Human Decisions*, pp. 111–15.

[9]Arnold Kaufmann, *The Science of Decision Making* (New York: World University Library, McGraw-Hill, 1968), pp. 127–30.

The situation may be different with decisions that can be approached by a formal study and where easily quantified payoff parameters such as return on investment are concerned. Nevertheless, even in these circumstances it is probably wise to investigate a number of analytical approaches and criteria for resolution of the decision process.

An Interesting Historical Diversion

Daniel Bernoulli discussed a number of cases in which the principle of maximizing expected monetary value (emv) does not seem to be appropriate. The most famous of these is the St. Petersburg Paradox. This concerns a hypothetical game in which one player proposes to toss a "fair" coin as many times as necessary to get a head. When a toss results in a head he stops. He agrees, as part of the game, to give a second player $1 if the head appears on the first toss, $2 if this occurs at the second toss, $4 at the third and so on. This can be stated generally as an agreement to pay 2^{n-1} if a head appears at the nth toss. The point of the game is to ask the second player how much he is willing to pay to take part in the game.

The second player argues as follows. The probability of a head at the first toss of the fair coin is $\frac{1}{2}$. This probability holds for each toss of the coin. Assuming that the coin tossings are independent events, the chance of a head occurring at the *second toss* is $\frac{1}{2} \times \frac{1}{2} = \frac{1}{4}$. In general form, the chance of a head occurring at the nth toss is $(\frac{1}{2})^n$. The various states of nature can then be regarded as a head appearing at each of the tosses from the first to the nth, where n can be assumed to become as large as is necessary to obtain a head. The second player has two options: to play or not to play. The expected value of not playing is zero. The expected value of playing is the sum of the products of the payoff and the probability of occurrence for each state of nature from 1 to infinity. This can be written as:

$$\sum_{n=1}^{\infty} (\tfrac{1}{2})^n \times 2^{n-1} = \sum_{n=1}^{\infty} (\tfrac{1}{2})$$

The right-hand side of this expression is the sum of an infinite number of terms each equal to $\frac{1}{2}$, which is infinity. The paradox is, therefore, that the expected value of the game is infinite. If the second player made his decision on the basis of maximizing his expected value he would choose to play and he would be willing to pay any price for the privilege. However, to pay such a high price would clearly be a bad decision if there is only one play of the game.

In discussing this paradox, Bernoulli suggested that the criterion used should be maximization of the expected utility of money. He argued that the increase in utility linked with an increase in an amount of money should be inversely proportional to the amount of money. The utilities of the larger amounts of money payable when no head appears in the earlier losses are then proportionately much less. Bernoulli's proposal is the same thing as assuming that the utility function is logarithmic, with a shape as shown in Figure 2-1. Under these conditions, the expected utility for the second player approaches a finite value as the number of tosses increases and the amount of money that he should be willing to pay should be limited in similar fashion. This rescues us from the dilemma of an infinite expected value, but it does not seem to solve the paradox. Nor does it provide support for general adoption of the criterion of maximum expected value in resolution of decision problems under conditions of risk.

The introduction of subjective probability throws a new light on the St. Petersburg Paradox. Bernoulli's explanation goes part way in that it points out that the value of playing the game to the second player is finite if a utility function such as he proposed is used. A further factor involved may be this player's subjective estimates of the probabilities of no head occurring in each of the tosses. The experience and information available to most people would suggest that the chance of no head appearing until say, the sixth or eighth toss is so small as to be essentially zero. Despite the very large payoffs associated with these rare events, therefore, the average player may be expected to neglect them altogether. He would then base his offered payment for taking part in the game on his subjective expected utility, taking into account the payoffs and probabilities in the first few throws only.

Decision Criteria Under Conditions of Uncertainty

In the case of decisions under conditions of uncertainty, there is no certain outcome of the choice of a particular option. For each choice there is a number of possible outcomes that may range from very bad to very good. Furthermore, under these conditions it is assumed that no firm estimate is available of the probability of occurrence of any outcome. Under these circumstances, the choice of decision criterion depends on the attitude of the decision maker to the uncertainty about the outcome. Certain individuals may be averse to taking the risk of a bad outcome; others feel that things are going their way and that a good outcome is bound to happen. Choice of a decision criterion under such circumstances depends on human behavior in the face of uncertainty and can be discussed initially under the headings of pessimism and optimism.

The Criterion of Pessimism

The criterion of pessimism, developed by Abraham Wald,[10] involves investigation of the worst that can happen in the case of each option and then selection of the option for which the worst outcome is most advantageous in the view of the decision maker. Put another way, the decision maker determines the minimum payoff for each of the available options and then selects the option that provides the maximum of these minimum payoffs. For this reason, this criterion is called *maximin*. Note that if the decision maker is endeavoring to minimize some quantity (such as cost), he would, under this principle, minimize the maximum cost, which may be called *minimax*. Conceptually, maximin and minimax are the same thing.

Returning to the plant expansion problem of Table 3-3, let us suppose that the manager has no information on the probabilities of low, medium and high markets occurring. He may then express his problem in a payoff matrix as shown in Table 3-5, where the elements of the matrix are meant to represent the change from the present situation.

Table 3-5   The Plant Expansion Problem

	Future States of the Market		
	Low	Medium	High
Manager's Available Options			
1. Stay with present plant	0	0	0
2. Build small extension	50	300	200
3. Build large extension	−500	100	600

[10]Abraham Wald, "Statistical decision functions which minimize the maximum risk," *Annuals of Mathematics*, 46, 265–280, 1945.

The worst that can happen for each of the available options is shown in Table 3-6.

Table 3-6   Minimum Payoffs for the Plant Expansion Problem

	Minimum Payoffs
Manager's Available Options	
1. Stay with present plant	0
2. Build small extension	50
3. Build large extension	−500

The manager following the maximin criterion, therefore, would decide to build the small extension. Maximin can be seen to be a conservative or play-safe criterion, which guarantees the decision maker a payoff at least as large as the minimum payoff for the strategy chosen. It also protects him from bad outcomes. It may, however, prevent him from taking advantage of some of the better outcomes provided under favorable conditions under the other available options.

Minimax can be applied equally well to situations where there is no quantitative parameter in which the payoff can be expressed. This can be illustrated by the simple problem of whether to carry a raincoat when leaving the house early in the morning when there is a threat of rain later in the day. The following payoff matrix can be constructed for this problem:

Table 3-7   The Raincoat Problem

	Future States of the World	
Options	*Rain*	*No Rain*
1. Carry raincoat	Dry and satisfied at judgment	Dry, but have carried raincoat unnecessarily
2. Do not carry raincoat	Wet	Dry without having carried raincoat

In this case, the worst that can happen if the decision maker selects the first option is that he may have carried the raincoat unnecessarily, while under the second option the worst outcome is that he gets wet. Assuming that the decision maker has a greater preference for remaining dry than for getting wet, the minimax criterion would select the option of carrying the raincoat.

The Criterion of Optimism—and Variations

The opposite to a feeling of pessimism is the conviction that the world is going our way. Hurwicz has suggested that if a decision maker feels lucky or if he has a conviction that he can choose the right path, he should select the option that provides him with the maximum payoff.[11] This can be done by writing down the maximum payoff for each available option and choosing the option that provides the maximum of these maximum payoffs. Not unnaturally, this criterion has been called *maximax*. The maximax option in the plant expansion problem considered earlier is, of course, to build the large extension.

Hurwicz went further, to suggest the positions between the extremes of optimism and pessimism could be represented by a coefficient of optimism that takes the value 0 at the criterion of pessimism and 1 at that of optimism. This degree of precision in the quantification of human behavior does not seem to be merited in practice. Managers are not observed saying to themselves, "I feel 60 percent optimistic today." Nevertheless, its mention is useful, if only to point out that a range of behavior is possible between the extremes that lead to the maximin and maximax criteria for selection of options.

The Criterion of Regret

A further criterion for selection of an option is closely linked to the concept of opportunity costs well known to economists. Savage suggested that a new matrix be constructed showing a quantity that he called *regret*. This is defined as the difference in payoff between what the decision maker receives with any option and the maximum that he could receive for a particular future state of the world.[12] The regret, therefore, represents the loss that the decision maker suffers because he did not know the exact future state of the world.

[11]Leonid Hurwicz, "Optimality Criteria for Decision Making Under Ignorance," Cowles Commission Discussion Paper, Statistics No. 370, 1951; discussed in Luce and Raiffa, *Games and Decisions.*

[12]L.J. Savage, "The Theory of Statistical Decision," *Journal of the American Statistical Association* 46 (1951):55–67.

In the previous example of a plant expansion problem, the regret matrix is as follows:

Table 3-8   Plant Expansion Problem—Regret Matrix

	Future States of the Market		
Manager's Available Options	*Low*	*Medium*	*High*
1. Stay with present plant	50	300	600
2. Build small extension	0	0	400
3. Build large extension	550	200	0

Savage suggested also that the idea of minimax be combined with regret to form a criterion of *minimax regret*. Note that the term minimax is used here because we are seeking to minimize the maximum loss. In the particular example chosen, the minimax regret solution is once again to build the small extension, since the minimum maximum regret that would be experienced is 400 units.

Regret may be linked with opportunity costs, which, in economics, are considered to be the costs of not having chosen the best opportunity. Minimax regret is therefore a criterion providing for the minimizing of maximum opportunity cost.

Chernoff has raised three criticisms of the minimax regret criterion.[13] First, he says that it is not necessarily true that equal differences in two values of the payoff parameter represent equal amounts of regret at different levels of that parameter. This is related to the subject of utility considered in the previous chapter. Second, he states that in certain circumstances a small advantage in one state of nature may outweigh a much larger advantage in another state. It is undoubtedly true that this can happen. Third, he points out that the criterion may cause the decision maker to select a different option if one or more of the available options suddenly becomes unavailable.

Luce and Raiffa suggest a method of overcoming the third objection.[14] This is simply to make paired comparisons between options rather than to compare one option with all others when assessing regret. The option selected should then be that which is

[13]Herman Chernoff, "Rational Selection of Decision Functions," *Econometrica* 22 (1954):422–43.

[14]Luce and Raiffa, *Games and Decisions*, p. 287.

preferred or at least equally liked compared with every other option. Even this procedure is ambiguous in some circumstances, such as in the following payoff matrix.

Table 3-9   An Ambiguous Regret Situation

	States of Nature		
Manager's Options	N_1	N_2	N_3
O_1	10	5	1
O_2	0	10	4
O_3	5	2	10

Comparison of the options in pairs shows O_1 preferred to O_2 in terms of regret when only these two options are considered; O_2 similarly preferred to O_3 and O_3 preferred to O_1. For the whole matrix O_3 is the option selected by the minimax regret criterion.

The minimax regret criterion should therefore be applied with caution and with due investigation of anomalies that can arise.

The Laplace Criterion

One other criterion of choice between options is described in the literature. It is, however, not closely linked to human behavior in decision making and is of little practical importance. It is included here for completeness. The criterion is the Laplace criterion, which is based on the premise that, under conditions of uncertainty, when there is complete ignorance about the probability of occurrence of the future states of the world, it should be assumed that all such states are equally likely. The decision problem is then transformed from uncertainty into what has been defined as risk, with equal probabilities for each state of nature.

It is seldom (if ever) that a manager finds himself completely ignorant about the probability of future events. Even if he were, his first action would be to try to obtain some information that would enable him to make a judgment. This criterion is therefore of little interest in the study of managerial decision making.

Decision Criteria Under Conditions of Competition or Conflict

The choice of a decision criterion under conditions of competition or conflict is not a simple matter. In some circumstances, when the competition is between two parties only, a version of the minimax criterion is recommended. However, such circumstances arise very seldom in practical situations. The whole subject of decisions under conflict is given detailed treatment in Chapters 4 and 5 and the question of choice of criteria, therefore, is left until that stage in the discussion.

The Principle of Bounded Rationality

A somewhat different approach to the choice between options has been put forward by Herbert A. Simon and James G. March.[15,16] This is called the principle of "bounded rationality." The word rationality is used here by Simon and March in a somewhat different sense from that discussed in Chapter 1.

The central feature of the principle of bounded rationality is the contention that what Simon calls "administrative man" does not follow an exhaustive process of evaluation of all the options open to him. Instead, he proceeds only far enough to find a course of action that is satisfactory or good enough. This Simon calls "satisficing" and he describes it in contrast to the actions of "economic man," who selects the best option from among *all* those available to him. This is the process of optimization familiar to students of operations research and the use of mathematical models.

The distinction between satisficing and maximizing describes the difference between the two main approaches to the study of decision processes over the past thirty years. These approaches have been described as belonging to the "Neo-Rationalist School" and the "Classical Rationalist School" respectively.[17] The classical rationalist believes that any decision process can eventually be modeled and an optimum solution found. The neo-rationalist holds that some measure of individual input to decision making is necessary in any organization and that the zone of ambiguity of difference of view thus created is essential to the functioning of the organization. This subject is taken up again in Chapter 7 in the context of organizational decision making.

[15]Herbert A. Simon, *Administrative Behavior* (New York: Free Press, 1965), pp. xxiv–xxvii.

[16]James G. March and Herbert A. Simon, *Organizations* (New York: John Wiley & Sons, 1958).

[17]Catherine Grémion, "Towards a New Theory of Decision Making?" *International Studies of Management and Organization* (Summer 1972).

The Minimization of Uncertainty

Individual managers are influenced in their decision making behavior by the policies and practices of the organization in which they work. Cyert and March contend that organizations avoid uncertainty by avoiding situations in which future actions depend on uncertain future events.[18] They state also that their studies show that organizations emphasize future courses of action over which management is thought to have the greatest degree of control. This is similar to the activities of some executives, reported by Argyris, in marshaling human and financial resources to make their decisions come true once they have committed themselves to a course of action.[19]

It seems clear, therefore, that one further possible criterion for selection of a course of action is the minimization of uncertainty about the outcome of the decision process. The manager may choose the option that he feels gives him the best chance of achieving the forecast outcome, either because the uncertainty surrounding that option is least or because he feels that he has the best chance of achieving his forecast outcome. This is similar in some respects to the minimax criterion in that it ensures to the greatest extent possible that the manager will be regarded by his colleagues in the organization as reliable and unlikely to get the company into trouble. On the other hand, the criterion of minimization of uncertainty can result in the selection of courses of action that are much less "safe" than those chosen under minimax.

The reduction in uncertainty may be achieved through the actions of the decision maker in implementing the decision, rather than during the decision process itself. This is in line with a theory concerning an effect known as "cognitive dissonance," in which it is argued that if a person knows things that are not consistent with one another, he will, if properly motivated, try to make them more consistent.[20] On the basis of this theory, it can be

[18]Richard M. Cyert and James G. March, *A Behavioral Theory of the Firm* (Englewood Cliffs, N.J.: Prentice-Hall, 1963), p. 119.

[19]Chris Argyris, "Management Information Systems: The Challenge to Rationality and Emotionality," *Management Science* 17 (February, 1971):B279.

[20]Leon Festinger, "Cognitive Dissonance," *Scientific American* (October, 1972):93–102.

argued that a manager wishing to be or appear successful in implementing a decision will fashion his actions in such a way as to make the outcome successful. This is likely to occur whether or not he was in agreement with the resolution of the actual decision process. This subject is discussed also in the context of organizational decision making in Chapter 7.

Summary

Decision processes can be classified in a number of ways. One of the most common is with regard to the conditions surrounding the decision process. Four such conditions described often in the literature are: certainty, uncertainty, risk and competition or conflict.

The choice of criterion for selection between available options depends on the condition seen as prevailing. Under certainty, little difficulty arises if a single objective is involved and the option can be chosen that maximizes the degree of achievement of that objective. Under uncertainty, however, the choice depends on the attitude of the decision maker toward the outcomes or possibly on his appreciation of his organization's attitude toward them.

If probabilities can be assigned to the occurrence of future states of nature, decisions that could previously be treated only under uncertainty can be treated under a condition called risk. A criterion of choice involving maximization of expected value has been proposed by many under these conditions.

Probabilities associated with future states of the world in such treatments may be subjective probabilities derived by the decision maker as a result of his experience, judgment and beliefs. A quantity called the subjective expected utility can be derived for each available option, which is in two senses particular to the individual decision maker.

There is some doubt whether maximization of expected value or subjective expected utility is a valid criterion in practical decision making. Arguments in favor of this contend that if preferences and best estimates are incorporated into the expected value or utility then no other criterion is defensible. In real situations, however, conversion of a decision situation from uncertainty to risk and the use of a criterion of maximum expected values are probably avenues of analysis that a manager may allow, but on which he would not place sole reliance.

A feature of the principle of bounded rationality is the contention that a manager does not follow an exhaustive process of evaluation of all the options open to him. Instead, it is held that he proceeds far enough to find a course of action that is satisfactory under the prevailing conditions. Some authorities contend that managers seek to minimize uncertainty about the outcome of their decision processes. Once the decision is taken, managers may tend to implement the necessary actions in such a way to bring about a successful outcome, whether or not they agreed with the original decision.

Discussion Topics

1/ Do you think decisions under certainty occur very often in the day-to-day work of your organization? Explain your answer.

2/ Do situations arise of complete uncertainty, where it is not possible to put estimates of probability on the possible occurrence of future events? Can you give examples?

3/ Under what conditions would you delay a decision under uncertainty? What might be the advantages and disadvantages of such a delay?

4/ Where in your operation would you expect to find decisions being taken using (a) the minimax criterion (explicitly or implicitly) and (b) the maximax criterion?

5/ Would you find Savage's criterion of minimax regret useful? What steps would you take to ensure that the objections raised by Chernoff to this criterion do not affect your decision making?

6/ Would you as a manager ever consider transferring a problem involving uncertainty to the condition we have described as risk? Under what conditions would you do this?

7/ Can you identify decision situations in your organization where the decision maker often selects the option giving the lower expected value?

8/ In assigning subjective probabilities to future events or states of the world, would you be influenced by your ideas of luck or your estimate of the skill of yourself or others?

9/ What are the arguments for and against the use of maximization of subjective expected utility as a decision criterion?

10/ Do you believe that managers "satisfice"? If so, what behavioral considerations do you think are behind this phenomenon?

11/ Is the minimization of uncertainty a real consideration in managerial decision making? What practical steps do managers take to minimize uncertainty? Is there any relation between success in management and successful minimization of uncertainty?

12/ You are in downtown Montreal and it is 4 P.M. You wish to go to downtown Toronto. The train takes five hours for the trip according to the schedule and is frequently up to an hour late. The complete trip by air (downtown to downtown) takes three hours. The only train leaves at 5 P.M. The next flight leaves at 5 P.M. and planes are scheduled at hourly intervals thereafter. The weatherman has mentioned a probability of fog at Montreal airport in the period 5 P.M. on. Analyze your decision problem of whether to take the train or plane, making a range of assumptions about the weather and your plans in Toronto. (Incidentally, is your car at the airport?)

13/ The plant in your factory is known to be deteriorating. Your choice is between ad hoc maintenance and re-equipping. The cost of ad hoc maintenance would be $50,000 and of re-equipping $300,000. A factory holiday is approaching during which you could re-equip: another such opportunity would not occur for one year. If the ad hoc maintenance fails and re-equipping has to be done outside the holiday period, the loss of production would be valued at $7,000,000. You can make a subjective assessment of the probability of this occurring. Analyze your problem and suggest what strategy would be appropriate under a range of conditions.

14/ I offer you a choice between two games:

(a) We will toss a fair coin ten times for a 50¢ stake on each toss. The expected utility to each of us is zero.

(b) I will sell you ten tickets at 50¢ each in a lottery. There are 125,000 tickets and the single prize is $50,000. I suspect you would choose (b). If so, why and if not, why not? Do you think others would reason as you do?

4

Decisions Involving Well-defined Quantitative Parameters

Introduction

Decision processes involving well-defined quantitative parameters are usually the easiest to understand and to analyze. Not unnaturally, they have attracted the greatest amount of attention from analysts and from those engaged in the development of analytical procedures. Much of the progress that has been made in recent years in management science and in operations research has been in the application of quantitative methods to operational and administrative problems.

The most straightforward of these methods are those applicable to decision situations under conditions of certainty with a single objective. These will be treated first in this chapter. The discussion then moves to decisions under certainty with more than one objective. Following that, methods that can be used under different conditions of uncertainty and risk will be described. The chapter ends with a short treatment of quantitative approaches to conflict situations.

Routine Administrative and Operational Decisions

Many of the routine administrative and operational tasks in an organization are examples of simple decisions under conditions of certainty with well-defined quantitative parameters. The preparation of the payroll or of company invoices are examples of such tasks. Each of these tasks consists of a sequence of simple decisions linked together into a procedure. Each step in the sequence is agreed upon by the individuals responsible prior to resolution of any particular decision of the type considered and this agreement is written into a specification. The process is then regarded as completely specified.

Such completely specified systems are usually decision processes at the lower levels of managerial involvement. They normally relate to administrative and operational tasks that have become routine in the organization. In many cases the writing of the specifications is done by staff at the lower levels. Once these have been agreed the process is often delegated to a computer. Senior managers probably use only summary information from the process and may have contact with it only if something major goes wrong.

These routine administrative and operational tasks are nonetheless important decision processes. The responsibility of managers in these processes is not in the resolution of the decision on each occasion. It lies in the monitoring of the results of repeated resolutions and the maintenance of the specifications of the process as appropriate to changing conditions. The manager is thus freed from the onus of repetitive decision making and can concentrate much of his attention on other decision problems that have not yet been completely specified.

Completely Specified Decisions Based on Mathematical Models

Many of the completely or partially specified decision processes in modern organizations include mathematical models as part of the specification. These models have been developed in recent years to describe processes that occur commonly in administration and in operations. The most commonly applied of these techniques is called *linear programming*.

Linear Programming

Linear programming is concerned with the problem of allocation of resources in a process that results in the production of goods or of a service. Typical examples of the application of this analytical method are:

FERTILIZER PRODUCTION

A factory producing fertilizers uses as ingredients a number of different types of ore taken from a pit some miles away. On any one day, up to three different types of fertilizer can be produced, although not more than 50 percent of the factory capacity can be used on any one day to produce any one type of fertilizer and not more than an additional 30 percent for any other. The three types of fertilizers are in different demand and are sold at different prices. The factory manager wishes to know what types of ore should be transported to his factory on any one day so that his production can meet demand and result in the most profitable operation.

SCHEDULING OF A TELEVISION STATION

A television station is planning its summer schedule. It is attempting to arrive at a balanced program schedule that will satisfy the constraints imposed by the company's objectives and available resources, while at the same time providing a certain mix of program types. The problem at hand refers to the Sunday evening schedule in which five hours are to be filled each week for twenty weeks. It has been decided that station policy requires that:

1/ there shall be not less than 35 percent and not more than 45 percent of information programming, and that the balance of time shall be filled with entertainment programming;

2/ a minimum of 50 percent of the entertainment programs shall be a new material (i.e., no more than 50 percent repeats). Also a minimum of 75 percent of the information programs must be new material;

3/ overall, at least 55 percent of the programs must be produced locally, with not less than 25 percent in information programs and 25 percent in entertainment.

The foregoing requirements can be averaged over the total period; they need not be satisfied each week. The different types of programs have different costs and may be expected to bring different amounts of revenue. The station manager wishes to find a program mix that satisfies the above content requirements and minimizes net program costs.

FEEDING OF LIVESTOCK

Livestock can be fed a number of diets each consisting of a mix of ingredients. Each ingredient provides certain nutritional needs at a certain cost. Over a period of time, specified nutritional standards must be met and it is desirable to know how these standards can be maintained at minimum cost.

These situations have the following characteristics in common:

– a product or a service is being produced to meet a demand;
– the product or service results from a mix of ingredients or resources;
– the ingredients and resources have a cost attached to them;
– there are certain conditions or constraints that affect the way in which the product can be produced;
– there is a desire to optimize a pay-off or "objective function," which usually concerns cost or profit.

The method of linear programming provides a means of arriving at an optimum solution to such problems. Strictly speaking, however, it is applicable only if two important conditions are met. Those are referred to as the conditions of *divisibility* and *additivity*.

The condition of *divisibility* requires that the amount of the product or service produced be proportional to the amounts of each input resource. Further, the amount of payoff (say, profit) must be strictly proportional to the amount of the product or service produced. This implies that each activity (for example, the production of a particular type of fertilizer) must be capable of proportional expansion or reduction and that the levels of activity and use of resources must be capable of assuming fractional values as well as whole numbers. The condition of *additivity* requires the total amount of each input resource used be equal to the sum of the amounts used in each individual activity and that the total payoff be equal to the sum of the individual payoffs for each of the activities. These conditions preclude the possibility of economies of scale.

These are serious restrictions in real-life situations. However, situations do occur in which the conditions can be assumed to be met. Furthermore, there may be situations where the deviations from the required conditions are judged to be sufficiently small to justify application of the method. However, this is an area of danger and temptation. The desire to apply an available and easily manipulated mathematical model should never override a judgment regarding its applicability to the situation being studied.

If the necessary conditions can be met the linear programming method provides a program (or plan) for the use of resources in production of a product or a service. For example,[1] suppose that a company has the option of using one or more of four types of process to manufacture a product from certain materials. It wishes to know which is the best process or combination of the processes to use. This problem can be described in the following way:

Suppose that:

a/ a company has the option of using one or more of four types of production process to manufacture a product;

b/ each unit of production by the four processes yields a net profit of 4, 5, 9 and 11 dollars respectively;

c/ the resources from which the product is made consist of

---

[1]Harvey Wagner, *Principles of Operations Research* (Englewood Cliffs, N.J.: Prentice-Hall, 1969), chaps. 2, 3, 4 and 5.

three materials X, Y and Z of which there are 15, 120 and 100 units respectively available;

d/ the four processes require different amounts of each of the three materials as shown in Table 4-1.

Table 4-1   Units of Materials Required

	Process 1	Process 2	Process 3	Process 4
Material X	1	1	1	1
Material Y	7	5	3	2
Material Z	3	5	10	15

The objective is to maximize profit. If we let x_1, x_2, x_3 and x_4 be the number of units of product made in each of the processes, then multiply these numbers by the unit net profits in (b) above, the total profit can be written as:

$$4x_1 + 5x_2 + 9x_3 + 11x_4$$

We wish to maximize this expression.
The constraints are the amounts of materials available. From (c) and (d) above, these constraints may be written as:

Material X	$1x_1 + 1x_2 + 1x_3 + 1x_4 \leq 15$
Material Y	$7x_1 + 5x_2 + 3x_3 + 2x_4 \leq 120$
Material Z	$3x_1 + 5x_2 + 10x_3 + 15x_4 \leq 100$

The fact that it is not possible to produce negative amounts of product requires that a solution be found for which x_1, x_2, x_3 and x_4 are all non-negative.

The solution procedure determines a set of values of x_1, x_2, x_3 and x_4 that define levels of production in each of the four processes. These levels, taken together, are, first, *feasible* (i.e., possible within the constraints represented by the available amounts of material) and second, *optimal* in the sense of maximizing profit. The optimum feasible solution in this example can be shown to be:[2]

[2]Wagner, *Principles of Operations Research*, Chaps. 2, 3, 4 and 5.

Number of units produced in each process

Process 1	$x_1 = 50/7$
Process 2	$x_2 = 0$
Process 3	$x_3 = 55/7$
Process 4	$x_4 = 0$

Amount of available resources unused
in optimal feasible solution

Material X	all used
Material Y	325/7 units unused
Material Z	all used

Profit obtained from optimal feasible solution

Value of the objective function $4x_1 + 5x_2 + 9x_3 + 11x_4$
at the optimal feasible solution = 695/7

The technique by which the solution is obtained has been described in a large number of texts. The reader is referred to those by Harvey Wagner,[3] Hillier and Lieberman,[4] and Donald J. Clough[5] for further details.

Variations of the Linear Programming Model

Variations of the linear programming model can be applied to a number of problems involving networks;[6] for example:

- the problem of distributing supplies from a number of sources (such as factories) to a number of other points (such as warehouses or retail outlets). Each source is assumed to have a certain supply and each receiving point a certain demand. The objective is to minimize the cost of distribution. This problem is usually referred to as the *transportation problem.*

- the problem of assigning a given number of agents, one each to the same number of tasks, when the cost of assigning a particular agent to a particular task may be different from

[3]Wagner, *Principles of Operations Research*, Chaps. 2, 3, 4 and 5.

[4]F.S. Hillier and G.J. Lieberman, *Introduction to Operations Research* (San Francisco: Holden-Day, 1967), pp. 127–207.

[5]Donald J. Clough, *Concepts in Management Science* (Englewood Cliffs, N.J.: Prentice-Hall, 1963), pp. 324–71.

[6]Wagner, *Principles of Operations Research*, chap. 6.

that of any other combination. It is required to assign one agent to each task in such a way as to minimize total cost. This has application to such problems as assignment of pilots and crews to airline flights.

– the problem of finding the shortest (or cheapest) route between two points on a network in which the length (or cost) of travel between any two points is known. This problem arises in the scheduling of complex projects. It occurs also in situations such as where maximum flow is required in a network of pipelines.

All the above problems can be approached by the use of variations of the standard linear programming technique, provided the required conditions are met. One of the most important conditions is that divisibility be possible in terms of the variables involved in the formulation of the problem.

Another development in mathematical programming allows situations to be studied where the variables can take only integer values. This development is known as *integer programming*. It can be applied to situations in which the amounts of resources or facilities can be measured only in complete units, such as airplane loads or tanker car capacities. The integer programming method restricts such variables to nonfractional values.

A second significant branch of mathematical programming covers situations in which economies of scale apply or in which there are nonproportional variations in the values of parameters involved in production processes. In such cases the assumption of additivity cannot be made and new techniques must be devised to handle the problem of finding the optimum solution. These techniques are generally known as *non-linear programming*. Both this and integer programming are well covered in the literature.[7]

Dynamic Programming

All the above models are primarily concerned with the solution of a problem occurring at one point in time and, therefore, may be regarded as static in nature. A further class of models deals with a sequence of decision processes. These models fall under the title

---

[7]Wagner, *Principles of Operations Research*, chaps. 13, 14, and 15.

of *dynamic programming*. One of the most important applications of dynamic programming is to the problems of inventory replenishment and the scheduling of production processes to keep pace with demands for the products. This demand may vary from one time period to another. Since there may be economies in batch rather than continuous production, it is often more economical to produce more than is needed immediately in any one production run. However, this results in a build-up of inventory and of costs associated with financing the inventory, storage, insurance and so forth. The objective is to plan the production in such a way that demand is met at all times, but total cost is minimized.

There are many variations on this situation covered by the method of dynamic programming.[8,9] The manner of solution involves a step-by-step process of consideration of alternatives in each of the time periods under review. For each such time period, the decision situation is defined in terms of a set of "state variables." These variables (or parameters) are chosen to represent the complete decision problem, but they may take different values in each of the time periods under study. A decision in a time period is then viewed as an opportunity to change the values of these state variables. For example, a decision to produce a batch of product at any time would change the values of the variables referring to the inventory, unsatisfied demand and cost.

Each change of state within a given time period brings a payoff, which can be positive or negative. The payoff in any time period depends only on the beginning and ending values of the state variables and the overall payoff therefore may be obtained by finding the sum of the payoffs in each of the periods. The solution procedure consists of a method of maximizing the total payoff for given initial values of the state variables and a fixed number of time periods. The number of time periods can, of course, be made as large as desired.

The Application of Mathematical Models

The various versions of mathematical programming just discussed provide models that are applicable primarily to the plan-

[8]R. Peterson and E.A. Silver, *Decision Systems for Inventory Management and Production Planning* (New York: John Wiley & Sons, 1975).

[9]Ronald A. Howard, "Dynamic Programming," *Management Science* 12 (January, 1966).

ning and direction of operations. The success that has been achieved in their application is evident from the number of decision processes that were considered to be complex and not well understood many years ago, but that are now treated as routine. Decisions that were once made by specialists after considerable analytical work are now treated by standard techniques and delegated to less highly trained personnel. It is not unusual today to find a technician monitoring a computer giving the same output that a very experienced manager provided a few years ago. It is not that the computer routine necessarily gives a better answer. In many cases it is less flexible and more likely to become confused if an unusual situation occurs. Good specification of the process allows for this and provides for human intervention when necessary. However, the burden of repetitive resolution of routine decision problems is transferred from the manager, thus freeing him for more productive tasks.

Decisions Under Certainty with Multiple Objectives

The mathematical models considered in the previous section have a number of properties in common that may restrict their use in many practical decision situations. One of the most important of these is that the models are applicable only to situations in which a well-defined, quantitative parameter exists, measuring progress toward fulfillment of a *single* objective.

Many decision situations are such that the decision maker must resolve his problem against a background of *multiple* objectives. If one objective of the multiple set can be assigned overriding priority in the circumstances surrounding the decision at hand the problem can be treated as if only a single objective existed. If that is not possible, consideration must be given to two or more objectives, which may be in conflict, one with another.

As an initial step toward a treatment of the multiple objective problem, let us assume that the decision maker can assign priorities to the objectives in the circumstances surrounding the decision at hand. Let us assume also, at first, that progress toward fulfillment of each of the objectives can be measured in terms of the same quantitative parameter. If a set of weighting factors $(k_1 \ldots k_n)$ can be derived from the priorities assigned to the individual objectives and if $(u_1 \ldots u_n)$ represents the utility for the outcome of an option relative to the objectives, then a composite utility for the outcome $U = k_1u_1 + . . . + k_nu_n$ can be derived, as mentioned previously in Chapter 3. The problem in this case would be to determine the option with the maximum value of U.[10] However, this approach may not be practicable in a large number of situations facing managers today, in which quantitative weighting factors and utilities are not readily available.

Suppose, as a second approach, that progress toward fulfillment of each of the objectives can be measured in terms of a quantitative parameter, but not necessarily the same quantitative parameter for each objective. Suppose, also, that the levels of achievement required for each of the objectives of the multiple set can be stipulated for the time period under review. Further, let us assume that priorities can be set on the achievement of those goals as between the various objectives.

Sang M. Lee has proposed an approach to this problem based on the method of *goal programming* devised by Charnes and Cooper.[11,12] Goal programming is an extension of linear programming. Instead of direct maximization or minimization of an objective function, goal programming provides a method of minimization of the sum of the deviations between each goal and what can be achieved toward fulfillment of each goal, within the restrictions set by the constraints appropriate to the decision problem. The procedure suggested by Lee consists of minimization of these deviations taking into account the priorities assigned to the objectives to which they relate. He provides the following example of its application,[13] reproduced here with his permission:

American Electronics Inc. produces color television sets. The company has two production lines. The production rate for line 1 is two sets per hour and for line 2 it is 1.5 sets per hour. The regular production capacity is 40 hours a week for both lines.

[10]Samuel Eilon, "What is a Decision," *Management Science* 16 (December, 1969), B172–89.

[11]Sang M. Lee, "Goal Programming for Decision Analysis of Multiple Objectives," *Sloan Management Review* (Winter, 1972), 11–24.

[12]A. Charnes and W. Cooper, *Management Models and Industrial Applications of Linear Programming* (New York: John Wiley & Sons, 1961).

[13]Lee, "Goal Programming."

The gross profit from an average television set is $100. The president of the firm has the following goals for the next week shown in descending order of priority:

A. Meet the production goal of 180 sets for the week. This can be expressed: $2x_1 + 1.5x_2 + d_1^- - d_1^+ = 180$
where:

x_1 is operation hours of line 1
x_2 is operation hours of line 2
d_1^- is underachievement of production goal
d_1^+ is production in excess of 180 sets

B. Limit the overtime operation of line 1 to five hours. The regular operation hours can be expressed as:

$$x_1 + d_2^- - d_2^+ = 40$$
$$x_2 + d_3^- - d_3^+ = 40$$
where:

d_2^- is underutilization of regular operation hours line 1
d_2^+ is overtime operation in line 1
d_3^- is underutilization of regular operation hours line 2
d_3^+ is overtime operation in line 2.

Thus, the limitation of overtime operation of line 1 to five hours will be: $d_2^+ + d_{21}^- - d_{21}^+ = 5$
where:

d_{21}^- is deviation between five hours of overtime and actual overtime
d_{21}^+ is overtime operation of line 1 beyond five hours.

C. Avoid the underutilization of regular working hours for both lines. Differential weights should be assigned according to the production rate of each line.

D. Limit the sum of overtime operation for both teams. Again, differential weights should be assigned according to the relative cost of an overtime hour. It is assumed that the cost of operation is identical for the two production lines.

Before the complete model is formulated, there are a few points to consider. First, the third goal implies that the company has a policy of no involuntary layoffs. Since the productivity of line 1 is two sets per hour, whereas it is only 1.5 for line 2, the president wishes to avoid the underutilization of regular working hours of line 1 a great deal more than line 2. The ratio will be two for d_2^- and 1.5 for d_3^-, or to assign integers, four to d_2^- and three to d_3^-. Second, the criterion to use for the differential weights in the fourth goal is the relative cost of overtime. The production rates ratio for the lines is two to 1.5. Therefore, the relative cost resulting from an hour of overtime for line 2 is greater than that from line 1. The relative cost of overtime ratio for the two lines will be three to four.

Now, the goal programming model can be formulated as:

$$\text{Min. } Z = P_1 d_1^- + P_2 d_{21}^+ + 4P_3 d_2^- + 3P_3 d_3^- + 4P_4 d_3^+ + 3P_4 d_2^+$$

$$
\begin{aligned}
\text{subject to} \quad & 2x_1 + 1.5x_2 + d_1^- - d_1^+ && = 180 \\
& x_1 + d_2^- - d_2^+ && = 40 \\
& x_2 + d_3^- - d_3^! && = 40 \\
& d_{21}^- + d_2^+ - d_{21}^+ && = 5 \\
& x_1, x_2, d_1^-, d_2^-, d_3^-, d_{21}^-, d_1^+, d_2^+, d_3^+, d_{21}^+ && \geqslant 0
\end{aligned}
$$

Lee gives a detailed method of solution of the problem,[14] and provides an optimum degree of achievement for the goals in the order of priority specified. This optimum represents the minimum total deviation from the goals set. It does *not* imply any relationship between the goals other than the stated order of priority. In particular it does *not* necessarily represent a minimum cost or maximum profit solution. In this respect, note that the objective function contains deviations expressed in different units (such as numbers of sets and hours) rather than all in the same unit.

Lee's method has considerable application to decision problems involving multiple objectives but it also has many implicit limitations. First, the method of solution requires the same assumptions of linearity necessary to the linear programming technique. Second, the approach requires consistent ordering of priorities between members of a multiple objective set. Third, it is necessary that progress toward each of the goals to be fulfilled be expressed in terms of a well-defined quantitative parameter.

[14]Lee, "Goal Programming."

Nevertheless, the technique provides a method of tackling a problem for which there is no other simple quantitative approach.

A First Introduction of Uncertainty— Sensitivity Analysis

The models just described are known as *deterministic* because it is assumed that the values of the parameters involved are known exactly. A first step in the introduction of uncertainty into these models is known as *sensitivity analysis*.[15,16] In this type of analysis the decision maker investigates the effect of deviations from the values assigned to parameters on his solution of the deterministic model. In the simplest cases this is done one parameter at a time. For example, in the linear programming problem discussed earlier in this chapter it is possible to investigate the effect on the continued feasibility and optimality of a solution of variations in (a) the profit contributed by a unit of production from any one of the four processes; (b) the curtailing of (or addition to) the availability of any one of the input materials; and (c) the addition of a new production process. In this example, it is possible to calculate that if the profit contributed by a unit produced by process 2 is increased by more than $3/7$ the solution reached originally would not longer be optimal. That is to say that a different mix of products would yield more profit if the unit contribution of Process 2 were greater than $5^3/7$. Similarly, it can be shown that the original solution would not remain optimal if the contribution to profit of a unit from Process 4 were greater than $12^4/7$.

By a similar type of analysis, it can be deduced that the optimal solution obtained originally ceases to be feasible if the amount of material Y available is less than $73^4/7$ units. Furthermore, if a new production process becomes available with unit profit contribution greater than 14 units a new feasible optimal solution can be obtained.

This type of analysis, therefore, provides useful information about the sensitivity of a solution to variations in important parameters. It is a most desirable check on any decision solution

[15]Wagner, *Principles of Operations Research*, pp. 129–43.
[16]Hillier and Lieberman, *Introduction to Operations Research*, pp. 163–66 and 490–504.

reached by use of a deterministic model, where uncertainty exists in respect to one parameter only. If two parameters are subject to uncertainty, the analysis must involve investigation of the effect of paired, simultaneous deviations from the original values of the parameters. This introduces considerable complexity into the calculations. In cases of simultaneous uncertainty about the values of many parameters, other methods of investigating the sensitivity of the deterministic solution to these uncertainties must be sought.

David Hertz has shown the possible dangers of the use of a deterministic model when the many parameters involved are subject to uncertainty.[17] He describes a capital investment decision problem concerned with the extension of a processing plant. Management has decided to use nine key input factors relating to the fixed and operating costs and has agreed on "best estimates" (or expected values) of these factors. A deterministic model using these expected values gave an expected return on investment of 25.2 percent. Management personnel were then asked to estimate the likely range of variation of each of the nine factors and probability distributions were derived for each of the factors based on this information. By studying the return on investment obtained from each of a very large number of combinations of values of the nine factors drawn from these probability distributions (using a technique known as *simulation* that will be described later in this chapter) a distribution of values of return on investment was obtained.

In Hertz's example, the expected value of return on investment obtained using the probabilistic information on the input factors was only 14.6 percent, compared with 25.2 percent in the deterministic model. Furthermore, the probability that the level of return of 25 percent would be obtained or exceeded was calculated to be only 12.6 percent. This is a striking illustration of the mathematical theorem that the expected value of a function of a number of variables cannot be assumed to be equal to the same function of the expected values.

Examples such as this do (and should) cause great uneasiness to those using deterministic models. It may cause those involved

---

[17]David B. Hertz, "Risk Analysis in Capital Investment," *Harvard Business Review* (January–February, 1964).

to bias their estimates of parameters in such a way as to give overemphasis to the less favorable outcomes. An extreme example of this tendency is encountered when a manager insists on making a decision on the basis of the least favorable estimate of the outcome. He feels that by taking this approach, he can be confident of choosing an option that has a very high probability of being successful. This may be true. However, the approach is extremely conservative, being based on a combination of values of parameters that has a very small probability of occurring. A greater acceptance of risk may lead to a much higher probability of a favorable outcome.

Models Involving Parameters Represented by Probability Distributions

One method of taking account of uncertainty in the parameters affecting a decision situation is in the construction of a *probabilistic* (or *stochastic*) model. In such models each parameter is represented not by a single value as in the deterministic case, but by a probability distribution representing all values that the parameter may take and their probabilities of occurrence. The solution procedures for such models take into account all possible combinations of values of the parameters involved by means of analytical manipulation of the probability distributions.[18] These combinations may be thought of as an infinite set of options on a continuous scale, as compared to the discrete sets of options considered earlier in the text. Such models, however, are inherently more complex and may be more difficult to apply than the straightforward deterministic versions. For example, it is quite rare that a simple modification of the deterministic linear programming model can be found to apply to a problem involving uncertainty. On the other hand, probabilistic models in dynamic programming are not significantly more difficult to solve than their deterministic counterparts.[19] In many cases in which such models are applied, however, the amount of computation required to produce an acceptable solution may be very great.

The output of a probabilistic model is in the form of a distribu-

---

[18] Wagner, *Principles of Operations Research*, pp. 639–835.

[19] Peterson and Silver, *Decision Systems*.

tion function of the payoff parameter, as illustrated in Figure 4-1. The distribution function indicates a range of possible values of the payoff parameter and the probability of each occurring. The expected value can be calculated from this information. In many cases, of course, the distribution function may not be as symmetric as that shown in Figure 4-1.

The application of a probabilistic model can be regarded as analogous to the solution of a decision problem under conditions of risk. Under these circumstances the argument can be made, as in the previous chapter, that the only criterion for selection between options is the maximization or minimization of expected value. This would imply that the only significance of the distribution of payoff parameter is in its contribution to the expected value and that the spread of the curve is of no importance. A manager might be faced, however, with a situation such as is illustrated in Figure 4-2. In this case, the narrower curve offers a greater certainty coupled with a lower expected value, the broader one less certainty of outcome but a higher expected value. The same argument may be advanced here as previously. If the decision maker is greatly concerned about the possibility of low values of the payoff parameter, then it may be that the utility of such outcomes has not been correctly assessed. A decrease in utility for these outcomes would bias the curve toward the left and reduce the expected value. At some point what is shown as the broader curve in Figure 4-2 might then produce a lower expected value than the narrower curve.

The question persists, however, of whether a manager would

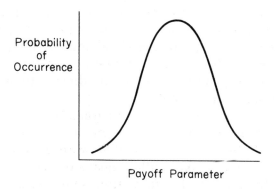

Payoff Parameter

Figure 4-1   Output of Stochastic Model

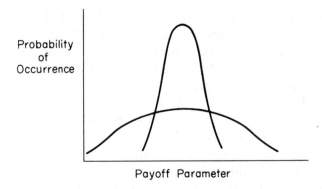

Payoff Parameter

Figure 4-2   Two Types of Distribution of Payoff Parameter

have the time or opportunity to ensure that an exact utility function had been used in the analysis. Faced with a situation such as that shown in Figure 4-2, he might well make his choice on a combination of criteria. This combination would probably include maximization of expected value. On the other hand, the minimization of uncertainty might be an important criterion used in the resolution of the decision problem.

Gathering of Data for Use in Probabilistic Models

In all applications of probabilistic models, there may be significant problems in obtaining sufficient data on the relevant parameters to allow proper determination of the type of probability distribution that should be used to represent the uncertainty observed. In such circumstances, there may be a temptation to use easily manipulated probability distributions rather than observed data to reduce the amount of analytical and computational work involved. Needless to say, this temptation should be resisted if there is any doubt that these probability distributions are appropriate to the problem at hand.

The search for data related to the parameters in a model may be thought of as a move toward the acquisition of *perfect information*. Perfect information, if it were obtainable, would provide the decision maker with a means of overcoming uncertainty. Unfortunately, such information is not available to mortal men. One course that is open in the effort to relieve uncertainty is to collect data on past developments that may be relevant to future conditions. This can usually be done only at a cost in money or resources and in time. When such data have been collected tests can be applied that allow a judgment to be made regarding the exactness of fit of the data to a particular probability distribution.[20] These tests are not exact; at best, they allow an experienced person to judge how close a fit has been obtained.

In some situations it may be sufficient to make use of special graph paper to test goodness of fit. It is possible, for example, to obtain a type of graph paper on which the cumulative distribution function of a normally distributed random variable will appear as a straight line. If this function of the data collected appears as a straight line on this paper, then there is reason to believe that the values of the parameter being studied are distributed, at least approximately, according to what is known as the normal probability distribution. Once again, however, the matter of closeness of fit is a matter of judgment.

Simulation

In situations in which the data collected can be judged to fit a well-known probability distribution, the analytical techniques associated with probabilistic models can be applied with some degree of confidence. Unfortunately, this is not always the case. Some sets of data cannot be said to fit such distributions. In such cases, it is most unwise to use the analytical models. The best recourse is to the technique of *simulation*.

The method of simulation has been covered extensively in the literature.[21-23] It consists of the formulation of a detailed model of the operation or system under study, containing the relationships between all the parameters and factors that are pertinent to the decision process at hand. The model may refer to a single time point or it may cover a number of time periods appropriate to a sequential decision process. All data available on the parameters and factors involved are stored in the model.

[20]Hillier and Lieberman, *Introduction to Operations Research*, pp. 116–17 and 626–27.
[21]Wagner, *Principles of Operations Research*, chap. 21.
[22]Clough, *Concepts in Management Science*, chap. 14.
[23]Hillier and Lieberman, *Introduction to Operations Research*, chap. 14.

Once the model is constructed, a series of "runs" of the decision process is undertaken. In each run a value for each parameter is sampled from the available data at random. These values are combined to arrive at a value of the payoff parameter. This single value of the payoff parameter represents one sample from the distribution of that parameter. This distribution is then investigated by a series of repeated runs of the decision process. Because this may involve a considerable amount of manipulation of data, the larger simulations are usually computer supported. Special purpose computer programming languages have been designed to facilitate these operations.

Large-scale simulations may be costly, especially if the statistical techniques involved require a large number of runs to produce the required degree of precision in estimating the distribution of the payoff parameter. However, simulation may be the only method available if the data referring to the parameters involved cannot be fitted to easily manipulated probability distributions or if analytical methods cannot be devised to represent the decision process under study. Alec Lee has provided some interesting examples of the application of simulation techniques to queueing situations.[24] In this informative and, at times, amusing book the author illustrates a most interesting combination of theoretical models, analytical techniques and practical problem solving.

The Use of Subjective Probabilities

Managers today face a great number of decision problems for which it is not possible or practicable to design a deterministic or probabilistic model. The scope of the problem may be too large or the parameters and the relationships between them may be too ill-defined. Alternatively, there may not be sufficient time before a decision must be made to construct a detailed model. Nevertheless, the manager may have significant information and experience that he wishes to bring to bear on the problem. This information may include subjective probability estimates with regard to future events and conditions.

To illustrate such a situation, let us consider the problem of estimating the outcome of the last game of the World Series of

[24]A.M. Lee, *Applied Queueing Theory* (New York: St. Martin's Press, 1966).

baseball. If one had time available and sufficient experience of the game it might be possible to define all the parameters involved: for example, those concerning the capabilities and reactions of the batters, pitchers and umpires would be important. Weather conditions might play a part and many other factors might have to be considered. Data could be collected on each of these parameters and, finally, a model could no doubt be constructed that would cover every possible play and combination of plays that could occur in the game. The task would be immense and probably would have to be abandoned.

On the way to the game, however, it is possible that one would meet a friend who would say, "I will give you 4 to 1 odds on the Reds." This can be interpreted as an expression of a subjective probability of 0.8 that the Reds would win. It is most unlikely that the friend had just completed an analysis of the type so recently abandoned. It is more likely that he arrived at his estimate of odds to be offered as a result of his experience, judgment and beliefs and such information as was available to him at the time.

A manager often finds himself in a position similar to the man offering the odds. He is faced with the problem of forecasting the outcome of a "game." Time and available resources do not allow the construction and use of a major model of the process, even if this were thought possible. Therefore, he is left with the alternative of using his experience and judgment in as logical a fashion as possible in the time available. Procedures developed by Raiffa and Schlaifer[25,26] and by their colleagues in the Bayesian school of probability provide a practical means of achieving this. This can be illustrated by reference to a simplified version of the plant expansion problem, considered earlier in the text. Further illustrations have been given by Newman[27] and by Magee.[28,29]

For simplicity at the outset, let us assume that the decision

---

[25]R.O. Schlaifer, *Analysis of Decisions Under Uncertainty* (New York: McGraw-Hill, 1965).

[26]H. Raiffa, *Decisions Analysis: Introductory Lectures on Choices Under Uncertainty* (Reading, Mass.: Addison-Wesley, 1968).

[27]J.W. Newman, *Management Applications of Decision Theory* (New York: Harper & Row, 1971).

[28]John F. Magee, "Decision Trees for Decision Making," *Harvard Business Review* (July–August, 1964).

[29]John F. Magee, "How to Use Decision Trees in Capital Investment," *Harvard Business Review* (September–October, 1964).

maker has before him a proposal to build a major extension of the plant. The net advantage to him depends on the future state of the market which, let us say, will be either high or low. (Much more complex problems can be approached using the same methods as for this simple problem.) Assume, further, that the net advantage in building the plant extension (compared with no additional advantage in staying with the present plant) is shown in Table 4-2 in thousands of dollars:

Table 4-2   The Plant Expansion Problem—Initial Consideration

	Future State of the Market	
	Low	High
1. Stay with present plant	0	0
2. Build major extension	−500	600

This decision problem can be expressed in a *decision flow diagram* or *decision tree* as shown in Figure 4-3. Note that the decision maker is placed to the left of the first decision node and does not cross that node. He is engaged in considering the question "What if I stay with the present plant or build a major extension?" At the initial decision node he has these two options, and he is considering the consequences of each before coming to a decision. After he has made his decision, the future state of the market will become known (high or low) and payoffs will result, as shown at the right-hand tips of the tree. Further to the right, the

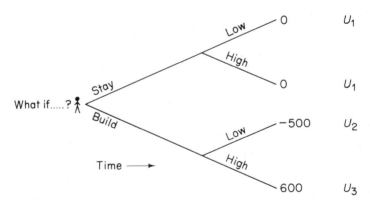

Figure 4-3   The Plant Expansion Problem—Initial Decision Tree

quantities U_1, U_2 and U_3 are shown to indicate the decision maker's utilities for these payoffs.

The problem as stated to this point is that of a decision under uncertainty. The decision maker will make his decision according to his personal approach to uncertainty and the policies of his company in this regard. Application of minimax would lead him to stay with present plant. Maximax would suggest building the major extension, as would minimax regret.

At this stage, however, the decision maker might possibly wish to investigate the effect of introducing into the analysis his opinions regarding the future state of the market. Let us assume that, initially, he feels that the probability of a high future market is 0.8 and of a low market, 0.2. These probabilities can be introduced into the decision tree as shown in Figure 4-4.

The problem has now been converted to a decision under what we have previously called conditions of risk. Expected values of the outcome can be calculated and are shown in the boxes on the appropriate branches of the tree. The values shown are expected monetary values. Expected utility values could be shown equally well, assuming that the values of U_1, U_2 and U_3 are known. The decision using the criterion of maximization of expected monetary value would clearly be to build the large extension. However, the decision maker might well be worried about the size of the loss if he chose that option and the market turned out to be low.

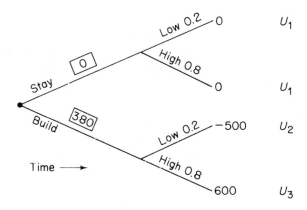

Figure 4-4   The Plant Expansion Problem: Introduction of Subjective Probabilities

Therefore, he might seek to delay the decision and to use the time gained to gather more information.

The Value of Information

The problem of determining the value of information in this decision situation can be approached first by considering the value of *perfect* information. This is the equivalent of calculating the value to the decision maker of exact knowledge of the future state of the market. In our simple case, this would be whether the market will be high or low.

Most attempts at gathering information about the future naturally provide only imperfect information, although some are more successful than others at the task of forecasting. The use of imperfect information still leaves room for uncertainty, so the value of imperfect information naturally cannot be as great as that of perfect information. The value of perfect information, therefore, represents the maximum value that can be expected from the process of information gathering during a decision process. Any practical process of information gathering will result in an increase of expected value less than that which can be attributed to perfect information. The expected value of perfect information thus represents an amount that can be used as a guide in committing resources to information gathering in any particular decision process.

Returning to the plant expansion problem, let us assume that the decision maker has temporarily postponed his decision and is about to embark on a program of information gathering. At this moment, a consultant enters the room and, saying that he has heard of the problem facing the decision maker, offers him perfect information on the future state of the market *at a price.* Consultants have been known to do this. The question now before the decision maker is what to offer for the consultant's information. Suppose that this information is contained in a sealed envelope shown to the left of the first decision node in Figure 4-5.

The decision maker can now reason in this way. "The consultant states that the envelope contains perfect information. If I open the envelope and find the word 'high,' I should build the extension and make $600,000. If the envelope contains the word 'low,' I should stay with the present plant. However, I cannot open the

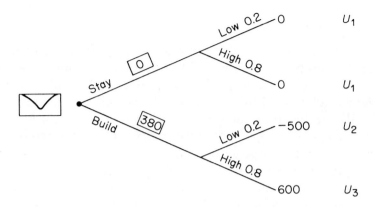

Figure 4-5   The Plant Expansion Problem: The Effect of Information

envelope without first paying for it. Holding to my subjective probability estimates of the future state of the market, I believe there is an 80 percent chance that the envelope contains the information 'high.' My *expected* payoff from opening the envelope and finding this information is therefore 80 percent of $600,000 or $480,000. My expected payoff from finding the information 'low' is, of course, zero." Note that, once having paid for the envelope, the outcome to the decision maker is $600,000 or zero, depending on its contents. Before having made the decision to pay for the envelope, however, the *expected* outcome from buying the information is $480,000, based on the previously stated values for the decision maker's subjective probabilities.

One further step gives the expected value of the perfect information contained in the envelope. Before the consultant entered the room, the decision maker had calculated an expected value of the option to build the extension as $380,000. The availability of perfect information increased the expected value of the decision process to $480,000. The *expected value of perfect information* is therefore the difference between these two figures, or $100,000. The decision maker can use this figure as a guide in deciding how much to pay the consultant for the envelope. Clearly, in a real life situation no information offered or gathered is likely to be perfect. The amount of resources allocated to information gathering should therefore be less than the expected value of perfect information.

The Effect of Increasing the Available Options

Faced with the possibility of paying the consultant for information and, even then, the possibility of incurring a loss, the decision maker may decide to search for other available options in his problem. Such an option may be to build a smaller extension. This can be illustrated in a decision tree shown in Figure 4-6.

In this situation, an expected value decision maker would still decide to build the large extension. In practice, however, a manager might well refer to the actual outcomes as the tips of the tree (essentially moving back to decision making under uncertainty) and decide to select the less risky (maximin) option of building the smaller extension, even though the *expected* outcome is smaller.

At this point, the question arises of the value of the consultant's perfect information in the new circumstances. The decision maker can argue as follows: "If I open the envelope and see 'high' I will build the large extension; but if I see 'low' I can now elect to build the small extension. My expected gain if I buy the perfect information is thus 0.8 × 600,000 + 0.2 × 50,000 or $490,000. The *expected* value of the perfect information now is therefore $490,000 less $380,000 or $110,000."

Note that the expected value of perfect information has changed with a change in the options considered. *Before committing resources to gathering information, therefore, the decision*

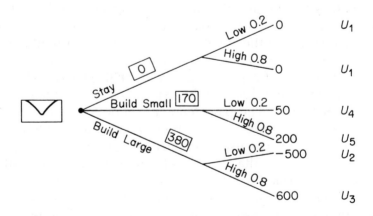

Figure 4-6   The Plant Expansion Problem: Addition of Another Option

maker should ensure that all available options have been consid-ered. Addition of an option may make a significant change to the value of gathering information.

The Value of Partial Information

In all practical situations, any information gathering will result in only partial information being available, and that at a cost. What then is the value of the partial information and is it worth the cost?

Let us suppose that our decision maker has decided to under-take some market research before committing himself to building the plant extension. To illustrate his problem, suppose that there are ten major markets for his product and that (for simplicity) his research can result in an estimated high or low market size in any area of the ten that he cares to cover. However, the cost of the market research in one area is $50,000, in two areas it is $90,000 and so on. Previous experience in this type of work suggests (say) that if the future market will be high, the research will report "low" in only one in ten of the major areas. Similarly if the overall market will be low, the research team will find "low" in six of the ten areas. The problem confronting the decision maker is the question of how much money to devote to market research. This is clearly linked to the value of the information gathered to him in his decision problem.

The use to which this information is put is essentially to con-firm or question the subjective probability values that the deci-sion maker put forward before the research is done. If the work suggests high future markets in one or more areas, the subjective probability of such a condition overall would probably be in-creased from the initial value of 0.8. If there is a suggestion of low future markets, it would probably be decreased.

A formula devised by Bayes links these *prior* (before) and *posterior* (after) probabilities in the light of previous experience in such information gathering studies (called the *likelihood*). This is explained in detail in Exhibit 4-1. Application of the formula shows that if research is done in one area and this indi-cates a high market, then the subjective probability of 0.8 should be changed to 0.9. Similarly if the research study indicates "low," the subjective probability of a future high market should be changed to 0.4. Similar calculations can be done to obtain posterior subjective probabilities in the case in which two or more areas are studied.

This application of Bayes' formula may seem to be somewhat mechanistic. Is it true that decision makers would in fact act in this manner in adjusting their subjective probabilities? Some experiments have been conducted to investigate this point.[30,31] These experiments show that the data gathered are likely to have less impact on the probability estimates than the Bayes formula requires. This is called the *conservatism effect*. In infrequent cases, however, the probability revisions were greater than required by the formula.

Notwithstanding these results, Bayesian probability revision provides some guide to the effect of information gathered on the subjective probability estimates of a decision maker. The posterior probabilities obtained can be applied to the decision tree of Figure 4-6 in order to obtain guidance as to whether the suggested market surveys should be undertaken. The new diagram is shown in Figure 4-7. In this diagram, the top portion is exactly that shown in Figure 4-6. The lower portion incorporates the posterior probabilities calculated in Exhibit 4-1. Note that the outcomes at the tips of the tree do not change. It is only the *expected values* (shown in the rectangular boxes) that are affected by the change of subjective probabilities.

On the basis of maximization of expected monetary value, some conclusions can be drawn at this stage. For example, if the market research in the one test area indicates "high," there is more reason to select the option of building the large extension. The expected value shown for this option after one test is $490,000. As more and more tests are done and as the revised subjective probability of a future high market approaches unity, this expected value would approach the actual outcome, $600,000. Again, if the first test indicated "low," the decision should be to build the small extension.

The question remains of whether it is worthwhile to embark on the market research in the one area. This can be approached in the

[30]Wayne Lee, "Choosing Among Confusably Distributed Stimuli with Specified Likelihood Ratios," *Perceptual and Motor Skills* 16 (1963):445–67.

[31]Wayne Lee, *Decision Theory and Human Behavior* (New York: John Wiley & Sons, 1971), pp. 253–54.

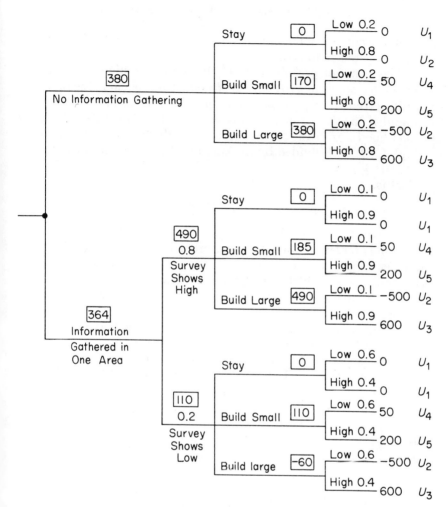

Figure 4-7   The Plant Expansion Problem Introduction of Posterior Probabilities: One Test

following fashion. If the market research indicates high, the expected value of the payoff is $490,000; if low, the expected payoff is $110,000. The expected value for the option of gathering information is therefore:

$490,000 × (probability of high indication in the market research)

\+ $110,000 × (probability of low indication).

EXHIBIT 4-1—Bayesian Probability Revision

In the context of the problem being considered, Bayes' formula can be stated as follows:

The *posterior* probability $(p(H|D))$ of a future high market (H) given that some data (D) have been collected is equal to the probability taken from previous experience that such data would be found if the future market was going to be high $(p(D|H))$ (the *likelihood*), times the *prior* probability of the future market being high $(p(H))$; all divided by the sum of all possible products like $p(D|H) \times p(H)$.

That is,

$$p(H|D) = \frac{p(D|H) \times p(H)}{p(D|H) \times p(H) + p(D|L) \times p(L)}$$

In the problem at hand, the *prior* probabilities $p(H)$ and $p(L)$ are the decision maker's original subjective probability estimates, i.e., 0.8 and 0.2 respectively. The likelihood, $p(D|H)$, is the probability in any one area of finding a high market if the future market is going to be high. From the previous experience mentioned above, this likelihood is 0.9, since the research will report "low" in only one of ten areas. Similarly, the likelihood $p(D|L)$ is 0.4.

The posterior subjective probability estimate of a future high market given that a high market is found in one of the ten areas (i.e., given D) can then be calculated as:

$$p(H|D) = \frac{0.9 \times 0.8}{0.9 \times 0.8 + 0.4 \times 0.2} = 0.9$$

Similarly

$$p(L|D) = \frac{0.4 \times 0.2}{0.9 \times 0.8 + 0.4 \times 0.2} = 0.1$$

Similarly if D' represents a low market indicated in one of the ten areas,

$$p(H|D') = \frac{0.1 \times 0.8}{0.1 \times 0.8 + 0.6 \times 0.2} = 0.4$$

and

$$p(L|D') = 0.6$$

Similar calculations can be made if research data are available from two or more areas.

These two probabilities can be calculated as follows:

probability of high indication = probability of high, given a
future high market
+ probability of high, given
a future low market

and similarly for the probability of a low indication in the market
survey. This leads to (using the decision maker's original subjective probabilities and the original likelihoods):

probability of high = $(0.9 \times 0.8) + (0.4 \times 0.2) = 0.8$
probability of low = $(0.1 \times 0.8) + (0.6 \times 0.2) = 0.2$

Note that these values are the same as the decision maker's original subjective probability estimates, but this is only by coinci-
dence. The expected value for the option of gathering information
is, therefore:

$$(0.8 \times \$490{,}000) + (0.2 \times \$110{,}000) = \$414{,}000$$

The net expected value, taking into account the cost of the market
research in the one area is $\$414{,}000 - \$50{,}000 = \$364{,}000$. This is
shown at the appropriate place in Figure 4-7 and can be compared
with the $\$380{,}000$ figure for the branch without market research.

The decision maker might argue, therefore, that the market
research (costing $\$50{,}000$) was not worthwhile, since, based on
his original subjective probability estimates, the expected value
of the market research course of action is less than that of no
information gathering. On the other hand, if he used any criterion
of choice between options other than maximization of expected
value, he might think an expenditure of $\$50{,}000$ to be well
worthwhile in terms of the information it provides.

Advantages of the Bayesian Method

The approach to decision making just described may seem to be
too detailed in its quantitative aspects and to take too little account of other factors that may be important in the situation under
review. It may be thought that such a detailed approach may not
be justified in view of the uncertainties surrounding the quantita-

tive values used. This opinion may well be justified. Certainly, it cannot be recommended that the approach be followed blindly. It does, however, provide one avenue of exploration of the consequences of selection one of the available options. Used in conjunction with other approaches available to a decision maker it offers the following advantages:

- it provides a logical method of linking together such quantitative data as are available and of investigating the consequences of those values of the parameters involved;

- it serves to clarify the decision problem, even if the decision is not made solely on the basis of the quantitative analysis;

- it provides a guide to the value of information and to the resources that should be committed to gathering information in a decision situation;

- it can be used to explore sequential decision processes in a series of logical steps similar to those described above;[32]

- it may serve to make manager's preferences and opinions more explicit during the course of discussions related to the analytical approach.

Decisions Under Conditions of Conflict

Decision making under conditions of conflict is a major part of the work of the modern manager. In the simplest of such decision situations, an actual opponent (or opponents) can be identified and there is open competition between the parties for a pay off. In more complex situations, the nature of the conflict may be less clear.

The theory of decision making under conditions of conflict has been developed to date to the point where only certain simple situations can be treated quantitatively. These situations do not occur often in the complex environment of modern decision making. Nevertheless, they are of interest as an introduction to the treatment of more complex conflict situations, discussed in detail in the next chapter.

---

[32]Magee, "Decision Trees for Decision Making."

A first distinction that can be made in treating decisions under conflict is whether only two "players" or parties are present or more than two players are involved. This distinction is made by the notation *two-person* or *N-person* in describing decision situations.

Another important classification is in terms of *zero-sum* and *non-zero-sum* situations. In the zero-sum category a gain by one player implies an equal loss by another; that is, the sum of gains and losses is zero in any one play of the game. In a non-zero-sum game this is not the case. One variation of this classification should be noted here. If the payoffs are expressed in the form of utilities it is necessary only that the payoffs to the players form a *constant-sum* since arbitrary transformations of the players' utilities are allowed, which can convert the constant-sum to a zero-sum.

The theory of two- and N-person, zero- and non-zero sum games was first described by von Neumann and Morgenstern in 1944.[33] This treatise has been basic to all discussions of the theory of games and the related subject of decisions under conflict since that time. In 1950, a layman's introduction to the subject was published that described the application of the basic ideas of the original treatise to situations in the game of poker, in business and in war.[34] An extensive bibliography of the early work in this area is given by Luce and Raiffa.[35]

Two-Person, Zero-Sum Decision Situations

Simple two-person, zero-sum decision situations can be described in terms of the payoffs to the players as a result of a choice of strategy by each of them. Consider the following payoff matrix that describes a conflict decision situation (or game) between two players, A and B. Both players have four available options or strategies. The elements of the matrix represent the results (or payoffs) to the players of choosing a particular pair of options. Where the payoff is positive it represents a gain to A and where

[33]J. von Neumann and O. Morgenstern, *Theory of Games and Economic Behavior*, 3rd ed. (Princeton, N.J.: Princeton University Press, 1953).

[34]John McDonald, *Strategy in Poker, Business and War* (New York: W.W. Norton and Co., 1950).

[35]R.D. Luce and H. Raiffa, *Games and Decisions* (New York: John Wiley & Sons, 1967). appendices 5 and 6.

negative it means a gain to B. Because the gain is zero-sum, these gains are matched by a corresponding loss to the other player. The question is which option should each choose. It is assumed that the choices are to be made simultaneously.

Table 4-3   Simple Two-Person, Zero-Sum Game Matrix

	B_1	B_2	B_3	B_4
A's Options A_1	−4	5	9	3
A_2	8	4	3	7
A_3	7	6	8	9
A_4	7	−2	4	−6

This matrix has been chosen for a first illustration because it has a particular characteristic. Note that the element 6 resulting from the choice of strategies A_3 and B_2 (the strategy pair A_3B_2) is simultaneously a minimum in its row and a maximum in its column. If A chooses A_3, he can assure himself of a gain of at least 6, whichever B selects. B's best strategy if he thinks A may choose A_3 is to choose B_2. By doing so he can limit A's gain to 6. Any other choice by B under these conditions would result in a greater gain to A. Any movement by A from strategy A_3 could result in a reduced payoff to him. The strategy pair (A_3,B_2) therefore represents a maximum of the minimum gains for A over all his available strategies. It also represents the minimum of B's maximum possible losses.

The strategy pair (A_3,B_2) is called a *saddle point* or *equilibrium*: it is the maximin strategy for A and the minimax strategy for B. It is interesting to note that if a saddle point exists in a matrix either party can choose his minimax strategy in a single play of the game and reveal this choice. The opponent's knowledge of this choice cannot cause him to have a smaller payoff. On the other hand, there is no advantage to either player in revealing this choice.

This situation may appear to be somewhat unlikely to occur in modern decision making and this is readily conceded. The situation is clearly unfavorable to B and he would probably act to change it. It might be, however, that B would be forced to accept the unprofitable situation for a short time to stay in the game for later gains. He might then wish to minimize his losses in the short term.

The payoff matrix describing a simple two-person, zero-sum game may not have a readily identified saddle point such as that in the matrix shown in Table 4-3. A more general situation is illustrated in Table 4-4.

Table 4-4   Two-Person, Zero-Sum Game Matrix Without Saddle Point

		B_1	B_2	B_3
		B's Options		
A's Options	A_1	2	−3	4
	A_2	−3	4	−5
	A_3	4	−5	6

In this matrix no saddle point can be detected. If either A or B chooses a single strategy, knowledge of this choice can be of assistance to the other. This is not of importance in a single-play, simultaneous-choice decision situation. In a multiple-play game, however, unsystematic choice of strategies can result in instability and possible loss to either player. For example, if A first chose A_2, B would choose B_3. A might then move to A_3, B might move to B_2 and so on.

A major contribution of the von Neumann-Morgenstern theory is that the equivalent of a single-strategy saddle point exists in such situations. This equivalent equilibrium situation involves the use of *mixed strategies*. Instead of selecting a strategy independently in each of a series of plays of the game, each player uses a predetermined mixture of his available strategies. This mixture can be calculated for each player and provides the equivalent of a saddle point. Furthermore, each player can reveal the strategies that are included in his mix. He cannot, however, reveal his method of choice of a strategy from the mix for any one play of the game, without risking a reduction in his payoff from that guaranteed by the equilibrium situation.

The method of determining the correct mixture of strategies is given in Exhibit 4-2. Note that this method also determines the *value* of the game to both parties. This is the *expected* payoff to each party in the game, assuming that strategies are chosen in the manner required to ensure that the equilibrium situation is maintained. In a multiplay game, the actual payoff to each player will approximate more and more closely to the product of the value and the number of plays, as the number of plays increases.

EXHIBIT 4-2—Determination of the Mixed Strategy for a Two-Person Zero-sum Game[36]

Consider a two-person, zero-sum game, where A has m strategies and B has n. Let the payoff matrix have elements a_{ij}, $i = 1 \ldots m$ and $j = 1 \ldots n$. Suppose A and B play their respective strategies with probabilities p_i and q_j respectively where $\sum_1^m p_i = 1$ and $\sum_1^n q_j = 1$. We need to find sets of mixed strategies $S_A^* = (A_i, p_i)$ and $S_B^* = (B_j, q_j)$ such that S_A^* guarantees A a payoff of at least ν (the value of the game) for any of B's strategies and equal to ν for his optimal strategy S_B^*; and similarly for B.

The average payoff for A's optimal strategy S_A^* against any strategy (B_j) of B is:

$$a_j = a_{1j}p_1 + a_{2j}p_2 + \ldots a_{mj}p_m$$

The requirement that a_j be not less than ν gives the following n conditions:

$$a_{11}p_1 + a_{21}p_2 + \ldots + a_{m1}p_m \geqslant \nu$$

$$a_{1n}p_1 + a_{2n}p_2 + \ldots + a_{mn}p_m \geqslant \nu$$

Since A wishes to maximize ν, the value of the game, the solution amounts to the following formulation:

Minimize $\displaystyle\sum_{i=1}^{m} p_i/\nu$ (i.e., maximize the value, ν)

Subject to $\displaystyle\sum_{\substack{i=1\ldots m \\ j=1\ldots n}} a_{ij}p_i \geqslant \nu$

This can be recognized as a simple linear program and solved accordingly. The values, p_i thus obtained provide the proportion of times that the ith strategy should be played in terms of the matrix elements a_{ij}. A similar analysis can be conducted for B.

[36]Luce and Raiffa, *Games and Decisions.*

118

To illustrate this analysis, consider the following two-person, zero-sum situation. Two retail outlets are the sole suppliers of a certain product to a community and they compete by offering special prices in the Thursday night paper. It is assumed that the two competitors disclose their price and learn of the other's price simultaneously. The price may be either high or low. What *A* gains in sales, *B* loses and vice versa. If the prices offered by each outlet are the same (i.e., both high or both low) outlet *A*, because it is more conveniently located, gains ten units from *B*. If *A*'s price is high and *B*'s low, *B* gains fifteen units from *A*. However, if *B*'s price is high and *A*'s low, *B* still gains five units from *A* because customers suspect *A* is selling off old stock. The payoff matrix describing this somewhat contrived situation is shown in Table 4-5 with gains to *A* being shown as positive:

Table 4-5   Conflict Situation Involving Two Retail Outlets

		B's Options	
		High	*Low*
A's Options	*High*	10	−15
	Low	−5	10

Application of the method outlined in Exhibit 4-2 shows that *A* should play "high" ⅝ of the time and "low" ⅜ of the time. *B* should play "low" ⅝ of the time and "high" ⅜ of the time. The value of the game is +⅝. This means that the *expected* value to *A* in a single play is ⅝. In a multiplay situation, the payoff to *A* is ⅝ times the number of occasions on which the "game" is played. The situation is, therefore, disadvantageous to *B*. If *A* correctly determines his mixed strategy, uses it and does not reveal his method of choice of a strategy for any particular play, the outcome in the long run is a gain for *A*. This is not immediately obvious from the payoff matrix in Table 4-5. On the other hand, if *A* does not follow the correct mixed strategy, *B* may have an opportunity to gain in spite of the inherent bias in the game in favor of *A*.

This example is, of course, very simple and many important factors that might influence the situation have not been included in the analysis. It does represent the only type of conflict situation for which a simple quantitative model is applicable. More complex situations of this type must be treated by other techniques. These are considered in the next chapter.

N-Person Games and Coalitions

The theory of N-person games is complex and difficult to apply to simple decision situations. Methods of treating many-player decision problems will be described in the next chapter. One aspect of the problem can be discussed here as a prelude to the later treatment. This concerns *coalitions*.

Coalitions are a natural feature of N-person games and decision situations under conditions of conflict. They come about when some of the players in such a game combine for the purpose of furthering a common objective and opposing another party with whom they are in conflict. For example, in a three-man poker game, it is not unusual to see two players combine against the third. Such coalitions may be transitory, however, and usually persist only so long as there exists an objective that is common to the combining parties. In business situations coalitions are common. For example, a consumer buying at a discount outlet forms a temporary coalition with that outlet against, say, a department store selling the same merchandise. Some coalitions between business organizations may be illegal, as for example in price fixing.

The von Neumann-Morgenstern theory suggests that players (that is decision makers) in a N-person game should continually consider the possibilities and advantages of coalitions with each of the other players in the game. To do otherwise is to risk a coalition being formed against their interests. The crucial questions arising in such situations concern the benefits and dis-benefits of the formation of any particular coalition and the problem of how the benefits from the association should be divided.

Coalitions are inherently unstable. Suppose that two parties in a three-party situation enter into a coalition (that is legal), and by virtue of this cooperation each grows strong relative to the third party. It is natural that the third party should attempt to form a coalition with one or other of two already cooperating. In the course of such negotiations the third party might offer an arrangement that would seem more attractive than the status quo.

Relative weakness is not necessarily a disadvantage in considering the possibility of a coalition. For example, many cases have existed of large and powerful organizations allowing weaker ones to stay in business to avoid the possible dangers of an apparent monopoly. Such coalitions may not be characterized by formal negotiations and may, in fact, be implicit and understood, rather than explicit. They are nonetheless coalitions and the price of maintaining the coalition should be continually assessed to determine whether it is greater or less than the cost of defection.

Summary

Decisions under conditions of certainty occur in many of the routine administrative and operational decision processes in modern organizations. Many of these processes consist of a sequence of very simple decisions linked together into a procedure or program, which completely specifies the process. Others may include mathematical models as part of the specification. The most commonly applied of these models is linear programming. Other applications are found of nonlinear, integer and dynamic programming. Under conditions of certainty these models are called deterministic. They are used in circumstances in which there is a single objective (usually maximization of profit or minimization of cost) or one objective of a multiple set is of prime importance. Where a number of objectives are of roughly equal importance, to use these models in relation to one objective is to risk sub-optimization. One method, by Lee, provides an approach to some aspects of the problem of decision making under multiple objectives.

A first approach to the introduction of uncertainty into deterministic models is by sensitivity analysis. By variation of one parameter at a time, information can be obtained on the sensitivity of the solution to this variation. This procedure is much more difficult to use if two parameters are varied simultaneously and almost impossible if more than two are involved. In such circumstances recourse must be made to probabilistic models in which each parameter is represented by a probability distribution. Major applications of probabilistic models are found in the area of dynamic programming.

In many situations under uncertainty it may be desirable to gather data before arriving at a decision. This can usually be done only at a cost. This gathering of data can be thought of as a search for information as a means of overcoming uncertainty. Sometimes the data collected cannot be judged to fit a well-known probability distribution that can be incorporated easily into an analytical model. Under these circumstances, the technique of simulation can be used.

There are a great number of decision problems facing managers today for which it is not possible or practicable to design a deterministic or probabilistic model. Nevertheless, managers have information and experience that can be brought to bear on the problem. This can be done by the use of subjective probability estimates in a decision flow diagram or decision tree. Using such methods the expected value of perfect information can be calculated. This provides a guide as to how much should be spent on gathering information in a decision process. The expected value of perfect information may change if the number of available options changes. The method also allows a means of assessing the worth in the decision situation of gathering partial information, such as from a program of tests or market research.

Decisions under conditions of conflict may be classified initially by reference to the categories two-person or N-person and zero-sum or non-zero-sum. Quantitative analysis can be carried out practically only for two-person, zero-sum decision situations. These do not occur frequently in practice. Coalitions are a feature of N-person games. Each player in such games should continually review possible coalitions open to him assessing the benefits and disbenefits of each and the manner in which the benefits would be divided. Coalitions are inherently unstable. Relative weakness as compared with the other parties is not necessarily a disadvantage in an N-person situation.

Discussion Topics

1/ Can the procedures designed to service routine administrative tasks really be considered as decisions under certainty? If not, why not?

2/ List the uses of deterministic models of operations in your company or department. Are there any in which where you think such models could be used but are not being used at the present time? Are there any models being used that are deterministic in spite of the fact that uncertainty exists in specifying values of the parameters?

3/ What is the relation between linear and dynamic programming? Could dynamic programming be applied to a problem that was being solved by linear programming, or vice versa?

4/ The method of Sang M. Lee in minimizing deviations from goals set with respect to multiple objectives does not necessarily provide an *optimum* solution as far as cost or profit is concerned. Why is this? (Note the form of the objective function.)

5/ What is the major limitation of sensitivity analysis if two or more parameters can vary simultaneously?

6/ Is the criterion of maximization (or minimization) of expected value appropriate to probabilistic models? Would minimization of uncertainty be more appropriate?

7/ Wagner has referred to simulation as a method that is adopted "when all else fails." Do you agree with this?

8/ What methods can be adopted to ensure that the cost of a simulation analysis does not exceed that justified by the results obtained? Is there a rough relationship between the number of runs in the analysis and the uncertainty contained in the results?

9/ How would you use a decision analysis involving Bayesian probability revision in your organization? Is there more than one particular class of problems (for example, capital investment) to which it applies?

10/ How would you use the expected value of perfect information in decision problems in your organization?

11/ Why does the expected value of perfect information change if more options become available to the decision maker? Can this value *decrease* if more options become available?

12/ What is the relationship of the expected value of perfect information to the expected opportunity cost?

13/ The likelihood in Bayes' formula has been compared to the calibration in scientific experiments. Do you see it in this way?

14/ Why do you think that most experimental subjects exhibit the conservatism effect in estimating posterior probabilities? Do practical managers act in this way too?

15/ Is adoption of Bayesian probability revision contrary to consistent managerial behavior?

16/ Could Simon's economic man (who maximizes) adopt Bayesian probability revision in his decision making? How about his administrative man?

17/ Do two-person zero-sum games ever occur in business and industry? Does the presence of government make all business situations N-person?

18/ How should consideration of the formation of coalitions affect managerial behavior under conditions of conflict?

19/ Would game theory be useful in considering the situation confronting a country in the area of international trade?

20/ What is the difference between the games of bridge and poker as seen from the game theoretic point of view?

21/ The von Neumann-Morgenstern analysis recommends mixed strategies in a two-person zero-sum game. This intuitively seems appropriate for multiplay situations. What is the effect of this conclusion on choice of strategies in a single play of such a game?

Problem

A company is in the market for an executive jet. It is interested in a plane from early production which sells for $5,000 less than a new one. The problem is that some of the planes from the early production have minor defects that are costly to remedy. There are two types of plane from the early production, type *A* and type *B*. It is known that planes of type *A* had defects in six of the ten major systems in the plane, while those of type *B* had defects in only one of the systems. It is estimated subjectively that twenty percent of the planes were type *A* and eighty percent type *B*. None of the planes has yet been flown and it is known that none of the defects has yet been remedied in any plane that is for sale. The cost of remedying one defect is estimated at $2,000 and the cost of repairing six at $10,000. The question is whether to buy the older or the newer plane. Minimizing cost is a major consideration.

Each plane has a serial number. By comparing this with a list, it is possible to determine whether the plane is type *A* or *B*. Unfortunately, the cost of obtaining this list is $1,250. Is it worthwhile to buy the list, based on the criterion of maximizing expected gain? (No.) If not, what is the maximum that should be paid for the list using this decision criterion? ($1,000.)

It is now discovered that the seller has a warranty plan on all planes sold. As far as a plane from early production is concerned, this warranty costs $3,000 and it covers fifty percent of the repair costs. However, if the total repair cost is greater than $5,000, there is no charge for *any* of the repairs. Should the plane be bought with or without the warranty, once again assuming maximization of expected gain and the criterion? (Without.) Should the list of serial numbers be bought for $1,250 at this point? (Yes.)

It is possible to have the plane tested before buying. Any one of the ten systems can be tested and for each test, it is possible to obtain the answer "perfect" or "defective." To test *one* system costs $450 and *two* systems $650. There is available, also, a two-stage test in which the second stage can be authorized after the result of the first stage is known. This costs $500 for the first stage and an additional $200 for the second stage. What should be the strategy now? (There is little to choose between no testing, one test, two tests and the two-stage test.) Should the list of serial numbers be bought for $1,250 after any one of the test sequences? If not, how much is it worth in any one situation?

The answers to the above questions depend on the decision criterion employed. How would your answers change if you used a criterion other than maximization of expected gain?

Further problems of this nature are contained in the following references:

Daley, J.C., and E.C. Johnson. "Emission Control Processes Selection," *Journal of Metals*, July, 1972.

Hammond, John S. "Better Decisions with Preference Theory," *Harvard Business Review*, November–December, 1967.

Magee, John F. "Decision Trees for Decision Making," *Harvard Business Review*, July–August, 1964.

———. "How to Use Decision Trees in Capital Investment," *Harvard Business Review*, September–October, 1964.

Newman, J.W. *Managerial Applications of Decision Theory.* New York: Harper & Row, 1971.

Raiffa, Howard. *Decision Analysis: Introduction Lectures on Choices Under Uncertainty.* Reading, Mass.: Addison-Wesley, 1968.

5

More Complex Decision Processes

Introduction

Many of the decision situations facing managers in modern organizations are considerably more complex than those discussed in the previous chapter. This complexity arises from the following factors:

– in many cases, the available options cannot be evaluated simply in terms of a single, well-defined quantitative parameter. It may be that only the *preferences* of the parties involved can be determined and that these preferences can be expressed only on a nonquantitative ordinal scale;

– the decision situation may involve multiple objectives (rather than a single objective). Priorities as between individual objectives may vary from time to time and one objective may not always be in the position of first priority. Preferences may therefore vary during the course of the decision process;

– there may be some difficulty in identifying the "opposition" in the decision situation; that is whether it is from purely natural forces, a clearly defined opponent, or a mixture of both;

– the decision situation may be unique and "single-play," rather than one that is repeated many times.

If one or more of these conditions exists the quantitative methods of the previous chapter may be difficult or impossible to apply. The purpose of this chapter is to outline methods of studying decision problems under these more complex conditions.

In the previous chapter the discussion was taken from deterministic models, through uncertainty to situations of conflict. This thread of argument will be reversed in this chapter. Because one of the most generally applicable methods of treating complex decision problems (the analysis of options) originated from study of conflict situations, this is where the discussion starts. By the end of the chapter, however, the argument will have led back to the treatment of decision situations under conditions of uncertainty.

Managerial decision situations can be related directly to games. In fact, some of the more intellectually challenging games that we play (such as chess, bridge and poker) contain many of the elements of everyday decision making found in business and in our personal lives. In such games, however, the rules and the payoffs are known exactly. The challenge arises from the very large number of combinations of plays and the need to select a series of plays designed to maximize payoff in the face of another player's opposition. Managerial decisions are seldom so well defined. Nonetheless, some insight can be obtained into the more complicated decisions by studying the conflict implicit in the simpler games. For this reason, this chapter starts with a brief consideration of conflict in the strictly competitive situations found in many games. This is an extension of the treatment of two-person, zero-sum games contained in the latter portion of the previous chapter. The discussion proceeds from there to the more general decision problems found in modern organizations.

Strictly Competitive Decision Situations

In the strictly competitive decision situations discussed in the previous chapter (two-person, zero-sum games), the gain to one player is exactly equal to the loss to the other. A number of options (or strategies) may be available to each player, but it is assumed that the players must make a choice of strategy simultaneously. Because of the strictly competitive nature of the situation no cooperation or communication between the players can be mutually profitable. Neither player can be assumed at the outset to know what the other's choice of strategy will be.

The "solution" to such conflict situations consists of rules governing the choice of strategies, originally described in complete form by von Neumann and Morgenstern.[1] These have been outlined in the previous chapter. In essence, these rules define strategy choices that bring about an *equilibrium* in the game.[2] This equilibrium is such that it is not to the advantage of one player to move away from his equilibrium strategy, *provided the other player does not*. The equilibrium strategies may consist of a *pure* strategy or a set of *mixed strategies* for each player. An equilibrium pair is not necessarily unique, although, if other equilibrium pairs exist, they all result in the same value of the game to the players.

The set of strategies providing equilibrium maximizes what may be characterized as the *security level* for the players engaged in the game situation. The outcome of the game using the equilibrium set may not be the best that either player could desire, but it does represent an outcome that he can be sure of obtaining. Any movement by one player away from his equilibrium strategy cannot cause a deterioration in the other's equilibrium position and may well cause an improvement to the player remaining at the equilibrium. In cases where a pure strategy equilibrium pair does not exist an equivalent equilibrium, providing the same type of security, can be obtained by the use of mixed strategies. In

[1] J. von Neumann and O. Morgenstern, *Theory of Games and Economic Behavior*, 3d ed. (Princeton, N.J.: Princeton University Press, 1953).

[2] R.D. Luce and H. Raiffa, *Games and Decisions* (New York: John Wiley & Sons, 1957), pp. 56–73.

two-person, zero-sum situations, therefore, rational decision makers can be assured of an equilibrium that represents a certain level of security that cannot be broken down by the other player.

In a number of experiments conducted by research organizations and summarized by Lee,[3] players were, in fact, found to search for and move toward equilibrium positions in decision situations involving both pure and mixed strategies. This tends to confirm that the approach to two-person zero-sum games suggested by the theory is likely to be adopted, at least in situations that conform closely to the strictly competitive characteristic of those games.

However, two major questions are outstanding: first, do two-person, zero-sum games ever occur in managerial decision making; and second, how does the mixed-strategy solution apply to a situation in which there is only a single play?

Do Strictly Competitive Situations Occur in Managerial Decision Making?

Dealing with the first question first, a number of simple examples of two-person, zero-sum games can be constructed and put forward as applicable to situations confronting managers. The scenario of the two stores engaged in competition discussed in the previous chapter is such an example. It can be argued, however, that managerial decisions are seldom that simple. Other factors almost always intrude and their intervention makes the simple model much less applicable. On the other hand, it is undoubtedly true that the investigation of a simple model can provide some clarification and elucidation of more complex situations.

Some authorities hold that the application of two-person, zero-sum theory to real life situations is unrealistic. For example, Nigel Howard states that it is hard to think of any real-life situation that is truly a two-person, zero-sum game.[4] He goes further by stating that a tendency exists to see conflict situations in terms of the zero-sum approach because it is thought to be ". . . hard-headed, tough minded and realistic." He sees this approach as interesting only insomuch as it is generally invalid

---

[3]Wayne Lee, *Decision Theory and Human Behavior* (New York: John Wiley & Sons, 1971), pp. 282–86.

[4]Nigel Howard, *Paradoxes of Rationality* (Cambridge, Mass.: The MIT Press, 1971), p. 152.

and points out that it applies only to such pursuits as parlor games and sports. This being the case, he says, it is unfortunate that these games are used from the earliest age to train people in conflict behavior.

Procedures in a "Single Play" Strictly Competitive Situation

Turning to the second question, is it appropriate to apply the mixed strategy "solution" to a conflict situation with no pure strategy equilibrium, for which there is only a single play? Let us consider such a conflict situation described by Conan Doyle in the adventures of Sherlock Holmes entitled *The Final Problem*.[5] Holmes is being pursued by Moriarty and catches a train from London to Dover with a view to escaping to the Continent. The train has one stop (at Canterbury). As it leaves the station, Moriarty catches a glimpse of the departing Holmes, who sees Moriarty arrive at the station in pursuit. Holmes reasons that if Moriarty catches up with him he will kill him and deduces that Moriarty will charter a train in pursuit. Holmes now has the choice between getting off at Canterbury or going on to Dover. Moriarty presumably has the same choices. The pay-off matrix can be written as follows:

Table 5-1   Payoff Matrix for Holmes vs. Moriarty

		Moriarty	
		Canterbury	Dover
Holmes:	Canterbury	1,2	2,1
	Dover	2,1	1,2

Note that this matrix has been written in terms of the *preferences* of the players in what is known as a *mutually ordinal* scale. Holmes' preferences are shown first and a larger number 2 is meant to describe a greater preference than the smaller number 1. Other than that the numbers have no significance. Note also that the "game" can be considered zero-sum, despite the fact that Holmes gets killed if the two meet and only a draw ensues if they do not meet. If interval scale utilities were assigned to the ordinal preferences shown in the table the arbitrarily assigned units and

[5]Sir Arthur Conan Doyle, "The Final Problem," included in *The Complete Sherlock Holmes Short Stories* (London: John Murray, Ltd., 1928), pp. 536–56.

zero points could be adjusted to ensure that the strict requirements of zero-sum could be met. Such situations are referred to as
"constant-sum" games.

The von Neumann-Morgenstern theory tells us that, since no
pure strategy equilibrium exists, a mixed strategy policy should
be adopted. Holmes should calculate the proportion of times he
should get off at Canterbury and the corresponding proportion of
times that he should go on to Dover. In a multiple play situation,
he should then play each of his available strategies in the correct
proportion. However, a problem arises in that Holmes is engaged
in a game in which a wrong choice will result in there being no
more plays. A manager involved in a major decision may face a
similar predicament if the outcome of his first choice of strategy is
unfavorable to his company.

Luce and Raiffa suggest that the mixed strategy solution can be
implemented by selecting a pure strategy for each play by a
simple physical experiment,[6] such as tossing a coin or throwing a
die. That is to say that, provided the experiment is designed to
give the same proportions to its outcomes as are desired between
pure strategies, the decision as to which strategy to employ in a
single play should be made on the basis of the experiment alone.
This procedure is intuitively acceptable in a multiplay situation.
It is, however, very difficult to accept that it should be used in
real-life decision making in a single-play situation. In any case, a
manager who is convinced that he should decide between two
options in such a situation by tossing a coin would be well
advised to do it in the privacy of his locked office.

In a single play of a two-person zero-sum game, therefore,
unless a pure strategy equilibrium exists, it is probably best to
avoid a decision for as long as possible. In practical terms this
means seeking delay to gain time for gathering information or
reassessing the decision situation and the available options.

As in the discussion in the previous chapter, the process of
gathering information is an endeavor to increase a player's knowledge of the situation. This can be thought of as moving as close as
possible to the possession of perfect information within the constraints imposed in terms of time and money available. Perfect
information in the simple example discussed above would be

[6]Luce and Raiffa, *Games and Decisions*, pp. 86–87.

knowledge of the other player's selected strategy. If Holmes knew that Moriarty was going on to Dover (for certain), his decision problem would disappear.

An intuitively acceptable procedure in a single-play, strictly competitive decision situation without a pure strategy equilibrium is to endeavor to gain knowledge of the other player's strategy choice before choosing one's own. The difficulty remains, of course, that if both players try to do this, one of them must make the wrong decision. There is no equilibrium that provides a security level to each in a single play of this type of game.

In the case of the two stores advertising simultaneously in the Thursday night's paper, the solution might involve advertising in a different medium (say, television) once the other store's announcement had been made. This procedure of relating a choice of strategy to the intentions of an opponent comes into prominence later in this chapter in consideration of other decision situations that are found to occur often in the operations of modern organizations.

Objective and Subjective Rationality

As a minor diversion, note that reaction to an opponent's strategy will be seen to be rational only if that strategy is known for sure. If the opponent's strategy choice is wrongly diagnosed (possibly as a result of a successful bluff on his part) reaction to his strategy will be considered to have been irrational. This raises the question of the relationship of rationality to the quality of information in the possession of the decision maker.[7]

For example, it is sensible in hurrying to take a plane to New York to inquire of an airline clerk whether the plane you are about to board is going to New York. If the clerk says yes, it is rational to board the plane on the assumption that you are in possession of information that is as near perfect in the context of the decision to board the plane as it is necessary to obtain. It can be argued, however, that until the plane actually arrives in New York the decision to board the plane can be considered as only *subjectively rational*. Suppose the clerk was misinformed and the plane was in fact heading for Montreal. It would still be subjectively rational to

[7]Howard, *Paradoxes of Rationality*, pp. 10 and 27.

board the plane on the basis of the clerk's (wrong) information. It would not, however, be *objectively rational*, for the simple reason that the plane did not in reality go to New York. If one defines a *stable* decision as one that would not be affected by additional information, then only an objectively rational decision would be a stable one for a rational decision maker. In practice, perfect information is rarely available before an event. Nevertheless, possession of the greatest practical amount of relevant information before a decision (including as much as possible regarding the opponents choice of strategies) is the best assurance of closeness to objectively rational decisions and the minimum deviation between desired and actual outcomes.

Decision Situations that Are Not Strictly Competitive

Most practical decision situations in modern life fall into the non-zero-sum category. Before discussing a simple example of such a situation, it may be useful to summarize the characteristics of zero-sum decisions, so that the distinction between the two sets of conditions can be made clear.

Zero-sum decision situations have the following characteristics:[8]

1/ It is never *advantageous* to make known to an opponent the equilibrium pure or mixed strategy that it is planned to employ. (Note that whereas nothing is *gained* by disclosure, nothing is *lost* by such an action, provided the equilibrium strategy is maintained.)

2/ There is no benefit to be obtained from communication or cooperation with an opponent prior to the play;

3/ Equilibrium strategies are equivalent (that is, give the same value of the game) and are interchangeable;

4/ If x is a maximin strategy and y is a minimax strategy then (x,y) is an equilibrium pair, and conversely.

Non-zero-sum decision situations have none of these characteristics. They always have a mixed strategy equilibrium pair, but the equilibrium and maximin strategies do not necessarily coincide.

[8]Luce and Raiffa, *Games and Decisions*, p. 90.

The fact that the strategies that form an equilibrium pair are not generally maximin makes them far less attractive than in zero-sum situations, since they do not provide a level of security. In fact, choice of the maximin strategy in a non-zero sum game is an invitation to the opponent to move toward his optimal strategy against the maximin strategy. This, in turn, would generally give reason for the original player not to choose maximin in the first place and so on, into a condition of instability.

A simple example of a non-zero-sum game is described by Luce and Raiffa under the somewhat distracting title "Battle of the Sexes."[9] In this game, a man (player 1) and a woman (player 2) each have two available options, to go to a prize fight (a_1 and b_1) or to a ballet (a_2 and b_2). The man prefers to see the fight and the woman the ballet, but they both prefer to go out together rather than go alone to the preferred entertainment. This game can be illustrated by the payoff matrix in Table 5-1. Equilibria are shown circled in the matrix.

Table 5-2   Pay-off Matrix: The Battle of the Sexes

		Player 2	
		b_1	b_2
Player 1	a_1	(2,1)	−1,−1
	a_2	−1,−1	(1,2)

Comparing the characteristics of this situation with those of a zero-sum game listed earlier, the following comments can be made:

1/ It may well be advantageous to announce a strategy before the play and announce also a determination to stick with it. Player 1 could say, "I am choosing a_1 and will not change my mind." Under these circumstances, player 2, following her preferences, would be forced to choose b_1. She has, in fact, been forced by the prior declaration of player 1 to act in *his* interests, while choosing according to her own preferences. Of course reaction to such a procedure on the part of player 1 could cause player 2 to alter her preferences, change the payoff matrix and initiate a new game situation. However, if she keeps to her *original* preferences, a prior communica-

[9]Luce and Raiffa, *Games and Decisions*, pp. 90–94.

tion benefits both the players, and particularly, the one who makes the declaration.

2/ The strategies (a_1b_1) and (a_2b_2) are both equilibrium pairs since each strategy in a pair is best in the face of the other in the same pair. However, these equilibrium pairs do not yield the same payoffs to the players as would necessarily be the case in a zero-sum situation. Furthermore, the equilibrium strategies are not interchangeable as in the zero-sum case; that is (a_1b_2) and (a_2b_1) are not equilibrium pairs.

3/ The pair of maximin strategies designed to provide a security level is not in equilibrium. It is to the advantage of each player to react to the choice of a maximin strategy by choosing a non-maximin strategy.

The Prisoners' Dilemma Situation

The above example illustrates the differences between zero-sum and non-zero-sum decision situations in what is clearly a rather contrived scenario. A non-zero-sum game that has much greater application to practical decision making is known as Prisoners' Dilemma. In this situation, two men decide to commit a crime but are caught in the act and separated by police before they have an opportunity to communicate. They are placed in separate cells as shown in Figure 5-1 and left to consider their fate. After some time, a police officer enters each cell in turn and discusses with each man his predicament. He says that the prisoner has two available options, to confess to the crime or not to confess and that he is going to make (or has made) the same explanation to the other prisoner. If both do not confess, each man will receive a moderate punishment on a minor charge. If both confess, they will be prosecuted on a major charge, but the police will recom-

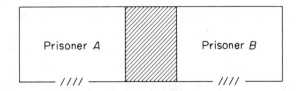

Figure 5-1   Prisoners in Separate Cells Without Communication

mend leniency. However, if one confesses and the other does not, the prisoner who confesses will receive a very light sentence, whereas the other will be treated very severely. The essence of each prisoner's dilemma is that he does not know how his partner will react (or has reacted) to the approach by the police officer.

The payoff matrix for the situation is as shown in Table 5-3. The elements of the matrix represent the preference orderings for the players, a larger number being more preferred and presumably referring to a shorter prison term. The preferences of A and B are shown for each outcome (thus, 4,1) meaning that this outcome is most preferred by A and least preferred by B. The problem for both A and B is to select a strategy from the two available to him.

Table 5-3   Payoff Matrix for Prisoners' Dilemma

			Prisoner B	
			Not Confess	Confess
			b_1	b_2
Prisoner A	Not Confess	a_1	3,3	1,4
	Confess	a_2	4,1	2,2

The prisoners' dilemma situation has been discussed extensively in the literature.[10-13] The paradoxical conclusion is that the rational strategy for each player to pursue to maximize his payoff is to confess. The argument of Prisoner A in reaching this conclusion is that if Prisoner B is going to confess, confessing also will bring the payoff with preference 2 rather than preference 1. If Prisoner B does not confess, for Prisoner A to confess brings a payoff with preference 4 rather than one with preference 3.

Each player can argue, therefore, that his best strategy is to confess, leading to the unique equilibrium pair of the game (a_2b_2) shown circled in Table 5-3.[14] Furthermore a_2 and b_2 are the

[10]Luce and Raiffa, *Games and Decisions*, pp. 94–111.

[11]Howard, *Paradoxes of Rationality*, pp. 44–48.

[12]Anatol Rapoport, *Two Person Game Theory* (Ann Arbor, Mich.: University of Michigan Press, 1966), pp. 128–44.

[13]Wayne Lee, *Decision Theory and Human Behavior* (New York: John Wiley & Sons, 1971), pp. 289–97.

[14]Note that the outcome 2,2 does not *necessarily* mean that the payoffs to the two players are equal. It merely indicates that each obtains his next-to-least-preferred outcome.

unique maximin strategies for prisoners A and B respectively. However, by deserting the rational strategies (a_2b_2) and selecting the pair (a_1b_1) both players are better off. The fact that if both players are irrational they do better than if they act rationally is what Howard has termed "the second breakdown of rationality." (The first breakdown he described as the fact that in some games both players cannot be objectively rational. This was seen to occur in the two-person zero-sum game between Holmes and Moriarty described earlier.)

It would be comforting if one could argue that situations such as Prisoners' Dilemma do not occur in real life; but, in fact, they do. Consider the competition between two firms, each supplying the same product, for which they must independently choose a price, say for simplicity, high or low. Let us assume that each firm would profit most by undercutting the other's price and would profit least by being undercut. Furthermore, assume that between both charging a high price and both charging a low one, each would profit more from the high price situation, although this profit level would not reach that achieved by undercutting the other. The payoff matrix obtained from this situation is exactly that shown for prisoners' dilemma in Table 5-3. The "rational" solution leads to the equilibrium pair of strategies in which both firms set low prices. However, if both act "irrationally" and set high prices both would be better off. A means of dealing with this situation (and other non-zero-sum games) is the subject of the next two sections of this chapter.

It is tempting to say that the solution to the prisoners' dilemma situation is for the prisoners to communicate, either in terms of a binding pact made before the expedition or after the arrest, possibly by a prearranged code. This does not alter the fact, however, that the rational choice of strategy for each of the players in the prisoners' dilemma situation is to break the pact and confess. Assuming that the sole objective of a player in this game is to maximize his payoff, the existence of a pact increases the temptation to confess because the chance that the other will not confess can be assumed to be greater. This may seem to be unethical and it is undoubtedly true that many persons finding themselves in a prisoners' dilemma situation would prefer to remain ethical. However, this changes the payoff matrix and the game. Under the

new conditions, illustrated in Table 5-4, each player most prefers
not to confess in order to keep to a previous binding agreement.

**Table 5-4   Game Derived from Prisoners' Dilemma
Assuming Ethical Players Who Prefer
to Keep to an Agreement**

		Prisoner B	
		Not Confess	Confess
Prisoner A	Not Confess	4,4	1,3
	Confess	3,1	2,2

The strategy pair in which both players do not confess is now
an equilibrium as long as the players prefer to keep to their
agreement. As pointed out above, however, there is a danger to
both players that one will prefer to break the pact, reverting to a
prisoners' dilemma situation and leaving the other vulnerable.
Situations such as shown in Table 5-4 are called *coordination
games.*

It is possible that players could be faced with repeated plays of
the prisoners' dilemma situation and the strategy that should be
employed in such circumstances should be explored. It can be
argued that over a passage of time one player could make it clear
to the other (even without explicit communication) that he would
not confess if the other did not confess. Having passed this mes-
sage he could then defect from the understanding and obtain his
highest preference as an outcome. This might be possible, but it
does not alter the fact that at any time each player is vulnerable to
the other confessing. The only rational strategy remains to confess
on the first play, assuming the conditions of prisoners' dilemma
are maintained.

The prisoners' dilemma type of situation is not limited to two
persons. It may be applied equally well to a situation involving
many people. Methods of treating prisoners' dilemma developed
later in this chapter are particularly applicable to decision problems involving coalitions of players, in which the temptation to
defect from a coalition to obtain greater benefit must be considered.

Lee has summarized the results of a number of laboratory experiments conducted by various researchers to study the reaction

of subjects in a prisoners' dilemma situation.[15] These experiments are generally inconclusive. Lee says that the subjects use both strategies in the game, but that the "confess" strategy typically predominates. Those involved in the experiments seemed relatively unaffected by the opponent's strategy and found a great deal of difficulty in interpreting it.

The major conclusion to be drawn from the study of prisoners' dilemma is that one cannot and should not rely on rational behavior from the opponent. Situations like prisoners' dilemma (and other many-person, non-zero-sum games) occur in everyday management. In such circumstances, to assume that a competitor will necessarily act in a rational manner may be misleading. It may, in fact, be an advantage to act irrationally oneself on occasion. Furthermore, the possibility that a partner in a coalition may break the agreement to seek greater benefit elsewhere should always be kept in mind.

An Approach to Non-zero-sum Decision Situations

The manager reading these pages might well throw up his hands in despair at this point saying, "I've been led to believe by my analysts over all these years that I should be rational and *optimize*. Now I'm told that this may not be to my advantage. What's to become of me now?"

The response to this valid question is that he should seek to be *objectively rational* in all situations rather than to pursue what superfically appears to be an optimum solution. To be objectively rational requires that the decision maker have perfect information, which is rarely possible. However, the approach of the decision maker should be to obtain as much information as possible (including that concerning the strategies of the others involved) before coming to a decision. Since the strategies of the other players are in turn likely to depend on their knowledge of those of the first, this appears to involve a vicious circle. Fortunately, there is a method of proceeding in such circumstances. However, before describing that method some further discussion of the structure of games is required.

[15]Lee, *Decision Theory*, pp. 291–97.

The Nature and Theory of Metagames[16]

The development that follows is based on Nigel Howard's approach to game theory contained in his book *Paradoxes of Rationality*[17] and in some others of his writings. The serious mathematical student is urged to consult these works. The following discussion provides just sufficient of the theory to allow the development of the method of *analysis of options* in the next section of this chapter.

The basis for metagame (Greek *meta*: after) theory is a recommendation by von Neumann and Morgenstern in their classical work on game theory that to study a given two-person, zero-sum game, the games that can be devised in which each player is able to predict the other's strategy should be studied also. Von Neumann and Morgenstern called these the majorant and minorant games. This involves studying player 1's reaction to player 2's strategy choice, player 2's reaction to player 1's reaction, and so on. Howard generalized this idea to many-person, non-zero-sum games and obtained an infinite tree of metagames based on any given game G. This illustrated in Figure 5-2. In this tree, the game 2G, for example, is the game in which player 2 can predict the strategies of all the other players in the game G.

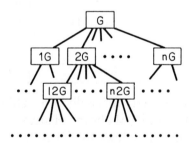

Figure 5-2   The Metagame Tree

[16]The material contained in this section is introductory to the development in the next section of the analysis of options. Whereas this material is necessary to the logical development, those interested only in the technique described in the next section may pass directly to it, at the risk, however, of a lesser understanding of the foundation on which the technique is based.

[17]Howard, *Paradoxes of Rationality*, pp. 60 ff.

The justification for studying the metagame (for example, the 2G metagame above) is that if player 2 wishes to be objectively rational he must choose (and attempt to follow) a strategy in the 2G metagame. Recall that objective rationality requires knowledge of the other players' choices of strategy, knowledge that is not available in the original game G. *It is, however, available in the metagame.*

The purpose of constructing the metagame tree is to investigate an equilibrium state that can be called *actual stability.* This is a state in which all players discern correctly what strategies the others will choose. Actual stability is of particular interest to the decision maker in that it provides a certain level of security in a competitive situation. A situation that is not actually stable cannot be expected to persist for long in a conflict situation.

To illustrate the construction of metagames, consider the earlier example, based on a prisoners' dilemma situation, of two firms engaged in a price competition. The payoff matrix in the game (which we can now call G) is as shown in Table 5-5. The outcome (2,2) is the unique equilibrium.

Table 5-5   A Pricing Problem

			Firm 2	
			Pricing Strategy	
			High (H)	Low (L)
Firm 1	Pricing Strategy	High (H)	3,3	1,4
		Low (L)	4,1	2,2

The game 2G is shown in Table 5-6. This shows Firm 2's possible reactions to an initial choice of strategy by Firm 1. There are four such possible reactions by Firm 2:

always high, whatever Firm 1 does
always low, whatever Firm 1 does
high against Firm 1's high, low against their low
low against Firm 1's high, high against their low.

These are shown in the 2G game as available strategies for Firm 2:

Table 5-6   The 2G Metagame Derived from Figure 5-6

		Firm 2		
	Always High	Always Low	High against High Low against Low	Low against High High against Low
Firm 1 High	3,3	1,4	3,3	1,4
Low	4,1	2,2	2,2	4,1

The preferences inserted in the payoff matrix for the 2G game shown in Table 5-6 are derived from Table 5-5. For example, if Firm 1 selects "High" and Firm 2 "Always Low," this results in the H/L outcome (1,4) shown in Table 5-5, and so on.

It is important to note at this stage that Firm 2, in constructing the 2G metagame, is not actually taking a decision. Rather it is indulging in an analysis of the question, "What if Firm 1 selects a particular strategy?" In its turn, Firm 1 can assess the question, "What if Firm 2 selects a particular reaction to my selection of a strategy?" This results in the construction of the 12G metagame shown in Table 5-7. In this metagame, Firm 1 can choose any one of the two strategies "High" and "Low" in reaction to Firm 2's choice of one of the four strategies (always high, always low, high against high and low against low, low against high and high against low). This results in sixteen strategies shown in Table 5-7. The strategy HLLH, for example, represents the reaction

> High against   Always High
> Low against   Always Low
> Low against   High against High and Low against Low
> and   High against   Low against High and High against Low

The elements in the 12G metagame matrix shown in Table 5-7 are assigned in the following manner. Consider Firm 1's strategies HLLH (the sixth from the bottom) against Firm 2's strategy (low against high, high against low) at the right-hand side. This results in a strategy H for Firm 1 against (low against high, high against low) for Firm 2, that is L for Firm 2. Referring now to the original game matrix in Figure 5-6, this results in the outcome (1,4), which is shown in the appropriate position in Table 5-7. The 12G metagame shown in Table 5-7, therefore, represents Firm 1's reactions to Firm 2's reactions to Firm 1's strategy choice. The

Table 5-7   The 12G Metagame

Firm 1	Firm 2 Always High	Always Low	High against High Low against Low	Low against High High against Low
HHHH	3,3	1,4	3,3	1,4
LLLL	4,1	(2,2)	2,2	4,1
LLLH	4,1	2,2	2,2	1,4
LLHL	4,1	2,2	(3,3)	4,1
LLHH	4,1	2,2	3,3	1,4
LHLL	4,1	1,4	2,2	4,1
LHLH	4,1	1,4	2,2	1,4
LHHL	4,1	1,4	3,3	4,1
LHHH	4,1	1,4	3,3	1,4
HLLL	3,3	2,2	2,2	4,1
HLLH	3,3	2,2	2,2	1,4
HLHL	3,3	2,2	(3,3)	4,1
HLHH	3,3	2,2	3,3	1,4
HHLL	3,3	1,4	2,2	4,1
HHLH	3,3	1,4	2,2	1,4
HHHL	3,3	1,4	3,3	4,1

strategies (low against high, high against low) and HLLH, for example, may be thought of as *policies* of the firms.

One might well ask what advantage is to be gained from a study of the metagames 2G and 12G. This can be answered by a simple example. First consider the game 2G shown in Table 5-6. Note, in passing, that we could equally well consider the game 1G, which is exactly the same, but with the roles of players reversed.

In the 2G game, the only equilibrium is still (2,2) resulting from the strategy pair (L, always L). The outcome (L,L), yielding (2,2), can be called the only *meta-equilibrium* from the metagame 2G. Nothing has been gained this far in terms of equilibria since the metagame 2G has yielded nothing new in this respect. However, something has been gained in terms of expanding the notion of a rational outcome.

Building on the definition of a rational outcome for a player as one that is the best attainable outcome for him given some strategy by the other player, we can define a *meta-rational* outcome for a player as one that yields a rational outcome for him in a metagame. In the 2G metagame, the outcome (3,3) is metarational for Firm 1 since it has become its best attainable outcome in response to the policy "high against high, low against low." However, the meta-rational outcomes for Firm 2 in the 2G metagame are simply the same as its rational ones in the original game. Proceeding to the 12G metagame, however, Firm 2's meta-rational outcomes now can be seen from Table 5-7 to include that defined by the strategy pair (H,H). This strategy pair yielding the outcome (3,3) is, in fact, an equilibrium in the metagame 12G (i.e., a meta-equilibrium), *even though it does not appear as an equilibrium in the original game.*[18] This arises because if Firm 2 chooses the policy (high against high, low against low) that can be interpreted as "I will cooperate if you will," it is Firm 1's interests to cooperate, that is to choose the policy LLHL. (Let us ignore any legal barriers to such cooperation at this stage.) At the same time, the policy LLHL, makes it in player 2's interests to choose the policy "high against high, low against low."

The foregoing is necessarily a simple example. However, it serves to show how a *new jointly rational outcome* can be discovered by a study of the appropriate metagames. This outcome does not appear as an outcome of rational choices of strategies in the original game. Moreover, it can be proved that, in the above example, the strategy pairs (H,H) and (L,L) are the only meta-equilibria from every metagame based on the original game, in which each player is named in the title (e.g., 12G) of the game at least once. Having discovered (H,H) as a meta-equilibrium, it is not lost in other metagames in the infinite tree. Furthermore, no other meta-equilibria will appear in these games. For proofs and discussions of these assertions, the reader is referred to the original work in this area contained in Nigel Howard's book, *Paradoxes of Rationality.*[19]

Application of Metagame Theory

The basic concepts of meta-equilibria and meta-rationality are those on which the application of metagame theory to managerial

---

[18]In searching for equilibria, it is perhaps helpful to remember that Firm 1's options are shown vertically in Table 5-7 and Firm 2's options are shown horizontally. By searching for an outcome in the directions ↕3, 3, it can be determined whether more preferred outcomes exist for any player, and thus, whether the original outcome is an equilibrium.

[19]Howard, *Paradoxes of Rationality,* pp. 60 ff.

decision making is based. The application consists essentially of considering, for each "player" in turn, the characteristics of the metagames in which he is involved. The procedure is as follows.

Let us assume that a manager wishes to consider the position of his organization relative to a particular situation, which we call a *scenario*. The scenario is described in terms of the options, positions or policies of those involved in the situation under study. Each player is interested in the *stability* of the scenario, which means, in essence, whether it can continue to exist as a result of some implicit or explicit agreement between all concerned. More generally, each may wish to know whether it can be a final position after all concerned have correctly assessed the other's strategy choices. Note that a scenario can be stable only if it can be stable for each player separately, so that stability must be investigated for each in turn.

To decide whether a scenario can be stable for a particular player involved in the decision situation we must ask whether it is rational for him. If it is and if the other parties involved continue to select the strategies described in the scenario, then it will certainly be stable for him. The stability of the scenario for the player concerned will be questionable only if there exists a strategy by which he can improve his position by acting unilaterally, assuming for the moment that the strategies of the others involved remain unchanged. Such a change of strategy can be called a *unilateral improvement* for him.

To determine whether a unilateral improvement exists for any "particular player" the options of that player are varied while keeping the positions of the others fixed. Each new scenario thus created is examined to determine whether it is *preferred* or *not preferred* by the particular player, as compared to the particular scenario chosen for analysis. A preferred scenario is a unilateral improvement, since it can be brought about by unilateral action on the part of the particular player. If no unilateral improvement can be found the original scenario can be considered as stable for the player concerned, *provided he believes that the other players will keep to their parts in it*. It is rational for the player to remain at this stable position (at least for the time being) since he has no means of improving his position by an action on his part.

A full analysis would, of course, consider all possible unilateral improvements from the original scenario available to all players. However, continuing to follow our particular player, let us assume that a unilateral improvement has been found for him. It is now necessary to consider what actions on the part of the other players would prevent him from taking advantage of the improvement, provided he believed that the other players would in fact take these actions. Any such action by any one or more of the other players is called a *sanction* against the player having the available unilateral improvement.

It is necessary to consider all possible sanctions against the particular player by the other players relative to the particular scenario being considered. This is done by varying the available options of the other players and deciding for each combination of their options whether the new scenario represented by each such combination is "preferred" or "not preferred" by the original player, *whatever course of action he takes*. If a particular combination of the other player's available options is "not preferred" whatever the particular player does, this is a sanction against him. This procedure is repeated until all sanctions have been found. The scenario being considered is then said to be stable for the particular player, as long as he believes that if he were to take one of his unilateral improvements the other players would react by implementing a sanction. If no sanctions exist against the particular player being considered, however, a further step is indicated.

This further step consists of looking for all *inescapable* (or *guaranteed*) *improvements* for the player from the particular scenario being considered. Such an improvement is better for him whatever the other players may do in terms of choosing from their stated available options.

The above procedure forms the basis for the *analysis of options* discussed in the next section. This type of analysis is firmly based on theory yet can be understood by nontechnical persons, as the examples given in the following sections will show. The procedure can be repeated for any particular player, any starting-point scenario, any coalition of players and any sets of options available to the players or the coalitions.

It is interesting at this stage to compare this procedure with that described by March and Simon[20] under the "principle of bounded rationality." Referring to this, Simon states in *Administrative Behavior*, that managers "satisfice," that is, look for a course of action that is satisfactory or good enough.[21] The inference is that

[20]J.G. March and H.A. Simon, *Organizations* (New York: John Wiley & Sons, 1958), p. 169.
[21]Herbert A. Simon, *Administrative Behavior* (New York: The Free Press, 1965), p. xxv.

instead of optimizing in the strict sense of proceeding to a maximum they consider all the constraints bearing on the decision situation and choose a course of action that is satisfactory to them. Given that many of the constraints are due to the actions of others, the agreement between the apparent behavior described by Simon and the procedure being described here is very close.

The Analysis of Options

The procedure described in the preceding section may now be formalized into a series of steps as follows:

Step 1/ List all the parties (players) involved in the decision situation and all their available options;

Step 2/ List details of the particular scenario to be evaluated. This is done in terms of the strategies of the players in that scenario. The particular scenario chosen need not be the current situation (status quo), although it might be. The general question to be answered is "What if we were in this particular situation: would it be stable?"

Step 3/ Select a particular player (or coalition) with respect to whom it is desired to evaluate the stability (or otherwise) of a particular situation (scenario) made up of potential choices of available options by the participants in the decision situation;

Step 4/ Find all the unilateral improvements from the particular scenario for the player or coalition selected. If none exists, proceed to assess the unilateral improvements available to all other players and coalitions in turn. (i.e., return to Step 3). If a unilateral improvement exists for the particular player or coalition proceed to Step 5. (Some combinations of options may be judged "infeasible" and can be neglected at this stage.)

Step 5/ Determine all the sanctions available to the other players against the particular player or coalition relative to the particular scenario. (Neglect infeasibilities). If a sanction exists against the particular player return to Step 2 or Step 3 and consider any other scenario, player or coalition. If no sanction exists proceed to Step 6.

Step 6/ Find all inescapable (or guaranteed) improvements for the particular player or coalition from the particular scenario. Return to Step 1 to consider different sets of options, or Step 2 to consider a different particular scenario or to Step 3 to consider a different particular player or coalition.

This procedure is illustrated in Figure 5-3.

The analysis of options methodology (sometimes called *metagame analysis*) has been applied to a number of practical problems in recent years and reports of these applications are beginning to appear in the literature.[22-26] The examples in the next section are necessarily less complex than many experienced in real-life situations, but will serve to illustrate the technique.

Examples of the Application of Analysis of Options

The first example given here is based closely on the pricing problem illustrated in Table 5-5. Suppose that we are the management team of a U.S. firm (Firm 1) that is presently selling a specialized product in both the U.S. and Canada. We are concerned that a Canadian firm (Firm 2), now selling the same product in Canada only, may lower its prices below ours, or make a significant intrusion into the U.S. market or do both. Firm 1 is considering lowering its own prices as a defensive measure. Generally speaking, a firm would be expected to gain if it alone lowers its prices, but not if both firms do so. The management of Firm 1 is anxious to know the effects of possible actions by Firm 2 and, furthermore, what actions it should take to counter any such actions.

Following the procedure outlined in Figure 5-3, the first step is to list the "players" and their available options. In this case, the

[22]Howard, *Paradoxes of Rationality*, pp. 106–7.

[23]Management Science Center, University of Pennsylvania, "The Analysis of Options: A Computer Aided Method for Analyzing Political Problems," Volume 2 of Report ACDA/ST149 prepared for the U.S. Arms Control and Disarmament Agency, Washington, D.C., 1969.

[24]Nigel Howard, "The Arab-Israeli Conflict: A Metagame Analysis Done in 1970," *Peace Research Society Papers XIX*, The Ann Arbor Conference, 1971.

[25]Howard, *Paradoxes of Rationality*, pp. 127–46.

[26]Nigel Howard, "Metagame Analysis of a Business Problem," *Canadian Journal of Operational Research and Information Processing (INFOR)* 13 (February, 1975).

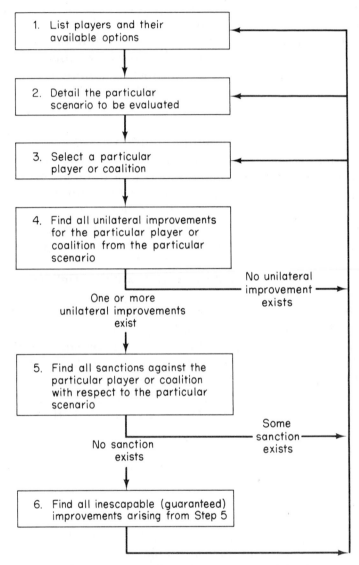

Figure 5-3   Procedure for Analysis of Options

available options consist of the actions that the firms could take to move away from the present position, which we will call the status quo. The players and options in this simple example are shown in Table 5-8.

We now introduce a simple convention. To indicate whether a player takes an option, a "1" is written against it if that option is

**Table 5-8   Players and Options in a Simple Example
of Analysis of Options**

Firm 1	Lower U.S. prices
(U.S.)	Lower Canadian prices
Firm 2	Lower Canadian prices
(Canada)	Invade U.S. Market: high prices
	Invade U.S. Market: low prices

taken and a "0" is written if it is not. A series of 1's and 0's written
against a player's options then represents that player's *strategy*
and a whole column of 1's and 0's represents a *scenario* in the
decision situation (or "game"). This is illustrated in Table 5-9.
The scenario represented in this Figure is that in which Firm 1
lowers its U.S., but not its Canadian, prices and Firm 2 invades the
U.S. market with high prices, but does not lower its Canadian
prices. We assume that Firm 2 cannot invade the U.S. market
simultaneously with high and low prices and therefore that any
scenario in which 1's occur against each of these options can be
regarded as *infeasible* and given no further consideration. The
situation shown in Table 5-8, therefore, has 24 feasible scenarios.
In a practical problem, the number of scenarios would be much
greater. Note that we do not assign any preferences to these
scenarios at the outset. Any necessary assertions about the preferences of the players for scenarios can be inserted into the analysis
as they are needed.

Table 5-9   Strategies and Scenario in Firm 1 vs. Firm 2 Situation

Firm 1	Lower U.S. Prices	1 }	Firm 1's
(U.S.)	Lower Canadian Prices	0 }	strategy
Firm 2	Lower Canadian Prices	0 }	Firm 2's
(Canadian)	Invade U.S. Market: high prices	1 }	strategy
	Invade U.S. Market: low prices	0 }	
		Scenario	

We now proceed to Step 2 and select a *particular scenario.*
Acting as we are on behalf of Firm 1, we are interested in whether
this scenario can be *stable* and if so, how. This involves an
analysis of the policies required of the players to bring about
stability or otherwise. Let us assume that Firm 1 is interested in

the stability of the status quo, that is the situation before any player makes a move.

Moving to Step 3, Firm 1 is naturally interested first in whether the status quo is stable for its rival, since it is concerned that Firm 2 may upset the status quo; Firm 2 is therefore selected as the *particular player*. Later in the analysis, different particular scenarios and players can be selected and the stability of these scenarios for these players examined. The first question, therefore, is whether the status quo is rational for Firm 2, since if it is, Firm 2 would have no reason to make a unilateral departure from it. This is approached by assigning each combination of Firm 2's options to one of three classes: "preferred to the status quo," "not preferred to the status quo" or "infeasible." This is illustrated in Table 5-10. Note that Firm 2's preferences shown in this table are, in fact, *Firm 1's estimates of Firm 2's preferences*, rather than exact information concerning the situation.

The blanks ("–") in Table 5-10 represent "either 1 or 0." A column containing blanks, therefore, represents more than one scenario. Column 1, for example, represents a scenario in which Firm 1's U.S. and Canadian prices remain high and Firm 2's Canadian prices are lowered. This is estimated by Firm 1 to be preferred by Firm 2 to the status quo, whether or not they also invade the U.S. market with high or low prices. Thus, Column 1 represents a *unilateral improvement* for Firm 2 from the status quo, (in Firm 1's opinion) being an improvement that Firm 2 can bring about by unilateral action. Since a unilateral improvement is seen to exist, it is clear that the status quo cannot necessarily be considered as stable for Firm 2 and that it is not seen as rational for Firm 2 to remain in the status quo situation.

A modified form of the tableau shown in Table 5-10 provides slightly more information. Against each blank in the tableau, a bracketed figure can be inserted (thus: (1)). Taken together, these figures represent the least preferred way of filling in the blanks from the point of view of Firm 2 (as estimated by Firm 1). This gives rise to the tableau shown in Table 5-11. If the least preferred way of filling in the blanks describes a scenario that is regarded as preferred to the status quo, certainly all the scenarios represented by the column must be preferred. If blanks occur in columns in the "Not Preferred" category, the bracketed figures must, of course, represent the most preferred way of filling in the

Table 5-10   Unilateral Improvements for Firm 2 from the Status Quo

		Firm 2's Preferences				
		Preferred to Status Quo		Status Quo	Not Preferred to Status Quo	Infeasible
Firm 1 (U.S.)	Lower U.S. Prices	0	0	0	none	—
	Lower Canadian Prices	0	0	0		—
Firm 2 (Canadian)	Lower Canadian Prices	1	—	0		—
	Invade U.S.: high prices	—	1	0		1
	Invade U.S.: low prices	—	0	1		1
	Column Number	1	2	3		4

Table 5-11   Modified Tableau Showing Unilateral Improvements for Firm 2 from the Status Quo

		Firm 2's Preferences				
		Preferred to Status Quo		Status Quo	Not Preferred to Status Quo	Infeasible
Firm 1 (U.S.)	Lower U.S. Prices	0	0	0	none	—
	Lower Canadian Prices	0	0	0		—
Firm 2 (Canadian)	Lower Canadian Prices	1	—(0)	0		—
	Invade U.S.: high prices	—(0)	1	0		1
	Invade U.S.: low prices	—(0)	0	1		1
	Column Number	1	2	3		4

blanks, since if the most preferred scenario is "not preferred" all scenarios in the column must surely be "not preferred."

It is important that *all* relevant scenarios be included in a tableau such as that shown in Table 5-11, so that nothing is overlooked. This should be checked at this stage by a simple procedure as follows. Note that in this tableau, only Firm 2's options have been varied. (The set of options varied in a tableau is called the omega set (Ω-set).) Firm 2 has three options, which would normally lead to eight scenarios. However, two options are infeasible together and when taken with the choice of lowering Canadian prices or not, this provides that two of the eight are infeasible. The six remaining scenarios can be checked as being made up of those represented by Columns 1, 2 and 3 (noting that some redundancy occurs in these columns). Having checked that all scenarios are accounted for, we may now proceed to Step 5.

Since the status quo is seen as not stable for Firm 2 (i.e., Firm 2 has a unilateral improvement), the question now arises of whether there are sanctions against Firm 2 for the status quo. To find such sanctions in this example, it is necessary to assign each combination of Firm 1's options to one of the three categories: (a) not preferred by Firm 2 to the status quo (in Firm 1's opinion) when blanks are written against all Firm 2's options (this denotes a *sanction*); (b) preferred by Firm 2 to the status quo (in Firm 1's opinion) when some combination of values is written against Firm 2's options (this is *not* a sanction) and (c) infeasible. This process is illustrated in Table 5-12.

Table 5-12   Sanctions Against Firm 2 for the Status Quo

		Firm 2's Preferences			
		Preferred to Status Quo	Status Quo	Not Preferred to Status Quo	Infeasible
Firm 1	Lower U.S. Prices	– (1)	0	– (0)	–
(U.S.)	Lower Canadian Prices	0	0	1	–
Firm 2	Lower Canadian Prices	1	0	– (1)	–
(Canadian)	Invade U.S.: high prices	0	0	– (0)	1
	Invade U.S.: low prices	0	0	– (1)	1
	Column Number	1	2	3	

Note that it is Firm 1's options that are varied in this new tableau and that the omega-set is made up of combinations of these options. All members of the omega-set are shown in the tableau.

The conclusion to be drawn from this tableau is that there does exist a sanction against Firm 2 with respect to the status quo. It is shown in Column 3 and it consists of Firm 1 exercising the option "lower prices in the Canadian market." This sanction is such that if Firm 2 really believed that it would be Firm 1's reaction to a unilateral move by Firm 2, it would suffice to deter Firm 2 from making such a move (based on Firm 1's estimates of Firm 2's preferences). The question of the *credibility* of the sanction is of fundamental importance. The use to which Firm 1 puts the above conclusion regarding the existence of a sanction must depend on its estimate of the reaction of Firm 2 to the moves comprising the sanction.

The fact that a sanction has been found to exist means that it is not necessary to proceed to Step 6. There can be no inescapable (guaranteed) improvements for Firm 2. We can now return to Step 2 or 3 and analyze the situation with respect to another scenario or player.

An Extension of the Firm 1—Firm 2 Problem

Let us suppose that Firm 1 wished to investigate the scenario in which both firms lower their prices in the Canadian market, but in which Firm 2 does not enter the U.S. market. This scenario is shown in Table 5-13.

Table 5-13 Scenario with Price War in the Canadian Market

Firm 1	Lower U.S. Prices	0
(U.S.)	Lower Canadian Prices	1
Firm 2	Lower Canadian Prices	1
(Canadian)	Invade U.S. Market: high prices	0
	Invade U.S. Market: low prices	0

From our knowledge of the analysis conducted to date, we know that a sanction exists for Firm 1 to deter Firm 2 from moving from the status quo (i.e., the scenario with all 0's shown against options). This sanction is "lower prices in the Canadian market." It is clear, however, that if both firms have lowered their prices, as in the scenario about to be investigated, this sanction is not applicable. This indicates that we should move to Step 6 of the analysis procedure and determine whether Firm 2 has any guaranteed improvements from the new scenario. Guaranteed improvements are strategies of Firm 2 that will guarantee an improvement from the scenario in question to Firm 2 (in Firm 1's opinion) regardless of Firm 1's reaction. This is illustrated in Table 5-14. Note that in this tableau, the omega-set (the options that are varied) consists of Firm 2's options.

A guaranteed improvement is shown in Table 5-14 in Column 1. This can be interpreted as follows: (in Firm 1's opinion) Firm 2 would have a guaranteed improvement if it simultaneously lowered its Canadian prices *and* invaded the U.S. market with low prices. Firm 1 can conclude therefore that the scenario considered in Table 5-14 is unstable—that Firm 2 would move from such a scenario to one more preferred.

It must be remembered that the entire analysis described has been conducted on the basis of Firm 1's opinions of Firm 2's preferences. These opinions would need to be checked in every way possible. Furthermore, the situation should be investigated from the point of view of all possible combinations of other players and scenarios.

The process of analysis is made considerably less onerous by use of a simple computer program, called MGAME. This program was developed originally at the University of Pennsylvania.[27] A version of it has been implemented on the IBM 370 computer system under CMS (Conversational Monitor System).[28] The use of the program starts with listing the players and their options, the particular scenario to be considered and the particular player or coalition. The program then allows a tableau to be constructed by entering preferences for scenarios and judgments regarding infeasibilities. A notification is received from the program if all combinations of the options being considered (the omega-set) have not been assessed. All tableaux can be stored and portions recovered and displayed at will as the analysis proceeds.

[27]Management Science Center, "Analysis of Options."

[28]M. Chandrashekar, "Analysis of Options: An Interactive Computer Program (MGAME)," Department of Systems Design, University of Waterloo, Waterloo, Ontario, January, 1974.

Table 5-14 Guaranteed Improvements for Firm 2 from the Price-War Scenario

		Firm 2's Preferences				
		Preferred to Price-War Scenario	Price-War Scenario	Not Preferred to Price-War Scenario		Infeasible
Firm 1 (U.S.)	Lower U.S. Prices	– (1)	0	– (0)	– (0)	–
	Lower Canadian Prices	– (1)	1	1	1	–
Firm 2 (Canadian)	Lower Canadian Prices	1	1	0	0	–
	Invade U.S.: High prices	0	0	– (1)	– (0)	1
	Invade U.S.: Low prices	1	0	– (0)	– (1)	1
	Column Number	1	2	3	4	

157

A More Complex Example of the Analysis of Options

A more complex example of the analysis of options concerns an imaginary corporation that we will call Delta, which manufactures a product.[29] Another corporation, Gamma, is an important customer of the Delta corporation. The local union has announced a strike against Delta and has called for a boycott of Delta's product. Gamma wishes to preserve its record of excellent industrial relations and is considerably embarrassed by the call for a boycott. In addition, Gamma is worried about Delta's ability to supply the product if the strike continues. A fourth "player," the international union is in full support of the local union's strike and also supports its call for a boycott of Delta. We can imagine ourselves in the position of Delta's management facing the question of how to handle the situation. An arbitrator has been called in and has proposed a settlement. This is a compromise between the local union's demand for a pay increase and the Delta management's position that it cannot afford to pay such an increase at the present time. To maintain production Delta has called in nonunion labor and this has been partially successful.

The available strategies of the four players in this situation are as shown in Table 5-15. These strategies do not necessarily represent all options available to the parties in such a situation. However, those shown are sufficient to illustrate the application of the method. Note that options 1 and 2 (of the local union) are dependent on option 5 of Delta and that options 3 and 6 are dependent on one another. The status quo is described by the right-hand column indicating the players' present strategies. The contents of Table 5-15 can be considered as the Delta management's assessment of the present position. This assessment may, of course, change as consideration of the problem proceeds. Thus options may be added or deleted if the Delta management considers this appropriate to the situation at any time.

We have now completed Step 1 of the analysis as shown in Figure 5-3. Players and their available options have been listed. The next step is to select a particular scenario that the party

---

[29] Howard, "Metagame Analysis of a Business Problem."

**Table 5-15   Options of Players and Initial Strategy
Choices in the Industrial Relations Problem**

Player	Available Strategies	Players Initial Strategy Choices
Local Union	1. Proclaim boycott (unless Delta meets union demands)	1
	2. Strike (unless Delta meets union demands)	1
	3. Settle (if Delta will settle)	0
Delta	4. Employ nonunion labor	1
	5. Meet union demands	0
	6. Settle (if union will settle)	0
International Union	7. Support local union	1
Gamma	8. Buy from Delta	1

conducting the analysis (in our case, Delta management) wishes to examine to assess its stability.

Suppose that the Delta management selects the arbitrator's proposed settlement as the scenario to be examined. Note that this is not the situation in which the players find themselves at the present time (the status quo), but a proposed future situation. Delta management is investigating the question, "What if we settle; would that be stable?" The proposed settlement is shown by column number 3 in the center of Table 5-16.

Proceeding to Step 3, it is necessary to select a particular player or coalition for which it is desired to examine the particular scenario. Delta probably would wish to examine the stability of the arbitrator's proposed settlement for all players and all coalitions. For the purpose of this discussion, let us assume that it is decided first to examine the settlement proposal as it affects the interests of the Delta corporation.

Step 4 involves finding all unilateral improvements for Delta from the arbitrator's proposed settlement. This is illustrated in Table 5-16. This tableau is formed by keeping the strategy choices of all players except Delta fixed at those required by the particular scenario being considered and varying Delta's choices of strategies. Each scenario thus obtained is placed in one of the three categories: "Preferred" or "Not preferred" (to the proposed settlement) or "Infeasible." This is done on the basis of the preferences of the Delta Corporation, as assessed by those conducting the analysis.

It can be seen from the tableau in Table 5-16 that Delta is assessed as preferring to employ nonunion labor regardless of whether a settlement was made (Column 1). Delta would also prefer to refuse a settlement whether or not nonunion labor was employed (Column 2) provided, of course, that the other players were constrained to their strategy choices contained in the proposed settlement.

On the other hand, Delta does not prefer the option of meeting the union demands over that of settling (Column 4), whether or not nonunion labor is used.

Having found that Delta has some unilateral improvements from the proposed settlement (and hence, that the settlement will not be stable unless sanctions exist against Delta), it is now possible to proceed to Step 5 and investigate these sanctions. Before doing so, however, it is necessary to check that the tableau shown in Table 5-16 does in fact contain all possible combinations of Delta's options (which it does).

Sanctions against Delta are shown in Table 5-17. Consideration of this tableau shows that a sanction exists that would deter Delta from using nonunion labor and/or refusing to settle. This is the possibility that Gamma would opt (or be forced to opt) to refuse to buy from Delta. Since a sanction exists, it is not appropriate to proceed to Step 6.

The conclusion from Table 5-17 leads Delta to consider a coalition (explicit or implicit) with Gamma. The Delta management, therefore, selects a Delta-Gamma coalition as the particular player for further analysis, while remaining with the proposed settlement as the particular scenario. Proceeding to Step 4, a tableau is prepared showing unilateral improvements for the Delta-Gamma coalition from the proposed settlement. This is shown in Table 5-18. A scenario is said to be preferred by a coalition if *all* coalition members prefer it, and not preferred if some member does not prefer it. Hence in this tableau, the least preferred choices for each member of the coalition must be shown against each option in the "Preferred" columns (Columns 1 and 2 of Table 5-18) since these columns are preferred by all coalition members. The "Not Preferred" columns (4 and 5), on the other hand, are not preferred by single members of the coalition.

Table 5-16 Tableau Showing Unilateral Improvements for Delta from Proposed Settlement

Player		Preferred by Delta	Proposed Settlement	Not Preferred by Delta	Infeasible
Local	1. Boycott	0	0	0	
	2. Strike	0	0	0	
	3. Settle	1	1	1	
Delta	4. Employ nonunion labor	1 – (0)	0	– (1)	
	5. Meet demands	0	0	1	1
	6. Settle	– (1) 0	1	– (0)	1
International Union	7. Support local	1	1	1	
Gamma	8. Buy from Delta	1	1	1	
	Column number	2	3	4	

Table 5-17 Sanctions Against Delta with Respect to Proposed Settlement

Player		Preferred by Delta	Proposed Settlement	Not Preferred by Delta	Infeasible		
Local Union	1. Boycott	– (1)	0	– (0)		1	1
	2. Strike	– (1)	0	– (0)	1	1	
	3. Settle	– (0)	1	– (0)	1	1	
Delta	4. Employ nonunion labor	1	0	– (1)			
	5. Meet demands	0	0	– (0)			
	6. Settle	0	1	– (0)			
International Union	7. Support local	– (1)	1	– (0)			
Gamma	8. Buy from Delta	1	1	0			
Column Numbers		1	2	3	4	5	6

162

Table 5-18 Tableau Showing Unilateral Improvements for Delta-Gamma Coalition from Proposed Settlement

Player		Preferred by Delta Gamma Coalition		Proposed Settlement	Not Preferred by Delta	by Gamma	Infeasible
Local Union	1. Boycott	0	0	0	0	0	
	2. Strike	0	0	0	0	0	
	3. Settle	1	_Delta Gamma_	1	1		
Delta	4. Employ nonunion labor	1	– [0] [1]	0	– (1)	– (0)	
	5. Meet demands	0 _Delta Gamma_		0	1	– (0)	1
	6. Settle	– (1) (1)	0	1	– (0)	– (0)	1
International Union	7. Support Local	1	1	1	1	1	
Gamma	8. Buy from Delta	1	1	1	– (1)	0	
	Column Number	1	2	3	4	5	6

It is important to remember at this stage that the judgments represented by "preferred" and "not preferred" are those of the Delta management alone based on their assessment of the situation. The opinions of the other players in the "game" are not sought or included in the tableau. However, the judgments by the Delta management are presumably based on as much information as they can obtain about the other players' preferences. These judgments may be expressed as follows (referring to Table 5-18).

   1/ Delta and Gamma would both prefer a scenario (Column 1) under which Delta continues to employ nonunion labor to the settlement proposed by the arbitrator; and would prefer still more that Delta employ such labor and refuse any settlement at all if at the same time the strike and the boycott were ended (Column 2). (Note the different views in the coalition about employing nonunion labor due to Gamma's embarrassment with regard to its own industrial relations.)

   2/ Delta's best prospect, given that the union demands must be met, is to continue employing nonunion labor and to continue to have Gamma as a customer (Column 4). From Gamma's point of view (as seen by the Delta management), not to buy from Delta is less preferred than the proposed settlement (Column 5).

The conclusion from the tableau shown in Table 5-18 is that Delta, by refusing to settle (whether or not it continues to employ nonunion labor), can foresee scenarios preferred to the proposed settlement provided the other players do not choose certain strategies in reaction to Delta's refusal to settle.

The analysis now moves to Step 5 and sanctions are considered against the Delta-Gamma coalition with respect to the proposed settlement. This is illustrated in Table 5-19.

The conclusion to be drawn from the tableau in Table 5-19 is that the coalition of Delta and Gamma can be deterred from taking the unilateral improvements shown in Table 5-18 if they believe that the reaction to such moves would be a strike and a boycott, backed by the international union (Columns 4 and 5). This sanction would, if credible, deter the coalition so that Delta would not be able to count on cooperation from Gamma. Once again, a

Table 5-19 Sanctions Against the Delta-Gamma Coalition With Respect to the Proposed Settlement

Player		Preferred by the Delta-Gamma Coalition		Proposed Settlement	Not Preferred		Infeasible			
		Delta	Gamma		by Delta	by Gamma				
Local Union	1. Boycott	0	– (1)	0	1	1	1	1		
	2. Strike	– (1)	– (1)	0	– (1)	– (1)	1	1		
	3. Settle	– (0)	– (0)	1	– (0)	– (0)			1	1
Delta	4. Employ nonunion labor	1	1	0	– (1)	– (0)				
	5. Meet demands	0	0	0	1	0			1	
	6. Settle	0	0	1	– (0)	– (0)				1
International Union	7. Support local	– (1)	0	1	1	1				
Gamma	8. Buy from Delta	1	1	1	– (1)	– (0)				
	Column Number	1	2	3	4	5	6	7	8	9

sanction against the coalition exists, so that the move to Step 6 to search for guaranteed improvements is not necessary.

The analysis can now be taken further by considering other players, coalitions and scenarios. Since this is done in the referenced paper[30] it is not necessary to repeat the details here. In the course of the further analysis, Delta is led to the point of analyzing the stability of a scenario representing the *conflict point* at which all players are carrying out their threats. This analysis is done from the viewpoint of all coalitions with the objective of finding a way out of the impasse.

A Critique of the Analysis of Options

In discussing the applicability of the technique of analysis of options to managerial decision making, it must first be said that there is no thought that the method should be applied to situations where well-defined and -understood models of the decision process and quantitative parameters exist. The analysis of options is complementary to the established methods of operations research and systems analysis. It provides a means of analyzing situations in which some doubt arises as to the applicability of an established method of analysis or in which the problem is new or unique, so that no general method of approach has yet been established.

One of the major characteristics of analytical methods is that quantitative parameters and "well-behaved" analytic functions must be found that are truly appropriate to the decision problem at hand. This is unnecessary in the analysis of options. All that is required is that the manager (or managers) involved in the decision problem make specific qualitative judgments concerning their preferences for particular scenarios. By this means, a great deal of important information, which cannot necessarily be expressed in quantitative form, is inserted into the analysis. In the example in the preceding section this information might concern sentiments of solidarity between two corporations against union pressure. This might cause Gamma to prefer that Delta should win the confrontation with the union, provided Gamma itself is not threatened. Such information could almost certainly not be

[30]Howard, "Metagame Analysis of a Business Problem."

framed in quantitative or analytic terms and would therefore be omitted in most model-building decision-making methods.

The analysis of options method is in essence a structured discussion of the decision problem. No attempt is made at the outset to encompass the whole problem. Understanding of the situation grows as the analysis proceeds and opportunities for solution of the problem emerge as more and more aspects of the situation are considered. The method does not, of course, offer a simple path to a unique, optimal solution. However, as Simon observed,[31,32] most managers faced with a decision problem do not seek such an optimal solution. They are more concerned with a course of action that they understand well and that they judge to be suitable to the situation as they see it.

The analysis of options has many advantages over other less-structured methods of approaching complex decision problems. First, it is firmly based on a theoretical approach to such problems, as embodied in metagame theory. Second, the method provides a means of considering all aspects of the problem as defined by a certain set of available options. During the course of the analysis any contradictions between assumptions and preferences made at any other stage can be detected, due to the explicit manner in which these assumptions and preferences are expressed. The fact that the problem is considered from many aspects encourages the introduction of new points of view. When no solution is found to be possible within one set of options, new options may be formulated that otherwise might not have been considered.

The advantages of the method over unstructured discussion are manifold. Repetition is avoided. The tendency in ordinary discussion to go round in circles is avoided by recording assumptions as they are made and conclusions as they become possible. In this way the analysis becomes cumulative rather than circular. This leads to relevance being established, making it possible to cut short time-wasting arguments that begin by discussing a relevant point, but then shift away from it. In ordinary discussions the prestige of a participant may become attached to his set of assumptions about the situation. Hence, when participants dis-

---

[31]Simon, *Administrative Behavior*, p. xxv.

[32]Herbert A. Simon, "Theories of Bounded Rationality," in C.B. McGuire and R. Radner, eds., *Decision and Organization* (North Holland, 1972), pp. 161–76.

agree it is often necessary to reach weak compromise conclusions. During an analysis of options, prestige becomes attached more to a participant's contribution in proposing that certain assumptions be tried out. If these assumptions prove unsatisfactory it is generally much easier for a participant to abandon them.

The analysis of options has a major advantage in that it can be a value-free approach. Although a manager in such an analysis maintains his own values that are reflected in his preferences, he is able, nonetheless, to stand back from the problem temporarily and consider the decision situation from an objective point of view that considers the opinions and likely preferences of all participants.

Perhaps the most important aspect of the analysis of options is that it is a method of analysis in which managers can participate with a minimum of formal analytical knowledge. Only an introduction to the procedure is required. Initiation into what may seem to be the difficult (and somewhat suspect) art of application of quantitative and analytical methods is unnecessary. Furthermore, the manager brings with him into the analysis, pertinent information in the form of his knowledge of the situation and his preferences for scenarios that might be lost in a narrower, analytical approach to the problem. He is, therefore, able to participate from the start in the attempt to find a solution to his problem, unencumbered by a feeling that methods are being used that he may not understand and probably does not trust. The manager and his analysts are brought together in a truly joint effort to solve the problem. The air of mystery associated with the use of mathematical model-building techniques disappears and all involved see the analysis of options as a common-sense (although curiously logical) discussion of practical matters, with which they are comfortingly familiar.

Applications of the Analysis of Options
to Decisions Under Uncertainty

The analysis of options is based on a theory of conflict between two or more participants. This conflict need not be such that one participant gains what the other loses (that is, it need not be zero-sum). Nature is regarded in the theory as a disinterested observer of the situation, taking no part from her lofty vantage point in the disagreements between men.

In many managerial decision situations, however, it may not be clear from whence the "opposition" arises. The actions of others, which are apparently unrelated to the decision problem at hand, may have a significant effect on the situation. In the raincoat problem discussed in Chapter 3, for example, the question was whether to carry a raincoat when leaving the house in the morning. The option selected depended in this problem on the decision maker's estimate of the probability of rain. The actual outcome of the decision situation depended on whether "nature decided it would rain." This was regarded as an option selected by nature in a manner completely unconnected with the decision maker's problem. The whole situation would be different, however, if, unknown to the decision maker, someone was rainmaking in the next county.

More realistically, in modern managerial decision making the situation may be affected by the actions of persons who are pursuing their own interests and who unwittingly intrude on a particular decision problem. This occurs often when a number of unassociated parties are unknowingly in competition for scarce resources. For example, suppose that it is essential to my business that I catch the 4:20 P.M. plane to a certain city. I call the airline and find that all seats are booked on that plane. I am in despair. How can I be certain that the 126 people booked on the plane took their decision to travel at that time based on considerations unconnected with my decision problem? I might suspect that a competitor had bought all the seats on the plane, specifically in order to defeat my purpose in traveling to the city in question. My assessment of the situation, of course, might depend on the degree of paranoia in my make-up at the time.

What we attribute to nature is usually what we do not understand completely and what we cannot readily attribute to the actions of others. The results of actions of an unknown competitor would be classified as the result of "an option selected by nature." In a complex decision problem, the "opposition" may well be a combination of natural and competitive forces. It seems intuitively natural, therefore, to consider applying a technique derived from the theory of conflict to situations where the "opposition" may not be solely from identifiable competitors. This has been suggested by the author as an extension of the areas of application of the analysis of options.[33] Let us first consider how this might be done and then discuss the validity of the extension of the technique to situations involving nature, that is decisions under uncertainty. Consider once again the plant expansion problem of Chapter 3.

Suppose that we are Firm A and that we have plans to take one or more of a number of initiatives which we judge will result in an advantageous move for our firm from the present situation. We realize, however, that there is some uncertainty surrounding our venture and we are not sure whether some of the uncertainty we feel is due to competition that we cannot identify (that is, we are not sure where we are on the spectrum between true nature and true competition). The initiatives that are available to us are shown in Table 5-20 alongside the present position (status quo). Each of the possible scenarios shown in Table 5-20 is the equivalent of a unilateral improvement in the analysis of options. There may be more such improvements within the possible 32 (2^5) combinations of the available options. Some infeasibilities may arise, such as those shown in Table 5-20. Preferences may exist for each of the scenarios, but those are not considered at this time.

Table 5-20   Some Possible Unilateral Improvements for Firm A

Available Options of Firm A	Status Quo	Some Possible Scenarios Involving Improvement			Infeasible
Build Large Plant	0	1	1	0	1
Build Small Plant	0	0	0	1	1
Lower Prices	0	1	1	0	1
Raise Prices	0	0	0	1	1
Expand Exports	0	1	0	0	

Let us suppose that there is no readily identified competitor. (If one appeared, the situation could be assessed in terms of the methods outlined earlier in this chapter.) The next step is to introduce into the analysis a "player" called "N," which is the embodiment of all (unidentifiable) opposition to Firm A's plans for an improvement in its position. In short, N represents the

[33]K.J. Radford, "An approach to Managerial Decision Making," paper presented to the Conference of the Operational Research Society (UK), Torbay, England, November 13–16, 1973.

source of the future states of the world. These states of the world are now shown as "options" of N in a tableau (Table 5-21) that is the equivalent of that described in the analysis of options (Figure 5-19) as showing sanctions against a player for a unilateral improvement from a particular scenario.

Table 5-21   "Sanctions" against Firm A's Improvements from Status Quo

		Firm A's Preferences				
		Preferred to Status Quo	Status Quo	Not Preferred	Infeasible	
FIRM A	Build Large Plant	1 0	0	–		1
	Build Small Plant	0 1	0	–		1
	Lower Prices	1 0	0	–	1	
	Raise Prices	0 1	0	–	1	
	Expand Exports	– (0) – (0)	0	–		
N	Government Ban on Product	0 0	0	1		
	Overseas Competitor enters Market	– (1) – (1)	0	– (0)		
	Recession	– (1) – (1)	0	– (0)		
	Column Number	1 2	3	4	5 6	

In the example shown in Table 5-21, a government ban on the product would certainly deter Firm A from taking any of the steps toward improvement from the status quo, as long as it was really believed such a ban was imminent. If no such sanctions exist the scenarios that are shown as preferred in a tableau such as that in Table 5-21 may be guaranteed improvements for Firm A. If more than one guaranteed improvement exists, preferences could be shown for each. These preferences could be based in part, on any quantitative work that was appropriate, such as calculation of the expected return on investment for each improvement.

The technique of analysis of options, therefore, can be applied to decision situations in which no identifiable conflict exists. In this respect it can be regarded as complementary to the other techniques applicable to decision making under uncertainty. In particular, it provides a means of inserting into such procedures managerial opinions that may not be quantifiable, so that all relevant information is brought to bear on the decision process.

A possible objection to the above procedure is that it ignores the derivation of the analysis of options from game theory. Since no preferences can be assigned to nature (it might be said) N cannot be regarded as a true player. Although this is true, it should be noted that nowhere in the suggested procedure are preferences in fact attributed to N. What is done in arriving at the tableau is to consider Firm A's preferences in the light of certain options being taken up by "player" N. This is exactly the same as the procedure discussed in Chapter 3 in which future "states of the world" were considered. Furthermore, to the extent that player N turns out to be wholly (or mostly) a true opponent, the procedure is justified on game-theoretic grounds.

More on Conflict Situations

To recapitulate, two basic conflict situations have been considered to this point. The first, the strictly competitive, two-person, zero-sum game, may not have a pure strategy equilibrium. In such a situation, players who wish to act rationally in choosing a strategy for a single play of the game cannot do so because no such equilibrium exists. Their only recourse in such a decision situation (other than endeavoring to change the game) is to try to discover the other player's strategy; that is, to try to obtain perfect information. Once that is obtained, the game is solved and the player obtaining perfect information is the winner. In multiple plays of this game, if perfect information is not available, the mixed strategy solution is the rational solution.

The second conflict situation that has been considered in the text to date is of the prisoners' dilemma type in which the equilibrium in the game is less preferred by both players than another strategy pair. This problem has been resolved by considering the metagames based on the game. It has been shown that an equilibrium that is jointly preferred by all players always exists in the complete metagame. Whereas the players cannot make a rational choice of strategies in the game, they *can* make a meta-rational choice in the metagame.

Inducement

A third type of conflict situation is not necessarily approached in this manner. These are situations in which *inducement* is possible. By inducement the following is meant. Suppose that in a two-person game, both players have preferences between two scenarios; if a player knows the other player's preferences, he can predict to some extent his rational behavior. The first player may then deliberately take actions that, if the other player reacts rationally, will have the effect of leading to a preferred outcome for himself. This process of forcing an opponent to make a move that leads to a preferred outcome for oneself is called inducement.[34]

Consider for example the situation represented by the payoff matrix in Table 5-22. The best strategy pair for both players is (A_1B_1). If A is at A_2, B, by choosing B_1, will try to induce A to move to A_1. Similarly if B is at B_2, A by choosing A_1, will try to induce him to move to B_1. No conflict exists between the players in this situation. Each will try to induce the other to move to a mutually preferred outcome, if this is necessary.

Table 5-22   Game With No Conflict Point

		B's Strategies	
		B_1	B_2
A's Strategies	A_1	3,3	0,0
	A_2	0,0	2,2

In the game illustrated in Table 5-23 however, the situation is different. There is no single rational outcome that is best for both players and the game is unstable. The players will continue to move about among the three outcomes (A_1B_1), (A_2B_2) and (A_2B_1). These consist first of the two outcomes that B and A respectively will try to induce and the outcome (A_2B_1) that can be called the conflict point. The conflict point is an outcome that neither wants, but both are liable to end up with unless a valid bargaining procedure can be set up. This is the point at which Delta, Gamma, Local Union and International Union can be shown to arrive if there is a bargaining breakdown in the industrial relations situation discussed earlier in this chapter.[35]

It is noteworthy, in passing, that the prisoners' dilemma game (Table 5-4) has no inducing moves. The outcome (3,3) cannot be brought about by inducement. The players inevitably arrive at the

[34]Howard, *Paradoxes of Rationality*, pp. 168–98.
[35]Howard, "Metagame Analysis of a Business Problem."

Table 5-23   Game With a Conflict Point

		B's Strategies	
		B_1	B_2
A's Strategies	A_1	3,4	2,2
	A_2	1,1	4,3

outcome (2,2). To obtain the outcome (3,3) that is the equilibrium in the metagames it is necessary to apply the concept of inducement in the metagames.

Inducement is interesting in respect of certain types of strategy choice, in particular the *sure-thing strategy*. A sure-thing strategy is a strategy that guarantees a rational (i.e., optimizing) outcome. A sure-thing strategy may or may not exist in a game, but such a strategy exists for some player in *every* metagame. For example, a sure-thing strategy exists in prisoners' dilemma—it is the strategy "confess." This is the strategy that is best for a player using it, whatever the others do. It might be asked, therefore, whether if a sure-thing strategy exists it is always a good policy to adopt it. Unfortunately, although there are decision situations (such as prisoners' dilemma) in which the sure-thing strategy is best, it generally leads to an equilibrium outcome that is best for the other player. Generally speaking, a sure-thing strategy should be adopted only if the best equilibrium for the other player is also the best equilibrium for oneself. If there is any possibility of a conflict between possible stable outcomes (for example, if there are two or more possible compromises, of which the one most favored by player 1 is not the one most favored by player 2) then to adopt the sure-thing strategy is to invite capitulation to the other side. This can be illustrated by reference to the game of "Chicken."

The Game of Chicken

Chicken is exemplified by a situation in which two "players" drive cars directly toward each other at high speed. Each player has the same two options, to swerve (S) or to go ahead (G). The situation is illustrated in the payoff matrix shown in Table 5-24. If neither swerves, the result is mutual destruction, least preferred by both. Each player prefers most to go ahead while the other swerves. If one swerves, he would prefer the other to swerve, rather than that he go ahead. There are two equilibria in this game, shown circled in Table 5-24. These equilibria are rational for both players: that is, a move away from each would result in a less preferred outcome for the player that moves. There is no sure-thing strategy in the game.

Table 5-24   Payoff Matrix for Chicken-Equilibria Circled

		Player 2	
		Swerve	Go-Ahead
Player 1	Swerve	3,3	(2,4)
	Go-Ahead	(4,2)	1,1

Situations such as Chicken exist in real life. The 1962 Cuba missile crisis is an example.[36] Many others exist in the world of international politics and trade. On a less spectacular level, it occurs between a buyer and a seller, bargaining over price. The situation can be analyzed by considering the metagames, as follows.

The 2G metagame is shown in Table 5-25. The policy by player 2 (Swerve if he Goes Ahead, Go Ahead if he Swerves) is a sure-thing policy. However, if it becomes known to player 1, it induces a win for him, as Mr. Chamberlain found out at Munich.

Table 5-25   The 2G Metagame for Chicken (Meta-Equilibria are Circled)

		Player 2's Strategies			
		Always Swerve	Always Go Ahead	Swerve if He Swerves Go Ahead if he Goes Ahead	Swerve if He Goes Ahead Go Ahead if he Swerves
Player 1's Strategies	Swerve	3,3	(2,4)	3,3	2,4
	Go Ahead	(4,2)	1,1	1,1	(4,2)

The 12G metagame is shown in Table 5-26, in the same format as shown earlier in Table 5-7. Again, in this metagame, a sure-thing rational counterpolicy (GSSG for Player 1) induces the most preferred outcome for the other player. A policy GGSG, which

---

[36]Howard, *Paradoxes of Rationality*, pp. 181–84.

might be described as a retaliatory counterpolicy for player 1, is necessary to achieve the compromise outcome (3,3), which appears for the first time as a meta-equilibrium in this metagame.

Table 5-26   The 12G Metagame for Chicken
(Meta-Equilibria are Circled)

		Player 2's Strategies			
		Always Swerve	*Always Go Ahead*	*Swerve if He Swerves Go Ahead if He Goes Ahead*	*Swerve if He Goes Ahead Go Ahead if He Swerves*
Player 1's	SSSSS	3,3	(2,4)	3,3	2,4
Strategies	GGGG	(4,2)	1,1	1,1	(4,2)
	GGGS	4,2	1,1	1,1	2,4
	GGSG	4,2	1,1	(3,3)	4,2
	GGSS	4,2	1,1	3,3	2,4
	GSGG	4,2	(2,4)	1,1	4,2
	GSGS	4,2	(2,4)	1,1	2,4
	GSSG	4,2	(2,4)	3,3	4,2
	GSSS	4,2	(2,4)	3,3	2,4
	SGGG	3,3	1,1	1,1	4,2
	SGGS	3,3	1,1	1,1	2,4
	SGSG	3,3	1,1	(3,3)	4,2
	SGSS	3,3	1,1	3,3	2,4
	SSGG	3,3	(2,4)	1,1	4,2
	SSGS	3,3	(2,4)	1,1	2,4
	SSSG	3,3	(2,4)	3,3	4,2

The conclusions that can be drawn from this analysis can be summarized as follows. In decision situations similar to the game of Chicken:

1/ for the compromise to be a stable outcome, both players must be ready to risk the least preferred outcome;

2/ if one player (and not the other) is willing to risk the least preferred outcome, that player wins;

3/ if neither player is willing to risk the least preferred outcome, no stable outcome is possible.

Extensions of this analysis are possible by introducing bluffing. A player bluffs when he declares that he will never "swerve," while secretly preparing to do so if necessary. By bluffing, a player hopes to avoid being induced into a losing situation, while at the same time inducing the other into such a situation, yet not actually risking disaster.

Summary

Many managerial decision problems cannot be considered in terms of a single objective and a single, well-defined quantitative parameter. It may be difficult to define the "opposition" in such problems and most such situations are unique and single play. Nevertheless, managers have preferences for options and scenarios in such situations. Some guidance in terms of desirable solutions to such problems can be obtained by studying simple game situations.

In strictly competitive conflict situations, as in all game situations, one or more equilibria always exist in terms of pure or mixed strategies. However, unless a pure strategy equilibrium exists, this is of little assistance to a decision maker in a single play situation. His only rational course of action is to try and change the game or to seek more information in an endeavor to move closer to the position in which he has perfect information. Perfect information in this case must include knowledge of his opponent's choice of strategy. With perfect information a decision maker can be objectively rational, a condition that all decision makers should desire, since in such circumstances no decision problem exists. In all other cases, and in most practical situations, a decision maker can be only subjectively rational. Many authorities think that strictly competitive conflict situations do not occur in real life decision making and that consideration of such situations in the search for desirable courses of action may be misleading.

A great number of real life decision problems arise in circumstances different from strictly competitive situations and are much less easily treated. In one commonly considered such situation (prisoners' dilemma) the rational strategy pair results in a less desirable outcome than an irrational strategy choice on the part of the players. The desire to resolve this seeming paradox leads to a study of metagames, in which the players' reactions to other players' strategy choices are considered. This reveals that the strategy pair that was seen as irrational (but desirable) in the original game appears as meta-rational in the metagame.

Metagame theory can be applied to practical decision making by means of a method known as the analysis of options. This method consists of a procedure of six steps by which the reactions of all participants (and all coalitions of participants) to the decision problem can be studied. The result of an analysis of options does not appear as a single, optimal course of action, as is the case in the application of quantitative analysis techniques. Rather, the analysis takes the form of a thorough review of all possible courses of action and of the decision makers' preferences for the available options. The result is a procedure related to that described by Simon as "satisficing." Use of the analysis of options has the major advantage that managers can bring their experience and preferences directly to bear on the decision problem. Discussion of available options and other characteristics of the decision problem is structured and logical. Managers take part directly and obtain a complete understanding of the situation as the analysis proceeds. Although the method of analysis of options was developed from a study of conflict situations, it can be applied equally well to decisions under uncertainty, where no "opposition" can be directly identified.

Another important type of decision problem arises in situations similar to the "game" of Chicken. Study of this game by metagame theory shows that for a compromise to be stable, both players must be prepared to risk the least desirable outcome. If one player (and not the other) is prepared to take this risk, that player wins. If neither player is prepared to take the risk, no stable outcome is possible.

Discussion Topics

1/ Do you consider proficiency in chess, bridge or poker to be an advantage in managerial decision making?

2/ Do strictly competitive conflict situations occur in business, government or industry? If not, why not?

3/ How does the concept of a "security level" brought out by the existence of an equilibrium strategy pair in a conflict situation relate to Simon's concept of "satisficing"?

4/ The von Neumann-Morgenstern mixed strategy "solution" to strictly competitive conflict situations applies to decision problems that are likely to be repeated many times. Does it have any application to single play situations? Would you toss a coin to resolve an important decision of this type?

5/ In non-zero sum game situations, the maximin strategy pair designed to provide a certain security level is not necessarily in equilibrium. What effect should this conclusion have on a manager who wishes to stabilize his position in such situations?

6/ Do prisoners' dilemma situations occur in real life? Can you give examples from your own experience?

7/ How is it that new rational outcomes not apparent in the original game can be discovered by study of metagames based on the game?

8/ In applying the analysis of options method, other players' preferences are assigned to scenarios. How is the analysis affected if these preferences are not estimated correctly? Is this related to the necessary step of making assumptions in any form of analysis and does it have the same pitfalls?

9/ The analysis of options is a method by which assessment of a decision situation can be undertaken in steps. This avoids the problem of assembling assumptions about all the parameters involved at the outset of an analysis. Is this of great advantage in managerial decision making?

10/ "The analysis of options is nothing more than what we do already in our discussions of problems." Do you support this criticism?

11/ "An important aspect of the analysis of options is that it can be applied to situations where some or all of the factors cannot be expressed in quantitative form." Is this a valid advantage of the method?

12/ Do you agree that the analysis of options can be applied to a decision problem under uncertainty? If not, why not?

13/ Does inducement occur in practical decision problems? Can you give examples of situations in which this has occurred?

14/ Have you ever encountered a business decision that can be likened to the game of Chicken? If so, did the outcome of that situation resemble that described in the text?

15/ How does bluffing affect the outcome of decision situations based on the game of Chicken?

16/ The authorities have decided to build a new jet airport in your neighborhood. Construct an analysis of options related to this situation. Players might be government, airlines, a committee of residents and local contractors. What purpose might such an analysis serve to each of the parties?

17/ You represent a member of the European Economic Community and important trade negotiations are imminent. Other countries outside the community are pressing for a removal of tariff barriers on a certain commodity. Can such a problem be approached by the analysis of options? If so, outline the likely form of the analysis.

18/ Oil is an important source of energy in world affairs. Some nations produce a surplus, some are self-sufficient in this respect and others need to import oil. A conference of producers and importers has been called to discuss supply and price. How would you prepare your government for such a conference, assuming you represented each type of nation in turn?

6

Joint Decisions by Two or More Parties

Introduction

Up to this point in the text, much of the discussion of decision making has been in the context of a single individual faced with the resolution of a decision problem. The decision maker has been assumed to be rational in that he selects the available option that he prefers or sees as best after some evaluation of the alternatives. Much the same approach is possible when more than one individual is involved in a decision problem, as long as it can be assumed that the group is single-purposed, at least with respect to the decision under consideration. Such a group acts in much the same way as an individual, seeking the solution that is judged best for the "team." Decisions can be taken on the basis of rationality for the entity that the group represents. Individual members act essentially as advisors to the group in the process of deciding what is best or what it should prefer.

Many decision-making groups do not have such a singularity of purpose. They are made up of members who find it appropriate to work together for certain purposes, but who also have other objectives. These other objectives may be secondary to the immediate purpose of working together, but they nevertheless exist and they are taken into account to varying degrees by each individual in the process of decision making on behalf of the group.

Individuals generally join together in a group to share the benefits and risks of a venture. For example, two businessmen may form a partnership to undertake a particular operation. An agreement between two organizations for cooperation in a venture involving risk is another example of the formation of a group. Once the group is formed the question arises of how it should make decisions and this is the main subject considered in this chapter. First, however, it is interesting to consider the conditions under which cooperation can be acceptable to the parties involved. This amounts to investigating how a risk can be shared so that each party is content with his portion of the benefits and risks. This can be treated explicitly if what is at stake can be expressed in terms of a well-defined quantitative parameter, and this is done in the next section. Some of the results obtained are then used as a guide in the study of group decision making when the outcomes in a situation involving uncertainty or conflict cannot be so clearly defined.

Risk Sharing

The subject of risk sharing can be approached first by considering an example of a simple venture in which there are two outcomes, a gain of $10,000 and a loss of $5,000. If the probability of each outcome is $\frac{1}{2}$ (for example), the expected value of the outcome in this decision (which is under the condition we have called *risk*) is positive and equal to $2,500. As has been discussed previously, however, the individual decision maker is influenced by his utility for the gain and his disutility for the loss involved in such a venture. Let us assume for the moment that the decision maker is willing to make his decision on a criterion of maximum expected value. If, then, his disutility for a loss of $5,000 is greater than his utility for a gain of $10,000, his expected utility for the risk is negative and he might well refuse to enter into the venture.

For such an individual and a given venture (for example a 50/50 chance of a gain of $x or a loss of $y) it is possible to construct a curve such as that shown in Figure 6-1. This curve joins all points (x,y) for which the individual's utility for a gain of $x is exactly equal to his disutility for a loss of $y. The curve represents a series of ventures of the type described above, for which the individual has zero expected utility. Following Raiffa's exposition,[1] the curve divides the diagram into two areas. The area below the curve includes all ventures of the nature considered that are acceptable to the individual (because the expected utility is positive). The area above the curve contains all ventures that are not acceptable, or are rejected, because the expected utility is negative. Note that a curve such as that shown in Figure 6-1 is particular to the individual and to the venture being considered. Other curves could be added to describe the reactions of other individuals and other ventures. Note also that the decision between "acceptable" and "rejected" is made on the basis of expected subjective utility for gain or loss, because in this simple case the decision is made under conditions described previously as *risk*. The concept of acceptable or nonacceptable ventures is later extended to situations in which the gains and losses cannot be expressed in a simple quantitative parameter and in which other decision-making criteria are employed.

It can be seen from Figure 6-1 that under the circumstances

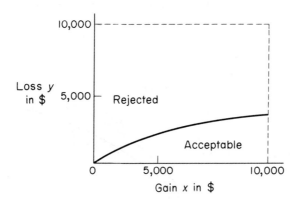

Figure 6-1   Acceptance and Rejection Sets for a Particular Individual in a Venture Giving 50/50 Chance of a Gain of $x and a Loss of $y

[1]Howard Raiffa, *Decision Analysis: Introductory Lectures on Choices Under Uncertainty* (Reading, Mass.: Addison-Wesley, 1968), pp. 190–92.

considered the individual concerned would not engage in a venture providing a 50/50 chance of a gain of $10,000 and a loss of
$5,000. However, suppose that this individual had an *option* on
such a venture. Would it be possible for him to find a partner with
whom to share the risk in such a way that each individual found
his share acceptable? Consider the situation shown in Figure 6-2.
The two individuals concerned have different acceptance and
rejection sets for the 50/50 venture, although the original $10,000
gain-$5,000 loss situation is acceptable to neither.

There are two ways in which this venture might be shared
between the two individuals. The first is that in which each takes
a *proportion* of the risk, thus maintaining the same ratio of possible gain to loss for each. It can be easily appreciated that all
proportions of the original venture lie on the line joining the
origin (in Figure 6-2) to the point representing the
($10,000-$5,000) risk. Most of these proportions are within the
acceptance set of individual 2, although only those involving up
to about sixty percent of the risk are acceptable to individual 1. In
these circumstances some arrangement for sharing the venture
could no doubt be worked out. For example, for the case shown in
Figure 6-2, the situation in which each partner assumes half of the
risk (that is each assumes a 50/50 chance of a $5,000 gain or a
$2,500 loss) would be acceptable to both.

Suppose, however, that the acceptance sets of the two individuals were as shown in Figure 6-3. No proportional share is
acceptable to individual 1. In such circumstances, it might be

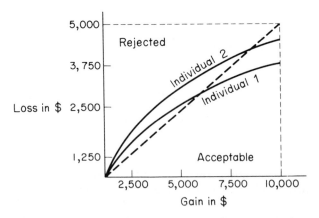

Figure 6-2   Sharing of a Venture by Two Individuals

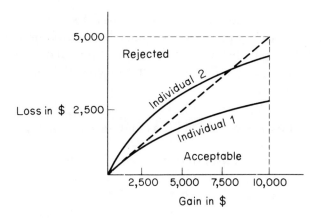

Figure 6-3   Nonproportional Sharing of a Venture by Two Individuals

possible to share the venture in a *nonproportional* fashion. For example, the risk ($5,000-$1,750) falls within individual 1's acceptance set and the complementary risk ($5,000-$3,250) falls within that of individual 2. It is easy to show algebraically that such a nonproportional sharing of the venture is equivalent to a proportional sharing of the risk *plus* a side payment from one individual to the other. In the above example, the side payment is $500 *from individual 2 to individual 1* and the appropriate proportion of the venture is 45 percent to individual 1 and 55 percent to individual 2. This is illustrated in Table 6-1.

Table 6-1   Proportional Sharing of a 50/50 Venture with Side Payment

	Individual 1	Individual 2
Gain	+ $500 + 45% of $10,000 = $5,000	− $500 + 55% of $10,000 = $5,000
Loss	+ $500 − 45% of $5,000 = − $1,750	− $500 − 55% of $5,000 = − $3,250

It may be thought that such a method of sharing is unfair to individual 2 who, in addition to assuming a less satisfactory ratio of possible gain to loss, is required to give a side payment just to take part in the venture. However, the total venture may not be available to individual 2. Even if it were, it would not fall within his acceptance set. It may be, for example, that the total venture represents an enlargement of individual 1's present business, which is beyond his present resources, but which he is prepared to share with a partner. Under these circumstances, it is reasonable for him to require a payment from individual 2 for a proportion of the venture.

Jointly Preferred Solutions and Pareto-optimality

The preceding discussion introduces the subject of risk sharing in a simple quantitative manner. Many situations cannot be discussed in such quantitative terms although the same general approach is permissible. Note that, up to this point, only the *feasibility* of risk sharing has been discussed. The problem of determining the *best* risk-sharing arrangement has yet to be considered. This involves a definition of the word "best," that is acceptable to the two or more parties involved. What is best for one may not be best for one or more of the others involved in the situation. What is required is an arrangement that is jointly considered as best by all the parties or, at least, that is jointly considered the best that can be obtained under the circumstances for all concerned.

Broadening the discussion slightly to investigate this point, let us assume that a number of different risk-sharing arrangements are possible between the parties involved. To simplify the discussion (and to allow a diagram to be drawn in two dimensions), let us restrict the consideration to risk sharing between two parties. The conclusions reached can easily be generalized intuitively to the case where more than two parties are involved.

Suppose that the two parties find themselves in a situation (called the status quo) and that some advantage will accrue to each from sharing in a venture. Suppose, further, that the utilities of the two parties for the outcomes of different sharing arrangements can be measured and that these utilities can be illustrated, as in Figure 6-4. The origin in this diagram refers to the status quo. A point in this diagram represents the *joint utility evaluation* of a particular risk sharing arrangement for the two parties involved. A point that is further along the axis for individual 1 (to the "east" in the diagram) is more to the advantage of that individual. Similarly, points further to the "north" are more to the advantage of individual 2. Generally speaking, points further to the "northeast" are more to the advantage of both individuals than is the status quo. There is, however, a limit to how far to the northeast the parties can go. This limit is set by restrictions on what sharing arrangements in the venture are achievable. The boundary to the northeast that represents the limit of all achievable sharings of the venture therefore divides the diagram into two spaces, achievable and nonachievable.[2] This boundary line is shown (arbitrarily drawn) in Figure 6-4. Any risk sharing arrangement that lies in the achievable region is preferable to both parties when compared with the status quo. Furthermore, proceeding in any direction between north and east from the status quo, the arrangement represented by the point on the boundary is the best achievable arrangement in that direction for the two individuals involved. The whole boundary is the set of best achievable arrangements over all possible directions between north and east, from the status quo. This boundary is called the *Pareto-optimal set*. It represents the set of best possible arrangements between the two individuals with respect to the status quo. This concept is easily generalized to situations involving more than two parties or individuals.

Whereas the Pareto-optimal set represents the best possible

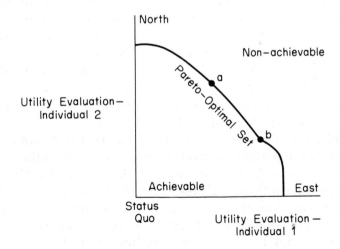

Figure 6-4 The Pareto-optimal Set for Risk Sharing Between Two Individuals

[2]Raiffa, *Decision Analyses*, pp. 196–208.

arrangements between the two parties, any point in the achievable region is an improvement with respect to the status quo for at least one of the parties. In general, therefore, a move from which *at least one party gains and no one loses* is called Pareto-optimal.

It is important to realize that, whereas the Pareto-optimal set represents improvements for both parties from the status quo, individual points in the set may be more preferred or less preferred by any one party than any other point in the set. For example, point *a* in Figure 6-4 would be more preferred by individual 2 than would point *b*; and vice-versa, for individual 1. The question arises, therefore, as to what point in the Pareto-optimal set should be chosen as a *jointly preferred* arrangement between the two individuals. If each seeks to maximize his own utility for outcomes the initial positions chosen by the two individuals might be far apart even though they both are improvements for both individuals from the status quo. The problem of deciding on a jointly preferred point in the Pareto-optimal set can be considered as a two-person game. The solution may involve negotiation or bargaining between the players prior to the choice of a joint strategy.[3]

In negotiations of this sort, each player has a security level that he can guarantee by selecting his maximin strategy. This security level may or may not be the status quo that exists before the game is played. Generally speaking, the subset of Pareto-optimal joint strategies resulting in outcomes for the players that are more preferred than the security level is called the *negotiation set*. This is illustrated in Figure 6-5. The choice of a solution from the negotiation set is what is normally at issue in bargaining, as, for example, in an industrial relations dispute.

Resolution of such problems would be relatively simple if the utilities of the parties for joint strategies were available in quantitative terms and, what is more, if the parties involved were willing to reveal these utilities in negotiations. These conditions are not always found in practical situations. However, it is one of the prime purposes of an arbitrator to discover the preferences of the parties and to assess these as best he can. He must then propose a solution that all parties consider "fair," however that might be defined.

[3]Wayne Lee, *Decision Theory and Human Behavior* (New York: John Wiley & Sons, 1971), pp. 301–3.

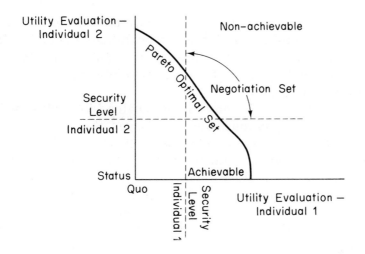

Figure 6-5   Negotiation Set for Risk Sharing Between Two Individuals

A specific approach to this problem has been proposed by Nash, for the case where the utilities of the parties are measurable. If u_1 and u_2 are the utilities of two parties for a proposed solution and if u_1^0 and u_2^0 are the corresponding utilities for the status quo, then the Nash solution proposes the choice of a joint strategy such that the product $(u_1-u_1^0) \times (u_2-u_2^0)$ is a maximum. This method of choice of a strategy pair with the security level as the status quo is called the *Shapley procedure*.

The Nash procedure has been thoroughly analyzed and discussed in the literature.[4] It has a number of characteristics that make it appear "fair." The solution is Pareto-optimal, and players in a game that appears the same from the point of view of one player or another receive equal payoffs. The procedure is not upset if new achievable joint strategy choices are made available, so the solution is not adversely affected by the introduction of irrelevant alternatives (or red herrings). The solution is not affected if arbitrary positive linear transformations of the parties' utilities are introduced. Further, the Nash solution is the only function that satisfies all these conditions.

The problem remains, however, that the Nash solution requires the availability of at least von Neumann-Morgenstern interval

[4]R.D. Luce and H. Raiffa, *Games and Decisions* (New York: John Wiley & Sons, 1967), pp. 121–34.

scale utility estimates of the parties involved for the joint strategy choices being considered. These may be difficult to obtain. However, if some indications of utilities are available, the method may at least give some guidance to an arbitrator in his search for a fair resolution of a problem.

Jointly preferred solutions can be obtained in another way if more than one play of the game is envisaged. Suppose, for example, that two joint strategy choices exist. In one of these, one player much prefers the outcome and the other much less prefers it, and in the other the situation is reversed. This is the case for the joint strategies represented by the points *a* and *b* in Figure 6-4 (and also for the joint excursions to the ballet and the prize fight discussed in the Battle of the Sexes game in the previous chapter). It might be possible to arrange a solution in these circumstances, in which the point *a* is chosen in the first play of the game and the point *b* in the second. If this were possible, it might be preferable to a prolonged wrangle, out of which neither party achieved what it really desired. Raiffa has given an example of a situation in which this cooperative procedure results in the practical achievement of a strategy choice that would be unachievable in a single play of the game.[5]

Wayne Lee has summarized some experimental work in which players were required to bargain for a contract, one acting as the sole manufacturer and the other the sole distributor of a product.[6] In these experiments, the players tended to arrive at arrangements in which the profit was split equally between them. As the status quo can be taken as the position before a contract is agreed, an equal split of profit would be in accordance with the Nash procedure. The less information available to the players about the conditions surrounding the contract, the more they seemed to deviate from this result.

Group Decision Making

In the preceding section, two ways were described in which a group may be formed. The first is as a result of those involved deciding to share in a risky venture. A simple example of a group

---

[5]Raiffa, *Decision Analysis*, p. 197.
[6]Lee, *Decision Theory*, pp. 303–7.

formed in this way is a partnership. A much more complex example is a company in business or a department of government, where a number of staff members have individually chosen to join the organization and to work to further its goals and objectives. In a large organization the risk is very diffuse and the benefits available to the staff members on joining the organization are much more standardized and assured than is the case with a small partnership formed to undertake a risky venture. Nevertheless, the same initial approach to group decision making can be taken in the case of both the large and small organizations.

The second way in which a group can be formed is as a result of negotiations between parties involved in a conflict situation. In such cases, the results of the negotiations between the parties involved act as the basis governing the formation of the group. An agreement between management and labor in a typical industrial relations situation is an example of such an arrangement. The process of bargaining in such cases is the means by which the parties decide how to move from the status quo in the northeast direction toward the Pareto-optimal set. The results of the bargaining are the basis for an arrangement that governs the future activity of the "group."

The groups that are formed in these ways are more or less stable depending on the circumstances in which they are formed. In a large organization, subgroups may be formed within the larger entity, and these subgroupings may shift with time and as circumstances change. In some circumstances the groups are relatively stable; in others, they are much more dynamic.

The Basis of Group Choice

Once the group is in existence, the question arises as to how decisions should be made on behalf of the group. Each of the members of the group presumably has his own preferences between available options in any decision situation. How should these individual preferences be combined to construct a means of defining group preferences?

A seemingly natural way to establish a group choice when the preferences of the individual members are known is by a simple majority. This works well when a choice between two alternatives is involved. However, in certain circumstances use of a simple majority role can lead to a paradoxical result. Consider a group consisting of three individuals 1, 2 and 3, and let there be three available options *A, B,* and *C.* Suppose individual 1 prefers *A* to *B* and *B* to *C* and therefore, assuming transitivity is maintained, *A* to *C.* Individual 2 prefers *B* to *C* and *C* to *A* and therefore *B* to *A;* and individual 3 prefers *C* to *A* and *A* to *B* and therefore *C* to *B.* The situation is illustrated in Table 6-2. It can be seen that a majority of the individuals in the group prefer *A* to *B* and *B* to *C.* The group could then be said to prefer *A* to *B* and *B* to *C,* if a majority vote rule were adopted. However, assuming transitivity is preserved by the group, this would mean that the group would be said to prefer *A* to *C,* whereas a majority of its members do, in fact, prefer *C* to *A.*

Table 6-2   Preferences of Individuals
in the Voting Paradox

Individual 1	Individual 2	Individual 3	Group Based on Simple Majority
A to B			A to B
B to C	B to C		B to C
therefore	C to A	C to A	therefore
A to C			A to C
	therefore	A to B	
	B to A		
		therefore	
		C to B	

It cannot be assumed, therefore, that a simple majority rule can be used universally to express group preferences. This being the case, we may ask if there are any other methods of formulating group preferences from those of the individual members that do not encounter similar problems? Several have been suggested. Many of them involve a function combining the individual utilities, measured in quantitative terms.

In the late nineteenth century, a group utility function of this nature was proposed in terms of the sum of the individual utilities.[7] Under this proposal, the group's utility for any available option is given as the simple sum of the member's utilities for that

---

[7] A function of this nature is discussed in A. Marshall, *Principles of Economics,* 8th ed., (New York: Macmillan, 1949), pp. 130–34 and 467–70.

option. While this may be intuitively appealing, several difficulties arise:

1/ there seems to be no reason why the *sum* of the utilities should be chosen rather than some other function, such as the sum of the squares of the individual utilities;

2/ the function that is chosen automatically dictates the relative weight that is given to any one individual's preferences;

3/ it is possible, at best, to measure individual utilities on an interval scale. On such a scale, the zero point and the unit of measurement can be chosen arbitrarily for each individual. Unless some means can be found for relating the utility scales of the individual members of the group, any utility function for the group based on individual utilities will automatically place a relative weighting on the preferences of the members.

The construction of a group utility function from those of the members in this fashion automatically embodies a value judgment with respect to the contributions of the preferences of the members of the group to that function.[8] This value judgment may or may not be deliberate and, furthermore, it may be changed arbitrarily by manipulation of the individual utility functions relative to one another. This problem has been discussed thoroughly in the literature under the heading of the *interpersonal comparison of utilities*.[9] The generally held view at the present time is that such an interpersonal comparison cannot be *assumed* to be acceptable. However, it may be acceptable under restricted conditions, such as by agreement between the individuals of like mind involved in a group decision problem. An example of such an agreement is given later in this chapter in the context of a corporate risk policy for capital investment decisions.

The Arrow Social Welfare Function

The fact that value judgments enter into the construction of a group decision function was a major consideration in one of the

[8]A. Bergson, "A Reformulation of Certain Aspects of Welfare Economics," *Quarterly Journal of Economics* 52 (February, 1938):310–34.

[9]Jerome F. Rothenberg, *The Measurement of Social Welfare* (Englewood Cliffs, N.J.: Prentice-Hall, 1961), pp. 51 ff.

basic contributions to group decision theory by Kenneth J. Arrow.[10] Arrow was interested in the method by which "social" choices can be made by a group acting collectively, when the members each have preferences for a series of available options. He assumed that each member respected transitivity in expressing his preferences. He specifically excluded consideration of measurable utility in his analysis and required only that the members of the group could express consistent ordering of the available options. He sought a rule of collective decision making that yields a consistent ordering and that is based on the preferences of the members of the group. He called this rule a *social welfare function*, because he was primarily concerned at the time with the economic problem of social welfare.

Arrow observed that the construction of a rule of collective decision making has been seen in previous work to depend on certain value judgments. He laid down what he considered to be five necessary conditions that a group decision-making rule should satisfy. He derived these from considerations of existing methods of making a group choice, such as voting, dependence on market forces, reliance on an agreement (or convention) and dictatorship.

Arrow's five "apparently reasonable" conditions can be stated as follows:[11,12]

Condition 1/ the group decision rule should give a true group ordering for a sufficiently wide range of individual orderings;

Condition 2/ if one available option rises or remains constant in the value scale of each member of the group, then it must rise or remain constant in the group ordering;

Condition 3/ if the individual orderings for any subset of the available options are unchanged, then the group

---

[10]Kenneth J. Arrow, *Social Choice and Individual Values*, Cowles Foundation for Research in Economics at Yale University, published by Wiley, 1951.

[11]Abram Bergson, "On the Concept of Social Welfare," *Quarterly Journal of Economics* 68 (May, 1954):233–52.

[12]Arrow, *Social Choice*, p. 59.

ordering for that subset should be unchanged also. This must be true even if there are changes in the individual orderings of the remaining options. The group ordering must be unaffected by the absence or presence of other options beyond those under consideration. This is referred to as the *Condition of Independence of Irrelevant Alternatives;*

Condition 4/ for any two available options under consideration, the group ordering must not be independent of the individual orderings. This is known as the *Condition of Citizen's Sovereignty;*

Condition 5/ the group ordering must not coincide with the ordering of one individual, regardless of the orderings of the other members of the group. This is the *Condition of Non-Dictatorship.*

Arrow's startling conclusion was that no criterion of group decision making can simultaneously meet all the above five conditions. By way of corollary, he concluded that no one group decision function has any *a priori* appeal. To state this important result in another way, a criterion of group decision making satisfying conditions 1, 2 and 3 above, must be either "imposed" in that it contravenes condition 4 or "dictatorial" in that it contravenes condition 5. A simple example of the Arrow conclusion is the paradox of voting described earlier.

The publication of this theorem in 1951 was followed by a great deal of research, publication and attempted rebuttal, from which Arrow's work emerged relatively unscathed. It was pointed out in the course of this ensuing discussion, that the conclusion was not important under certain specific conditions. For example, if the preferences of all the members of the group coincide, the fourth condition (non-dictatorship) is not applicable. All the other conditions would be satisfied if the orderings of one individual were taken to represent those of the group. However, in the general case in which there is no restriction on the orderings of members of the group, no group criterion can satisfy the five stated conditions. Blau put forward some counter-examples that seem at first sight to disprove Arrow's theorem; but these counter-examples are close to conditions of dictatorship, so that little harm is done to Arrow's original conclusion.[13,14]

Detailed summaries of proposals by which Arrow's conclusion might be circumvented have been given by Luce and Raiffa[15] and by Rothenburg.[16] These center on one or both of (a) a means of rejecting or relaxing one of the conditions and (b) imposition of additional restrictions on the group members' orderings of options in order to find areas in which a group decision criterion *can* be constructed.

The condition most often selected for discussion is number 3 above, the independence of the group ordering to the introduction of irrelevant alternative options. Procedures have been suggested for incorporating *strengths of preference* into the analysis. However these procedures require that some means of dealing with the problem of interpersonal comparison be introduced in terms, for example, of establishing a common unit of utility and/or a base of reference for the utility scale. Much of the work has concentrated on the formulation of restrictions on the individual orderings of options. For example, Luce and Raiffa discuss restrictions to be placed on the profiles of individual rankings, such that the simple majority rule always leads to a consistent group ordering.[17] However, many of the restrictions imposed in these proposals are difficult to relate to practical group decision making; some appear to be unnatural and arbitrary.

Raiffa has described work done in an endeavor to formulate a set of axioms that would allow a group of individuals who are all dedicated to maximization of expected utility to combine their utility functions and subjective probabilities in such a way that the group could act as a maximizer of group utility.[18] He shows, for example, that if each member of the group has a utility function that can be represented in exponential form, then the group utility function is also in exponential form. However, he points out that under conditions of risk sharing, a group utility function that depends on the individual members' utility functions cannot

[13]Julian Blau, "The Existence of Social Welfare Functions," *Econometrica* 25 (April, 1957), 302–13.

[14]Rothenberg, *Measurement of Social Welfare*, pp. 26–30.

[15]Luce and Raiffa, *Games and Decisions*, pp. 340–70.

[16]Rothenberg, *Measurement of Social Welfare*, pp. 44–52.

[17]Luce and Raiffa, *Games and Decisions*, pp. 353–57.

[18]Raiffa, *Decision Analysis*, pp. 207–37.

always be assumed to exist. Furthermore, he shows that there is no generally applicable method of combining individual subjective probability estimates to arrive at a group decision making procedure, even if the members of the group agree on utilities for available options. This conclusion is reached also by Fishburn in a study of various group choice functions that are generalizations of the simple majority rule.[19] In this work he finds no satisfactory way of establishing a rule for developing a consistent group utility function.

The main concern with regard to Arrow's theorem is the apparent reasonableness of his conditions. Conditions 2 and 3, noted above, provide for a relationship between the individual and group orderings that is hard to argue against. It is also difficult to accept that a criterion for group decision making that respects these two conditions must necessarily be "imposed" or "dictatorial." However, much of the force of Arrow's argument is lost if the preferences of the individual members of the group are similar. This suggests that the problems encountered in group decision making depend greatly on (a) the composition of the group and the characteristics and preferences of its individual members; and (b) the process by which the group reaches a decision. These two aspects of group decision making are now dealt with in turn.

The Characteristics of Decision Making Groups

A classification of groups that is useful in considering decision making behavior was first proposed by Marshak.[20,21] He considered such groups in terms of teams, foundations and coalitions.

In a *team*, each member has the same group-oriented interests. For this reason, a team demonstrates cohesiveness and solidarity and a definite organizational entity can be envisaged. For the purpose of decision making the members consider themselves as a part of this entity. In a *foundation* the identity of purpose is less strong. The individual members still subscribe to a group purpose, but individuals see the accomplishment of group objectives

---

[19]P.C. Fishburn, "A Comparative Analysis of Group Decision Methods," *Behavioral Science* 16 (1971):538.

[20]J. Marschak, "Towards an Economic Theory of Organization and Information," in R.M. Thrall, C.H. Coombs, and R.L. Davis, eds., *Decision Processes* (New York: John Wiley & Sons, 1954).

[21]J. Marschak, "Elements for a Theory of Teams," *Management Science* 1 (1955):127–37.

to a certain extent in terms of a means of achieving their own objectives. Members of a foundation do not identify themselves absolutely with the purpose of the group and the possibility of conflict within the group is correspondingly greater. In a *coalition* individual members do not necessarily subscribe to a group objective. They are drawn together into short- or long-term relationships by virtue of the advantages to them of such arrangements in the pursuit of their own goals and objectives.

In the case of a team, it is meaningful to speak of group objectives, purposes and preferences. The group objectives and preferences are easy to infer from those of the individual members of a team, because there is substantial identity of purpose among the members. In a foundation, the group purpose is not as easily inferred by observing the preferences and behavior of individuals or of a small group of members. This must be done by taking into account the organizational structure of the foundation and its functioning with respect to the decision processes it faces. In a coalition there is no obvious group objective and the interests of the members are not similar. The advantages of entering a coalition lie in the various arrangements that govern the behavior of members toward one another and toward the outside world. These arrangements are not necessarily permanent and members may seek to change them at any time as their individual interests dictate.

Types of Groups Found in Organizations

Examples of these three types of groups are found in different types of modern organization, both in business and in government. The owners of a manufacturing firm, for example, may constitute a team insomuch as they identify very closely with the success of the firm and their own personal success is dependent on that of the firm. By contrast, many of the employees may regard the firm more as a foundation. They may have no strong loyalty to the particular firm, especially if employment elsewhere is reasonably easy to get. For the time being, however, they are prepared to perform services useful to the firm so that they can receive benefits that are helpful to them in achieving their own objectives. These benefits may be in both quantitative and nonquantitative forms. Salary, pension rights and health-care benefits can be described quantitatively, whereas such rewards as authority, status and working conditions cannot be described in such a form. For the most part, the satisfactions of such employees are obtained outside the firm. Work done for the firm is regarded as a necessary means of achieving these satisfactions, but this satisfaction is postponed temporarily while the employee is on the job.

In organizations that have lost a sense of purpose employees may be more in a coalition than acting as members of a foundation. In such circumstances, the interests of the organization are secondary to the personal interests of the individual members. Many of these personal interests may lie in work done within the organization, which has little or no relation to the organization's purpose and serves only to provide satisfaction for the employee while on the job. Employees in such an organization operate in a loose coalition of individuals or subgroups of individuals. The purpose of this coalition is to maintain an arrangement suitable to each individual while he pursues objectives that may not be related at all to those of the organization.

The nature of an organization at any one time may resemble that of any of the three types of groups, depending on the condition of its management and the circumstances in which it operates. When an organization is in the early stages of its operation, or when it has been substantially reorganized, the sense of purpose may be very strong. Direction of the enterprise is in the hands of a group of men who work together singlemindedly to promote its success. Tasks are delegated to subordinates who are similarly inspired and all may work together as a team. Unless this atmosphere is maintained by successful management, however, the diffusing effects of growth, frustration by external conditions and conflicts between personalities may cause the organization to resemble more closely a foundation after some initial period of time. If the diffusion of purpose continues the pattern of a coalition may emerge.

Any particular group may contain subgroups of different types and, furthermore, the make-up of these subgroups may change rapidly as conditions change. It is entirely possible to find within a group a loose coalition of a number of closely knit teams. The distinguishing characteristic of any subgroup is the degree of identity between individual or subgroup goals and those of the larger group. Formations of subgroups may break up at any time and new alignments may emerge. The factor most often causing such realignments is frustration and dissatisfaction regarding the rewards gained or to be expected from the existing arrangement.

Decision Making Behavior in Groups

From the point of view of decision making, the task of constructing a group-decision rule is least difficult for a group acting as a team because of the greater identity of view and preferences between members of such a group. When members of an organization agree on a *policy* they are, in fact, acting as a team.[22] A similar condition prevails when the staff members concerned agree on the details of a completely specified decision process. Under such circumstances, the specification, or the policy, acts as the convention for group decision making required by Arrow's theorem. More difficulty arises in group decision making as the characteristics of the group become less like those of a team and more like those of a foundation or a coalition as a result of the lesser degree of agreement between individual views and preferences in the latter types of group.

A basic factor determining the behavior of a decision-making group is the degree of conflict existing between the individual members or subgroups. The less the degree of conflict, the greater the agreement between the members of the group and the greater the likelihood of construction of a group-decision rule. Conflict is seen, therefore, as a major contributor to differences in individual preference orderings, which limit the ability of a group to arrive at a choice between options.

Some aspects of the effect of conflict on group decision making were investigated by Bower.[23] He postulated that the effect of an increase of conflict between members of a group should be a decrease in the quality of group decision-making performance. Therefore, if a foundation and a team have the same group objectives, and conflict exists within the foundation, the group decision making performance of the team should be superior. Bower sought to obtain evidence of this effect in experiments with groups of subjects faced with investment projects characterized by profit, sales and risk.

[22]Carl S. Spetzler, "The Development of a Corporate Risk Policy for Capital Investment Decisions," *IEEE Transactions on Systems Science and Cybernetics* SSC-4 (September, 1968):279–300.
[23]Joseph L. Bower, "The Role of Conflict in Economic Decision Making Groups: Some Empirical Results," *Quarterly Journal of Economics* 79 (1965):263–77.

He found that the process of group decision making was essentially different in the two types of group. The basic problem in a team was to share information. In a foundation, however, the individual members needed to bargain with each other to reach a group choice. Describing the decision process as consisting of three activities—search for information, analysis of available options and choice between options[24]—Bower found that when conflict was present in the group the process of search for information was improved both in quantity and quality. He suggested, therefore, that the quality of the search process is related to the amount of conflict and to the degree of necessity felt by each individual to present to the group information in support of his point of view. In the same manner, the quality of analysis appeared to increase with the degree of conflict because each member of the group was careful to evaluate his position fully before presenting it for discussion and possible criticism. However, Bower's experiments indicated, as might be expected, that the probability of the group reaching an agreement on a choice between available options decreased as the amount of conflict within the group increased. He concluded generally that some conflict within a group was beneficial, but that too much conflict was detrimental to group decision making.

Much of the research and experimental work concerning group decision making has necessarily been done using easily available groups (such as students) and simplified decision problems. This has one advantage in that it provides a controlled environment for the experiments and a decision-making situation that can be studied repeatedly. A summary of this work has been provided by Shaw.[25] After giving details of the experiments, he put forward a series of what he called "plausible hypotheses" concerning the difference between individual and group decision making processes. These include the hypothesis that judgments made by a group are generally more accurate than those made by individuals, probably because of the wider range of knowledge in the group and the influence of more confident individuals in the group. Data from a number of studies show that groups arrive at a wider range of solutions to problems than individuals working alone and that many of these solutions are better than those of the

[24]Herbert A. Simon, *The New Science of Management Decision* (New York: Harper, 1962).

[25]Marvin E. Shaw, *Group Dynamics: The Psychology of Small Group Behavior* (New York: McGraw-Hill, 1971), pp. 59–83.

individuals. However, groups usually require more time than do individuals to arrive at a sequence of solutions.

Shaw quotes from studies that support the hypothesis that groups learn faster than individuals. On the other hand, experienced individuals may be more efficient in many decision-making situations than groups of less-informed persons. Groups are more effective than individuals on tasks requiring the combination of a number of steps in a definite order or when a number of different contributions must be combined. Groups are generally more effective when solution of the problem requires learning, but not necessarily when the task requires the use of judgment. As a summary, the question of whether groups or individuals are more effective in problem solving depends upon the type of task involved, the past experience of the individuals taking part and on how the term "effective" is interpreted. In all cases, the use of a group in decision making or problem solving is less efficient in terms of the amount of effort expended per problem resolution.

The Risky Shift Phenomenon

One notable phenomenon that has been observed under many experimental conditions is known as *risky shift*. This effect concerns the fact that decisions made by groups are generally more risky than those that would be advocated by individual members of the group prior to group discussion of the problem. Research workers studying this effect conclude that it is the activities within a group faced with a decision involving risk that tend to support a more risky solution than would be chosen by individuals acting alone. The shift toward a more risky solution may also be due to the presence of risk-taking individuals in the group, who feel less personal responsibility when advocating a risky solution within a group.

Dominance Within a Group

A theory of group decision behavior has been put forward by Clarkson and a simulation study to test the theory has been reported in the literature.[26] The theory endeavors to take into account the leadership and influence relations that emerge in a group faced with a decision problem. It touches on the notion of

[26]G.P.E. Clarkson, "Decision Making in Small Groups: A Simulation Study," *Behavioral Science* 13 (1968):288–305.

dominance that arises in a group when the solutions advocated by individuals are not the same. This dominance is a result of the interpersonal influence factors resulting from discussion and other interactions during the course of the group decision process. Earlier research had suggested that the dominant member in a group was usually the more conservative. The role of such a dominant member increases in importance as the degree of variation between individual members' solutions to the problem increases.

Experimental Evidence from Within Organizations

It is very difficult to obtain experimental results on the above phenomena from an organization operating in the day-to-day world. Most managers and members of decision-making groups, while perhaps sympathizing with the long-term objectives of the research, are more concerned with the pressing problems of their day-to-day work. Furthermore, the more important decision problems with which these managers are concerned are not likely to be repeated many times. Also, they may be regarded as confidential by those involved and they may be vital to the organization and to the status in the organization of those involved. Those circumstances are not the most favorable for the research worker bent on conducting experiments under real-life conditions. The number of detailed studies of group decision processes in organizations is therefore not large.

One study that relates to the existence of conflict among executives who would normally be concerned with decision making on behalf of the organization has been reported by Argyris.[27] He studied the behavior of 165 senior executives in six major companies in a large number of group decision-making meetings. The proceedings of the meetings were recorded on tape for later analysis and in most of the sessions, an observer was present to take notes. The subjects covered in the meetings were investment decisions, introduction of new products, manufacturing problems, marketing and pricing strategies and administrative and personal issues.

The results quoted by Argyris are a compendium of antagonism and distrust. He noted for example that the behavior of executives

[27]Chris Argyris, "Interpersonal Barriers to Decision Making," *Harvard Business Review* (March–April, 1966):84–97.

in the decision-making groups studied did not coincide with their individually stated views about effective managerial behavior. This tends to create interpersonal barriers to openness and trust that restrict effective decision making in groups of executives. As a result of the observations, Argyris prescribes a number of remedies for more effective managerial behavior in such groups.

A more optimistic view of executive behavior is reported by Spetzler in a study of the development of a corporate risk policy for capital investment decisions.[28] Spetzler interviewed 36 executives of a particular company, each of whom was either a senior officer, line manager or staff member involved with major capital expenditures. In a first set of interviews the attitude to risk of each of the individuals (when acting on behalf of the firm) was investigated and a utility function was developed for each on the basis of his reactions to a standard set of decision situations. The results of this first set of interviews was reported in general terms to the managers involved in order that the group could follow the development of the project. In a second stage, the managers were again interviewed to learn their reactions to a corporate utility function to be used on a trial basis. As a result of these discussions an agreement was reached on a policy for risk taking in capital investment decisions in quantitative terms.

Spetzler found that the group decision function derived by this process was markedly different from the average of those of the group members. At all levels of investment, the group consensus was in favor of more risk taking than the average of the individuals involved. This appears to confirm the risky shift phenomenon noted in a number of other studies. Unfortunately, Spetzler does not report what benefits were obtained by the company from the exercise, except in general terms such as increased awareness of the need for risk policies on the part of executives. If actual results were obtained, they would probably have been confidential and not publishable in the open literature. This does not, however, lessen the value of the approach in terms of the movement toward the complete specification of a group decision process.

Decision Making in a Committee

It has been said that a committee is a group of people who individually can do nothing, but who can meet together and

[28]Spetzler, "Development of a Corporate Risk Policy," pp. 279–300.

decide that nothing can be done. This is perhaps a little cynical, but it reflects a widespread disillusionment and frustration with group decision making. These feelings on the part of committee members are succinctly expressed in a light-hearted but penetrating article by Bruce Old on the mathematics of committees, boards and panels.[29] In a calculated example of the worst type of analytical approach, Old assigns quantitative measures to the ability of a committee to perform work. His conclusions are most entertaining. For example, his analysis shows that "whereas elastic bending occurs under stress, no work is performed by certain types of committee." Perhaps the most significant result in the whole of this tongue-in-cheek article is the "finding" that the relation between the efficiency of output from a committee and the number of persons on the committee reaches a maximum at seven tenths of a person. Old's conclusions may be closer than even he would have claimed for the results of his analysis.

When the members of a committee act as a team they approach decision problems in the same manner as an individual. Under these circumstances, there is a minimum of conflict within the group and maximum effectiveness in the decision making process. As Bower has pointed out, however, the quality of decision making may suffer under these conditions because of a reduction in the search for information and analysis of available options in a group that is already in substantial agreement.[30]

Effectiveness in decision making decreases as the committee acts more and more like a foundation or a coalition. In the latter case, only those decisions directly related to the purpose of the coalition have any chance of being resolved. The introduction of conflict into the group may improve the quality of decision making up to a point. Beyond some point, however, the chance of reaching a decision in the group becomes small and the committee ceases to be an effective vehicle for decision making.

The manner in which a committee acts is not static. In a short period of time the individual members may swing from a loose coalition to a team under the influence of events, information or the subtle direction of one of the members. Much of the work of a committee is not concerned with decision making itself, but with

[29]Bruce S. Old, "On the Mathematics of Committees, Boards and Panels," *Scientific Monthly*, August 1946, reprinted in R.G. Brown, ed., *Source Book in Production Management* (Hinsdale, Ill.: The Dryden Press, 1971).

[30]Bower, "Role of Conflict," p. 269.

the interaction between members and subgroups prior to the decision-making process. This interaction can take many forms.

The most common interaction between individual members of a committee consists of the passage of information. In some cases, those in which the committee is not working from an established data base, much of the initial interaction centers around the question of what information is to be used within the committee. Individual members may present different versions of data relating to the same subject or the same quantitative parameters. Resolution of the question of which set of data is valid for the decision problem at hand can take up a great deal of time. This, incidentally, is one of the most compelling reasons why any organization should establish a common data base for use in such decision making.

A second common set of interactive processes in a committee consists of discussion, elucidation and persuasion between the members. These serve to inform individual members of the opinions of the others and are foremost in determining the behavior of members of the committee at the time when the decision process is initiated. During these discussions, members may sound out others on the committee with regard to certain proposals without actually committing themselves to supporting a final course of action. Subgroups may be formed that are in conflict with each other, making the ultimate decision process much more difficult to achieve. On the other hand, a dominant member or subgroup may emerge that can recruit others to a team. The emergence of a leader of this sort in such proceedings has been observed and documented in experimental research.[31]

Many committees are merely facades behind which the proposal of a dominant member or group is presented for acceptance. In such cases much of the discussion and persuasion may have taken place outside the actual committee, in lobbies or in side conversations. The committee then acts as a foundation or a coalition. Individual members have the opportunity to assess the effect of the proposal of the dominant member on future progress toward their own objectives. If all members are in agreement the committee becomes a team for the purpose of the particular deci-

[31]H.J. Leavitt, "A Collective Problem Solving in Small Groups," *Journal of Abnormal and Social Psychology* 46 (1951); reprinted in M. Alexis and C.Z. Wilson, *Organizational Decision Making* (Englewood Cliffs, N.J.: Prentice-Hall, 1967), pp. 40–55.

sion process under consideration and resolution of the problem is agreed on the terms proposed by the dominant member of the subgroup. If a significant number of members oppose the proposal of the dominant member or subgroup, and if the weight of these members within the committee is substantial, the situation may come to resemble a two-person (or an N-person) game.

Under such circumstances a great deal depends on the ensuing discussion and negotiation. During the course of this discussion individual members may be convinced that it is in their own interests to join the dominant group. On the other hand, members of that group may defect and another dominant group may arise. At the time of decision nears, each member still in opposition must consider the usefulness to him in terms of his own objectives of remaining opposed to the dominant group. If he remains adamant, he can be considered as having left the group for the purpose of the decision problem at hand, with whatever consequences for him that this may imply. If he considers these consequences as outweighing the value to him of opposing the dominant group, he may join the group for the purpose of the particular decision, thus creating the semblance of a team for that occasion.

One type of interaction during this negotiation phase that has received some attention in the literature is called *logrolling*.[32] This refers to an arrangement between two or more individuals or groups by which one agrees to support the other's position in one decision process in return for support in another decision problem. Much of this type of negotiation may be implicit, rather than explicit, within the discussions. Those who have studied behavior such as logrolling in committees faced with decision problems point out that such behavior arises from the fact that single decision problems are seldom considered in isolation. Normally more than one decision is before a committee and it is considered natural that some type of trading of support between decisions would occur.

The process of "decision making" by committees, therefore, is seen more as a process of discussion, communication and negotiation with the objective of forming a team for the particular decision problem under review. It is in this precise context that the method of analysis of options is valuable. This method pro-

[32]Gordon Tullock, "A Simple Algebraic Logrolling Model," *American Economic Review* 60 (June, 1970):419–26.

vides a vehicle within which the necessary interaction may take place in a structured manner. It cannot, of course, guarantee that a committee can reach agreement on a particular decision. It does, however, allow opinions and preferences for available options to be considered in the light of the conflict or uncertainty that forms the background to the decision problem.

Summary

Decision-making groups are formed when two or more parties decide to cooperate in a risky venture. The composition of such groups ranges from a two-man partnership to the employees of a large organization and even to cooperative arrangements between organizations.

Each party in a venture has a set of risks that can be accepted and a set that cannot be accepted. The boundary between these risks may be known explicitly or may be only vaguely appreciated. A risk that is outside the acceptance sets of all individuals in a group may be partitioned in such a way that each individual receives a share of the risk that is acceptable to him. The process of partitioning the risk between the individual members of a group may involve side payments between the members to compensate for disproportionate sharing of the total risk.

Once the group has been formed and the arrangements governing the sharing of risk agreed, the question arises of how the group should make decisions, acting as a group rather than as individuals. One intuitively attractive rule for group decision making is that the group should act so that at least one member of the group gains and no member of the group loses. This is known as Pareto-optimal behavior. The problem remains, however, of which members of the group should gain (rather than not lose) and of how much each should gain relative to each other member of the group. This is the problem that is faced in many bargaining situations. A procedure for use by an arbitrator in such situations has been proposed by Nash. In many ways, two or more parties involved in a conflict situation can be considered as a group seeking a jointly acceptable way of resolving their differences.

Other intuitively attractive approaches to group decision making, such as simple majority rule, give rise to paradoxical results in certain circumstances. The proposal that a group utility function should be the sum (or some other combination) of the individual utility functions requires that a weighting of each individual's contribution to the group function be agreed. A group utility function can therefore be constructed only by such agreement between the group members. This is a necessary preliminary to adoption of a policy governing action by the group and of the complete specification of a group decision process. A theorem proved by Arrow shows that a group decision making rule cannot be generally assumed to exist. It can be constructed by agreement or imposed by a dominant member of the group. Much of the force of this theorem is lost, however, if the preferences of the members of the group are not greatly dissimilar.

Decision making groups can be classified according to their behavior into teams, foundations and coalitions. These three classifications essentially represent points on a spectrum. At one end of this spectrum a team consists of members with only group-oriented interests. At the other end a coalition consists of members drawn together by virtue of mutual advantage into a short- or long-term arrangement. The behavior of a group is dynamic and can change quickly during a decision-making process. In addition subgroups can form within the group with different characteristics. Conflict of opinion within a team is much less than within a foundation or a coalition, so that the ease of reaching a decision within a team is greatest. However, some degree of conflict of opinion in a group may improve the quality of decision making at the expense of the ease of reaching a decision.

The proceedings of committees formed to make decisions consist more of interaction between members than of actual decision making. This interaction is a preliminary to the formation of subgroups. The committee decision is usually that presented by a subgroup or individual member who reaches a dominant position during this process of interaction.

Discussion Topics

1/ Risk sharing is easy to understand in the context of a simple quantitative venture. Can the concept of risk sharing usefully be applied to the decision of a staff member in joining an organization?

2/ In a Pareto-optimal solution to a decision problem, no member of the group loses and at least one gains. Where does that gain come from?

3/ Can two parties involved in a two-person, non-zero sum game achieve a Pareto-optimal solution? In this sense, are the parties acting as a group?

4/ Do you think the Nash solution to a bargaining problem is "fair"? What are its major advantages? Can you propose a better procedure?

5/ The simple majority rule in group decision making can result in an apparently paradoxical outcome. Are there any conditions under which the effects of this paradox are lessened?

6/ Arrow's theorem requires that a group decision-making rule be constructed or imposed. What are the implications of this result on group decision making?

7/ Under what practical conditions do you think it would be possible to construct a group utility function?

8/ How would you go about reaching a decision in a group, the members of which have dissimilar preferences for the available options? Would you press for a quick decision?

9/ If the group of which you were a member appeared to be reaching a quick decision, would you introduce some conflict of opinion, with a view to improving the quality of the decision?

10/ Do you believe that the phenomenon known as risky shift actually occurs in practical decision making? If so, under what circumstances and is this a useful or dangerous phenomenon?

11/ If you were the only member of a group opposed to a particular decision, under what conditions would you join the dominant subgroup and when would you continue to oppose the decision? If you agreed to the decision, would your utility function have changed?

12/ Do you think logrolling is a useful procedure in terms of group decision making? If so, why? If not, why not?

7

Decision Making in Organizations

Introduction

Much of the theory developed on the subject of organizational decision making in the late nineteenth and early twentieth centuries was concerned with economic factors. Decisions regarding pricing, output, mixes of products, resource allocation and other economic matters were the main subject of attention of those interested in how an organization should make a decision. This was an attractive approach because it dealt with the important matter of efficiency and its relation to profit. The major factors considered in these studies were easily measured in terms of dollars as the unit of profit and cost.

This type of approach was reinforced by the introduction of powerful mathematical techniques into business decision making after World War II. These techniques allowed a much more sophisticated approach to optimization than had been possible previously. They provided a means for specifying an optimum design and operation for many of the basic processes in business

211

and industry. A number of problems, such as those concerned with queues and dynamic allocation of resources to a production process that had been regarded as too complex to treat analytically, were brought into the realm of quantitative analysis by the use of powerful mathematical methods.

Decision processes in organizations to which these mathematical and quantitative techniques apply are those that have been called "completely specified" earlier in the text. These are treated first in this chapter. The discussion then proceeds to organizational decision processes that cannot be completely specified and to a discussion of managerial and organizational behavior in resolution of these decisions. The role of the special systems group is considered and some recommendations are made that should allow greater support to senior management in decision processes at the high levels of the organization. Finally, a brief treatment is given of the role of an information system in support of organizational decision making.

Completely Specified Decision Processes

The decision processes to which well-developed mathematical and quantitative techniques apply have an important role in modern organizations. They exist in organizations that produce a product and in those that produce services. However, the fact that these processes are sufficiently well understood to be completely specified has caused them mostly to be relegated to the lower levels of an organization where they are monitored by middle- and lower-level managers.

In addition to the completely specified decision processes involved with the efficiency of *operational* tasks, there are, in most organizations, a number of such systems serving *administrative* tasks. The number and complexity of such tasks has grown significantly in recent years. What used to be a simple matter of paying staff a wage or salary has now grown into a payroll system, which makes deductions for tax and a number of employee benefits. Complete personnel records are kept and the pension plan is often a major system in an organization. The operational and administrative systems that are typically served by completely specified decision processes in a modern organization are shown in Table 7-1. As mentioned previously in the text, some of these tasks may be served by partially specified systems in which a major part of the process is specified, but the final decision is left to the responsible decision maker.

Table 7-1 Typical Tasks Served by Completely or Partially Specified Decision Processes

Personnel	: maintenance of personnel records
	: administration of pension plans
	: industrial relations services
Finance	: payroll and deductions from pay
	: accounts receivable and payable
	: general ledger accounting
	: cost accounting
	: internal audit
Distribution	: scheduling of deliveries
	: maintenance of inventories
	: order control and shipping
Production	: scheduling and control of production
	: purchasing and procurement
	: control of stocks of resources
Sales	: market research
	: sales planning
	: order processing

Each completely specified decision process, when fully implemented, contains a *monitor* function that allows those responsible to check that the process is operating within its specifications.[1] If these specifications are exceeded in any way the monitor provides a warning that some sort of remedial action is necessary.

Another important function in a system supporting a completely specified decision process is called the *interface*. This function provides an output that summarizes the operations of the process over a given period of time and provides information that may be useful in other related decision processes in the organization. For example, this summary information may be the number

[1]K.J. Radford, *Information Systems in Management* (Reston, Va.: Reston Publishing Co., 1973), pp. 57–59.

of units produced or the total salaries paid during a given time period.

As in the case of a process control system in a modern production facility, a completely specified system may produce physical output such as cheques, invoices or packages of goods. Because these decision processes are well understood and have become a routine part of the work of the organization there is sometimes a tendency to consider them less important or less challenging than others that are less straightforward. The completely specified decision processes are, however, a vital component of the decision-making capability of an organization.

Decisions That Are Not Completely Specified

Many types of decisions in a modern organization are not completely specified. These are the ones that managers may tend to regard as the "real" decisions, as compared with the more routine completely specified processes.

A decision process that cannot be completely specified is simply one for which it is not possible or desirable at any particular time to write down an agreed, detailed method of arriving at a resolution of the problem. It may be that the process is not sufficiently understood at the time to merit complete specification. Individual managers may have different approaches to the problem and may wish to apply their own personal experience, knowledge and beliefs in its resolution. There may be no means available of judging which approach is best. The pressure of modern-day affairs may not allow decisions to be delayed until an agreed specification is obtained.

Organization decision processes that involve uncertainty or conflict are not usually completely specified. These processes are those that managers tend to regard as the ones to which their judgment and experience should be applied. However, some progress has been made in introducing analytical procedures and support to managers engaged in these decision processes, as indicated by the methods described in chapters 4 and 5.

Particular factors that may result in a decision process not being completely specified are the following:

- the background to the decision is a multiple objective set and no agreement exists with regard to the relative priorities and weightings of the individual objectives;

- the decision impinges on the personal objectives of members of a group charged with resolution in such a way that the group is prevented from acting as a team with respect to the problem;

- no agreement exists with regard to the perception of the problem, its formulation or the model of the actual decision process involved;

- the decision process cannot be described in terms of a single, well-defined quantitative parameter, either because there is no agreement on the objective against which the decision is to be made or because the parameter to be considered in relation to an agreed objective cannot be specified;

- there is no agreement on preferences for available options between members of the group charged with resolution of the decision problem and no means of structuring discussion within the group to arrive at agreed preferences;

- no agreement exists with regard to the criterion of choice between available options.

If one or more of these conditions exists, it is unlikely that the decision problem can be completely specified, although in some cases it may be partially specified.

It may happen that a manager retains a decision process under his personal direction and uses his judgment to resolve problems that could, in reality, be completely specified. This may be due to unwillingness on the part of the manager responsible to undertake the process of specification, possible from fear of losing control of what he regards as an important part of his work. In such circumstances staff members may work long hours and overtime, personally undertaking decision processes that could be completely specified and delegated to a lower level. This reluctance to undertake the process of specification may cause a significant decrease in overall efficiency. In some such cases, the introduction of a completely specified system may be resisted strongly and employee morale may be affected if the matter is not approached with full consideration of the feelings of the staff members involved.

The question of whether to introduce a completely specified decision process, therefore, is one requiring considerable atten-

tion. One of the major mistakes that can be made in dealing with organizational decision processes is to force a specification upon managers who do not feel ready to accept it for reasons associated with their own judgment and experience. The failure of some computer applications can be laid to the introduction of completely specified systems before the managers responsible felt able to accept the specification as truly representing the problem facing them. For this reason, it is most desirable that the process of specification of a decision process be one in which the responsible managers take an active, if not a leading, part.

Managerial and Organizational Behavior in Decision Making

Satisficing versus Optimizing

The classical departure from economics and statistical decision theory as a basis for managerial decision making was made by Herbert A. Simon[2,3] and James G. March.[4] In their treatment of organizational decision processes they first separated out "programmed" decisions (those that we have called completely specified decision processes). They assumed that these could be approached in a rational manner by selecting the option that appeared as best to the decision maker.

March and Simon then postulated that some decision processes that could not be completely specified were approached by managers in a different fashion, which they called *satisficing*. Such decision making is not concerned with optimizing in a rational manner, but with finding a satisfactory solution that meets certain criteria set by the individual or the organization. As soon as a manager finds a satisfactory solution that is feasible within the constraints under which he must work, (according to March and Simon), he discontinues his search and adopts this satisfactory solution.

Most managers would no doubt prefer to optimize if this were possible. Maximizing a quantity that measures the achievement

[2]Herbert A. Simon, *Administrative Behavior* (New York: The Free Press, 1965).

[3]Herbert A. Simon, "The New Science of Management Decision," reprinted in L.A. Welsch and R.M. Cyert, eds., *Management Decision Making* (Baltimore, Md.: Penguin Modern Management Readings, 1970), pp. 13–29.

[4]James G. March and Herbert A. Simon, *Organizations* (New York: John Wiley & Sons, 1958), pp. 137–71.

of a desired objective is usually the desire of a rational individual. Why then do managers satisfice? One of the major reasons given for this type of behavior is that satisficing requires much less effort than optimizing and significant savings in time and resources can result. Simon offers as another explanation the fact that managers often have insufficient information on which to optimize.[5] Furthermore, in the time available for making the decision there may be little opportunity to gather more relevant information. Another constraint limiting the amount of information available may be the cost of gathering additional data pertinent to the decision process.

Eilon points out that satisficing often occurs where a decision must be made against a background of multiple objectives.[6] He gives the example of a manager operating in a part of an organization to which certain performance objectives have been assigned. Such a manager may make no attempt to assign priorities to the individual objectives or to resolve conflicts between them. He may be interested only in finding a solution to his problem that is feasible within the constraints that the multiple objectives impose upon him. If he were of a quantitative turn of mind he might resort to an analysis of the type proposed by Sang M. Lee,[7] which was discussed in Chapter 4. This provides a means of minimizing the total deviation between planned and achieved performance toward a number of goals, as distinct from an optimum solution to a decision problem. In such circumstances, Eilon argues, with some justification, there is no difference between goals and constraints.[8] He says that all constraints imposed on the solution of a decision problem within an organization can be considered as goals because they represent desirable or undesirable modes of operation. In the same way that priorities may be assigned to the satisfying of objectives, some constraints may be considered as more important to observe than others.

Another factor that may induce satisficing rather than optimizing is the difficulty that is experienced in many decision situa-

[5]Simon, *Administrative Behavior*, p. 81.

[6]Samuel Eilon, "Goals and Constraints in Decision Making," *Operational Research Quarterly* 23, pp. 2–15.

[7]Sang M. Lee, "Goal Programming for Decision Analysis of Multiple Objectives," *Sloan Management Review* 14 (Winter, 1972–73):11–23.

[8]Samuel Eilon, *Management Control* (New York: Macmillan, 1971).

tions in defining a quantitative parameter with which to measure progress toward the achievement of a goal. Money measured in dollars or some other currency is a highly satisfactory parameter for optimizing in economic decisions involving profit or cost. Many other decisions are concerned with matters for which it is considerably more difficult to define a suitable measure of performance. Without a suitable quantitative measure, managers are at a loss in optimizing and may resort consciously or unconsciously to satisficing as their only possible behavior in decision making. Satisficing may, in fact, occur under many of the same conditions where decision processes cannot be completely specified. This is not to say, however, that a decision problem that cannot be completely specified must necessarily be approached on the basis of satisficing.

The tendency to satisfice may be embedded in the structure of the organization in which a manager operates. In such cases, the various components of an organization may have their own set of goals and objectives. The individual managers working in each component may be judged on the basis of their progress in achieving these goals. In many cases, the goals may be generated from below rather than imposed from above. This may be done partially as a defense mechanism and partially as a bargaining ploy in the goal-setting process. Over a period of time, such goals may impose tighter and tighter constraints on the decision making behavior of managers, leading to a greater tendency to satisfice rather than optimize. In extreme cases, the goals may preclude a feasible solution and some sort of crisis in management may result.

The Minimization of Uncertainty

Satisficing does not provide a unique criterion for decision making.[9] Many of the available options in a decision situation may be satisfactory to the manager concerned. In such cases, a manager may still be faced with the problem of choice between two or more satisfactory courses of action. In such circumstances managers may implicitly or explicitly resort to a criterion of choice between options that minimizes uncertainty in the out-

[9]Brian J. Loasby, "The Decision Maker in the Organization," *Journal of Management Studies* 5 (1968):361.

come of the decision process. In similar fashion, the desire to have the outcome match closely what has been predicted at the time of making the decision sometimes influences managerial behavior in the action taken to implement a decision. As mentioned in Chapter 3, Argyris found evidence in studies conducted in an organization suggesting that executives marshal human and financial resources after the decision has been made in order that the outcome can be satisfactory.[10] The reduction in uncertainty is obtained, in such circumstances, by appropriate actions of the decision maker to implement the action required by his decision.

A number of studies have shown that organizations tend to avoid uncertainty in decision making if this is at all possible.[11] One result of this sort of organizational behavior may be an emphasis on short-term decision problems and a neglect of longer-term problems with their inherent greater uncertainties. This may result in a style of management in which preparation of short-term policies is preferred to work in long-range planning. The more thoroughly the short-term policies are prepared and implemented, the greater the probability that long-term decisions will be neglected.[12]

Another way in which organizations have been seen to minimize uncertainty is by endeavoring to exercise as much control as possible over the environment in which they operate. The greater the control that can be exercised, the less the future uncertainties that can be caused by events and the actions of others. In acting in this manner, organizations hope to achieve a stable environment in which the deviation between what has been predicted in a decision process and the actual outcome is kept to a minimum. At the same time, they emphasize decision making in areas where plans and decisions can be made self-confirming by future actions under the control of the organization.

To reduce uncertainty, many organizations endeavor to *negotiate* an environment in which they can operate. One method of achieving this is by means of industry-wide conventions gov-

---

[10]Chris Argyris, "Management Information Systems: The Challenge to Rationality and Emotionality," *Management Science* 17 (February, 1971):B279.

[11]Richard M. Cyert and James G. March, *A Behavioral Theory of the Firm* (Englewood Cliffs, N.J.: Prentice-Hall, 1963):118–20.

[12]Brian J. Loasby, "Managerial Decision Processes," *Scottish Journal of Political Economics* 14 (1967):248.

erning "good practice." Many other types of agreements between organizations that are nominally competitors provide a stable and predictable environment for operations without necessarily contravening legal barriers to collusion. Cyert and March quote agreed rate of mark up and standard costing procedures as examples of such agreements. The parties to an agreement of this sort essentially enter into a loose and unwritten coalition for the purposes of reducing the uncertainty surrounding their operations.

Another method of reducing uncertainty often employed by organizations is that of breaking down important decision problems into a sequence of lesser component decisions. Only the most pressing of these component decisions are made immediately. Others in the sequence are treated only as necessary, in the light of the latest available information. If a particular decision problem does not appear to be suitable for breaking down into a sequence of lesser decisions, every effort is made to modify the original decision or the environment to which it refers so that it can be treated in this manner. This organizational decision making behavior has been described as similar to the procedure of building operating and revising, prevalent in many branches of engineering.[13]

The Relationship of Decision Making to Organizational Structure

There have been many studies of the relationship of organizational structure to managerial behavior in decision making. March and Simon took the view that the structure of organizations is derived from the characteristics of the decision making within the organization.[14] Tannenbaum linked authority and influence with the fact that decisions made by managers affect the behavior of their subordinates, both directly, through authority, and indirectly, through influence.[15] Simon has stated as an important principle of organizational design that programmed activity

[13]Julius Margolis, "Research of the Theory of the Firm: Sequential Decision Making in the Firm," *American Economic Review* 50 (1960):526–33.

[14]March and Simon, *Organizations*, p. 169.

[15]Robert Tannenbaum, "Managerial Decision Making," *Journal of Business* 23 (1950): 30–21.

tends to drive out nonprogrammed activity.[16] He concludes that, ". . . special provision must be made for nonprogrammed decision making by creating special organizational responsibilities and organizational units to take care of it."

Blankenship and Miles have reported a study of the relationship between organizational structure and managerial decision making.[17] Their study concerns three structural properties of an organization—size, hierarchical level and span of control—as possible determinants of managerial behavior in decision making. The results they report are based on the decision behavior of 190 managers from eight organizations engaged in light manufacturing. They found that hierarchical level is strongly and consistently associated with a manager's decision-making style. Managers at the upper levels appeared to be freer of close control by their superiors and at the same time seemed to involve their subordinates more in the decision-making process. On the other hand, lower level managers seemed to be subject to much greater direction by their superiors at all stages in decision making, while consulting less with their subordinates. This suggests that if an organization wishes to encourage participation of subordinates at all levels of decision making, a substantial degree of delegation of responsibility will be necessary.

The Systems Group and the Special Project Team

As more and more complex decision-making techniques have been introduced into organizations there has been a natural move to set up a separate group to handle this specialized work. In some cases, this has been achieved by an expansion of an existing Systems and Procedures group and by its elevation to a higher position in the organizational hierarchy. Such groups have often been staffed by persons highly qualified in quantitative analysis.

Many of the early authors of works on operational research advocated the establishment of such groups and recommended that they report to the highest levels in the organizations. A great deal has been achieved by these groups in recent years. Many

---

[16]Herbert A. Simon, "The New Science of Management Decision," pp. 13–29.

[17]L.V. Blankenship and R.E. Miles, "Organizational Structure and Managerial Decision Behavior," *Administrative Science Quarterly* 13 (1968):106–20.

large operational problems have been tackled with the result that substantial improvements in the efficiency of routine operations have been achieved. These have been reported in areas as diverse as the operation of toll bridges, the shipping of oil by pipelines, distribution of goods over networks of retail outlets and the operation of major manufacturing and processing plants. With all this success, however, there has remained a significant set of decision problems that have not yielded to the techniques of quantitative analysis, which are the speciality of many such systems groups. These difficult problems arise at the higher levels in the organization. They have been called non-completely-specified earlier in the text.

Not unnaturally, the efforts of the specialized groups have been concentrated on the problems for which there was hope of solution and chance of success. This concentration has been accentuated and assisted by the advent of the computer as an organizational tool. Since the computer is by nature a quantitative device, it is natural that it should have been used with greatest priority and greatest success in support of organizational decision problems with the greatest quantitative content. The result has been, however, that the specialist groups have come to apply themselves over the years to the problems that are the prime responsibility of the middle and lower levels of management in the organization. The senior manager still finds himself substantially without support from these groups. Moreover, he may be somewhat disillusioned by the fact that the help that he was promised in his most difficult decision-making problems appears not to have materialized. To be sure, many complex problems that previously required senior managerial input have been completely specified and delegated to lower levels of management. Nevertheless, the fact remains that many of the more significant decision problems in an organization are still resolved by managers, with little or no assistance from the specialized groups.

These higher-level decision processes are often not approachable in quantitative terms. At best, only a portion of the problem may yield to quantitative analysis. A major factor in their resolution is the exercise of the experience and judgment of the managers who have been involved with similar problems over many years of work within the organization.

It is in precisely this type of decision process, however, that the analysis of options (described in Chapter 5) can be used. The major value of this technique is that it can provide a method for structuring discussion of a decision problem. Managers can then take part in an analysis of the problem on the basis of their own experience and without lengthy initiation into difficult quantitative methods. The major inputs into an analysis of options are the opinions and preferences of the managers concerned. The role of the analyst is to *conduct* the analysis, using managerial inputs as the major factors leading to a recommended course of action. In this way the skills of the analysts and managers are blended in a joint solution of the problem. The danger that the manager may become discouraged by the complexity of a mathematical approach is averted, as is the possibility that the preferences and judgments of the analyst, rather than the manager, become the major inputs to the study.

This suggests, therefore, that many of the more complex decision processes found in organizations should be approached by formation of a team of managers whose combined experience covers all aspects of the problem. A special project team of this nature can be assisted by a skilled analyst who has the experience and judgment necessary to avoid regression to more easily manipulated, but less appropriate, quantitative techniques. This is not to say that the use of quantitative techniques should be banished from the organization. They have a rightful place in support of important decision processes that can be completely specified. They are likely to be useful also in portions of the more difficult decision processes that can be partially specified.

The project team that is likely to be most successful operates as a joint effort of managers and analysts, with the managers leading the work by virtue of their greater experience of the problems involved. The role of the analyst is one of the support and of introducing specialist skills as they are needed in the solution of the problem.

The Information System in Support of Decision Making

One of the major constraints under which managers operate in decision making is the lack of information relevant to the problem. If perfect information were available, most decision problems would be easily resolved. Managers are generally in possession of imperfect information and are faced with the problem of searching for more information within the constraints of the time and cost involved in gathering this information. The purpose of an information system is to assist managers in their search for information pertinent to their decision problems. In this respect, the information system must serve and support the managerial decision-making process, rather than be an independent system in its own right.

The question of how an information system should be designed has been the subject of considerable controversy in recent years.[18,19] Unfortunately, the arguments have become entwined with those concerning the introduction of computers into organizations and with the promotion of the computer as a major aid to organizational decision making. Most, if not all, of the texts purporting to describe the design and implementation of management information systems that were published in the late 1960's were, in fact, devoted primarily to the implementation of *computer based systems*[20-22] rather than to the desirable characteristics of the *information system*.

Authors of that time appear to have overlooked the early work of Norbert Wiener, who saw the information system as an integral part of an organization, much in the same way as part of the brain and the nervous system act as an information system in the human organism. Wiener expressed his beliefs in his book *Cybernetics:*[23]

">. . . any organism is held together . . . by the possession of a means for the acquisition, use, retention and transmission of information."

Building on this and others of Wiener's ideas,[24] the author pro-

[18]Russell, L. Ackoff, "Management Misinformation Systems," *Management Science* 14 (December, 1967).

[19]Alfred Rappaport, "Management Misinformation Systems—Another Perspective," letter to the Editor of *Management Science* 15, no. 3, pp. B133–36.

[20]Sherman C. Blumenthal, *Management Information Systems* (Englewood Cliffs, N.J.: Prentice-Hall, 1969).

[21]Perry E. Rosove, *Developing Computer Based Information Systems* (New York: John Wiley & Sons, 1968).

[22]W. Hartman, H. Matthes, and A. Proema, *Management Information Systems Handbook* (New York: McGraw-Hill, 1968).

[23]Norbert Wiener, *Cybernetics* (Cambridge, Mass.: The MIT Press, 1969), p. 161.

[24]Norbert Wiener, *The Human Use of Human Beings* (New York: Avon Books, 1970).

posed the following broad specifications for an information system to serve the decision processes in an organization:[25]

- It must encompass formal and informal components.

- It must include sensors of all types necessary to capture data on internal and external conditions related to situations that confront the organization (or may confront it in the future).

- It must provide communication channels from the sensors to the decision making centers (people, groups of people and machines controlled by people).

- It must include storage facilities for data not immediately required or that may be required to be used more than once.

- It must have facilities for aggregating and collating data to convert them into information bearing on the decision processes necessary to the organization.

- It must provide channels of communication to the persons responsible for carrying out the necessary activities.

- It must provide output information in a readily comprehensible form to those persons and machines involved in the activities of the organization.

These broad specifications were used as a basis for generic design of an information system, with the following components:

- *Administrative and operational systems* serving routine (completely specified) decision processes in the organization such as personnel administration, production scheduling, and so forth.

- *The management reporting system,* which provides periodic and structured reports to managers based on summary data from the administrative and operational systems.

- *The common data base,* which acts as a store for data and information used by more than one part of the organization.

- *The information retrieval system,* from which historic data

---

[25]Radford, *Information Systems,* p. 10.

and information may be retrieved for use in planning and decision making.

– *The data management system*, which arranges and controls the flow of data and information between components of the information system.

These components of such an information system are shown in diagrammatic form in Figure 7-1.

The Operation of the Information System

The operation of such an information system can be described briefly as follows. Routine administrative and operational decisions are supported by completely specified systems (represented by the peripheral circles) that receive data and information from internal and external sources. The functioning of these systems is

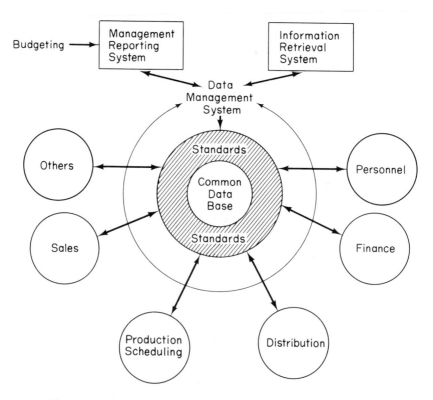

Figure 7-1   Generic Diagram of an Information System

reviewed when necessary by the managers responsible for them on the basis of information available at a monitor. Data and information required by other functions or for reporting to other levels of management appear at interfaces in the completely specified systems, which are connected to the common data base. These data and information must conform to established standards to gain admittance to the base and to be passed therefrom to other components of the system.

Reports for management are compiled from data and information in the common data base. Those that are structured and periodic are provided by the management reporting system; information not included in structured and periodic reports can be provided on demand by the information retrieval system. Flow of data and information is controlled by a data management system. Data and information in the system, and that it is desired to retain for future use, are placed in an historic store from which they can be retrieved, if this is found necessary to support future decision processes. The contents of the common data base are also transferred regularly to an historic store to provide a continual record of the affairs of the organization and also to safeguard against loss or destruction of the current base.

The basic generic design is applicable to a system for the whole organization or for any portion of it. Parts of an organization that are geographically separated or semi-autonomous in operation can set up their own information systems to the same general design, each with its own common data base. Data and information that are of common concern to two or more such parts of the organization (or to one part of the organization and head office) are then exchanged between the common data bases. Under these circumstances *the degree of formal communication achieved between the parts of the organization is in direct relation to the degree of standardization of data descriptions, formats and codes that has been achieved.*

This can be illustrated by the following diagram. At one end of the spectrum, the information systems in the various parts of the organization are completely independent; at the other end, one single system is used throughout the whole organization. The direction from left to right in the diagram is the direction of increasing standardization among the information systems in the various component parts of the organization. It is also the direc-

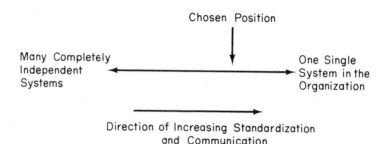

Figure 7-2   Relationship Between Information Systems in Different Parts of Organization

tion of increasing formal communication between those components through the medium of the information systems.

This approach to information system design allows the responsibility for the completely specified administrative and operational systems to remain in the hands of the managers concerned. Decisions with regard to computer support can be taken separately for each individual system on the basis of costs and efficiency of operation. This is particularly appropriate at the present stage of development of computers for support of such systems. Small micro- and mini-computers that can be dedicated to individual administrative and operational systems are increasingly available at modest cost. Their introduction into organizations will tend to bring computing capability back to the location of the system being served. Large central computers will become less common and the information system will be supported by a network of distributed mini-computers linked together in a logical diagram similar to that shown in Figure 7-1.

The redesign of the completely specified systems and their fitting into an overall design such as that shown in Figure 7-1 is a task that should be given early attention in the design and implementation of an information system.[26] It is also a reasonable initial approach to try to increase the proportion of decision processes that can be completely or partially specified.

The Information System in Support of Non-Completely-Specified Decision Processes

The task of designing that portion of the information system that must serve the non-completely-specified decision processes is

[26]K.J. Radford, "Information Systems and Managerial Decision Making," OMEGA, The International Journal of Management Science 2, no. 2, 1974.

much more difficult. No agreed requirements for data and information may be available with respect to such decisions. Individual decision makers may have widely differing requirements for information in support of a particular decision process. In this respect, managers may be thought of as persons trying to complete a complex jigsaw puzzle (representing perfect information). Each manager has completed a different part of the puzzle. The part completed relates to his personal knowledge of the situation, derived from experience and past acquisition of information. Each manager's requirements for data to complete the puzzle may be different. What is a vital piece of information to one manager may be already in the possession of another.

Determination of the information requirements of managers involved in complex decision problems represents an important area of research in which much remains to be done. Some of the more obvious approaches to this problem have not yielded appreciable results. As Daniel said in 1961, ". . . seldom is the open approach of asking an executive what information he requires successful."[27] Many executives find it difficult to be precise in defining information requirements. One particularly significant study in this area showed that people prefer to receive the kinds of information they consider to be most *useful to them*. The usefulness of a specific type of information in this study was found to depend in part upon the *reversibility* and the *consequences* of the decisions under review.[28]

In these circumstances, probably the best approach to information system design in this area at the present time is to make the contents of the common data base freely and easily available to managers who have the need to use the information. This can be facilitated by compiling a directory to the data and circulating this to those concerned. At the same time, records can be kept of the use of information in major decision processes, both in the form of withdrawals from the common data base (and its associated historic store) and of requests for new categories of information. (See Fig. 7-2.) Study of patterns that arise in these requests for data and information may throw more light on to the

---

[27]D.R. Daniel, "Management Information Crisis," *Harvard Business Review* (September–October, 1961): p. 93.

[28]Rosemary Hayslowe and Ivan D. Steiner, "Some Effects of the Reversibility and Consequences of Decisions on Post-Decision Information Preferences," *Journal of Personality and Social Psychology* 8 (1968):172–79.

difficult question of managerial requirements for information in complex decision making.

Summary

Early approaches to organizational decision making were based on considerations of economics. This type of approach, which was in terms of factors that could be easily expressed in qualitative form, was reinforced by the introduction of the powerful mathematical techniques of operational research into organizational decision making. These techniques apply mostly to decisions that can be completely specified and that serve important administrative and operational tasks in modern organizations.

Many of the decision processes facing managers in modern organizations cannot be completely specified for one or more reasons. Organizational decision processes that involve uncertainty or conflict are not usually completely specified. Managers engaged in non-completely-specified decision making are observed not to optimize. Instead, they choose a satisfactory solution that meets certain criteria and that is within the constraints set by the individual or the organization.

Both individuals and organizations tend to try to minimize uncertainty in organizational decision making. Individuals do this by choosing courses of action over which they feel they have most control and by managing resources after the decision in such a way as to make the chosen course come out best. Organizations reduce uncertainty by concentrating on short-term problems. Also, complex decisions are broken down into a sequence of smaller decisions that are tackled one at a time and at the latest possible time. Organizations try to exercise as much control as possible over the environment in which they operate in order to reduce uncertainty.

Systems groups set up to aid in organizational decision making have concentrated on the more tractable decisions involving well-defined quantitative parameters. They have consequently, tended to deal with decision processes that arise in the middle and lower levels of management and for which quantitative techniques and the use of computers in support of decision making are appropriate and successful. Senior management still receives little support from such groups. This can be redressed by the formation of special project teams to undertake major decisions, in which managers play a leading role and analysts provide support. Such project teams can make good use of the analysis of options technique, discussed in detail in Chapter 5.

Much of the discussion of management information systems to date has been, in reality, concerned with the introduction of computers into the organization. A different approach is possible based on the ideas of Norbert Wiener, in which the information system is regarded as a vital component of the organization, similar in role to that of the brain and the nervous system in the human body. In this approach the completely specified systems operate semi-autonomously in support of administrative and operational tasks in the organization. Information of interest to other parts of the organization is made available in summary form at interfaces between the components of the information system. The generic design is particularly appropriate in the light of the present trend toward distribution of computer power throughout the organization, rather than its concentration in a central facility.

The task of providing information to managers involved in non-completely-specified decision processes is difficult and this represents an important area for future research. Probably the best approach at the present time is to make the contents of the data base (present and past) freely and easily available to managers who have the need for such information and to record their use of it.

Discussion Topics

1/ What are the functions of the *interface* of a completely specified system? How do these differ from those of the *monitor*?

2/ How would you approach a manager who appears to be retaining a decision process that might be more efficiently approached by complete specification?

3/ How is *satisficing* related to non-complete-specification in a decision process? Do managers satisfice when they do not have sufficient information to optimize?

4/ How are constraints related to objectives in organizational decision making?

5/ What steps can be taken to minimize uncertainty in organizational decision making? Is it common for managers and organizations to act in this manner?

6/ Does the nature of the decision-making process in an organization influence its structure?

7/ How can the systems group best assist with senior managers with the decision problems at the higher levels of an organization?

8/ The role of the systems group is in support of the manager in his decision making tasks. True or false and why?

9/ Information system design has been unduly influenced by the availability of computers. True or false?

10/ Does the decision-making performance of a manager improve if he has the information he needs? Can he be overloaded with information?

11/ Who should control an information system, the manager or the systems specialist? Give reasons for your reply.

12/ How is the design of the information system related to the degree of formal communication within an organization?

13/ How will the trend toward small capable micro- and mini-computers affect information system design?

14/ How would you plan to discover the information needs of a manager engaged in a complex decision process?

Index

A

Absolute scale of measurement, 42–47
Acceptance set, of risks, 183–86
Ackoff, Russell L., 5, 224
  and Emery, F.E., 5
Actual stability, 142
Additivity, condition of in linear
  programming, 86–89
Administrative and operational
  decisions, 84, 212–14
  systems for, 225
Alchian, A.A., 4
Analysis of options, 141, 147–72, 207,
  223
  application to decisions under
  uncertainty, 168–72
  critique of, 166–68

Arbitrator, purpose of, 188
Argyris, Chris, 11, 78, 203, 219
Arrow, K.J., 53, 193–200
Assignment problem, 89–90

B

Bargaining, 188–90
  in groups, 201
  Nash solution to, 189–90
Battle of the sexes, 135–36, 190
Bayes' formula, 109
Bayesian school of probability, 103
Benefit, measures of, 32–35
Bergson, Abram, 194
Bernoulli, Daniel, 62, 70–71
Bernoullian utility, 37–38

Blankenship, L.V. and Miles, R.E., 221
Blau, Julian, 195–96
Bluffing, in "Chicken," 176–77
Blumenthal, Sherman C., 224
Bounded rationality, 77, 147–48
Bower, Joseph L., 200, 205
Breakdowns of rationality, 138

C

Canning, R.G., 24–25
Central nervous system, in humans, 5
Certainty, decisions under, 3, 57–59
  with multiple objectives, 92–96
Chandrashekar, M., 156
Charnes, A., and Cooper, W., 93
Chernoff, Herman, 75
Chicken, game of, 174–77
  bluffing in, 176–77
Choice between options, 3
Christenson, Charles, 8
Churchman, C. West, 4, 44
Clarkson, G.P.E., 202
Closed systems, 6
Clough, Donald J., 89, 101
Coalitions, of staff members, 11
  in an analysis of options, 160–66
  in committees, 206–7
  in groups, 197–200
  in N-person games, 120–21
Cognitive dissonance, 78
Committee, decision making in 204–8
Common data base, 206, 225–28
Communication prior to play in a
  game, 134–36
Competition, decisions under (see
  Conflict)
Completely specified decision
  processes, 21–22, 200, 212–14
  interface in, 213
  monitor function in, 213
  specifications of, 22
Complex decision problems, 1–2, 14,
  127–80
Computer, use in decision making, 2
Conan Doyle, Sir Arthur, 131

Condition of citizen's sovereignty, 195
Condition of non-dictatorship, 195
Condition of independence of
  irrelevant alternatives, 195
Conflict, decisions under, 57, 61,
  127–80, 214–16
  negotiations between parties in, 191
Conflict, in a group, 198–204
Conflict point in a decision situation,
  166, 173
Conservatism effect, 110
Consistency of preferences, 35–36
Constant-sum games, 132
Constraint, caused by one objective on
  another, 8
  types of, 16–17
Coordination games, 139
Cost of information, 3
Credibility of a sanction, 155
Criteria of choice between options, 13,
  19
  relation to attitude to risk, 19, 21
Customary wealth, 40–42
Cybernetics, 224
Cyert, Richard M., 4, 11, 13, 78, 219

D

Daley, J.C., and Johnson, E.C., 125
Daniel, D.R., 229
Data gathering, 100–101
Davidson, D., and Marschak, J., 52
Decisions (see also Decision
  Processes), nature of, 1–5
  administrative and operational, 84
  background to, 6–12
  component parts in sequence, 2, 220
  group, 4
  outcome of, 13
  repeated, 2, 15, 22
  stable, 134
  under certainty, 3, 57–59, 92–96
  under conditions of conflict, 57, 61,
  114–21
  under risk, 57, 59–61, 99, 182–83

Decisons (*Contd.*)
  under uncertainty, 3, 57–61, 105,
    168–72
  unique, single-play, 2, 15, 131
Decision criterion, under conditions
    of certainty, 62
  under conditions of conflict, 76–77
  under conditions of risk, 62–71
  under conditions of uncertainty,
    71–76
Decision flow diagram, 104–14
Decision making group,
    characteristics of, 197–208
Decision making, rationality in, 19–21
  group, 181–210
  organizational, 211–32
  personalistic involvement in, 19–21
  relationship to organizational
    structure, 220–21
Decision processes (*see also*
    Decisions)
  action to implement, 13
  completely specified, 21–22,
    212–16
  iterative nature of, 14
  model of, 13
  nature of, 5
  non-completely specified, 23–24,
    214–16, 222
  organizational, 24–25
  partially specified, 22–23, 213–15,
    223
  programmed, 21
  resolution of, 13
  sequential, 61, 90–91, 101, 114, 220
  steps in, 12–19
  types of, 21–24
Decision tree, 104–14
Delay in taking decision, 3
Deterministic problems in operations
    research, 58, 96
Divisibility, condition of in linear
    programming, 86–89
Dominance, in a group, 202–3
Dominant member of a committee or
    group, 206–7
Dorfman, Robert, 32

Drucker, Peter F., 13–15
Dynamic programming, 90–91

E

Effectiveness, measures of, 31–32
Efficiency, measures of, 31–32
Eilon, Samuel, 4, 13, 23, 35, 93, 217
Equilibrium, in game situations, 116,
    129–40
Evaluation
  of outcomes of options, 18
  of planned operations as part of
    management, 12
Expected value
  maximum as decision criterion,
    62–71
  of perfect information, 107–8
  relation to utility function, 40

F

Fayol, Henri, 12
Festinger, Leon, 78
Fishburn, P., 197
Foundation, 197–200, 206–7
Frequency school of probability 66
Friedman, M., and Savage, L.J., 38–40

G

Game (*see* two-person or N-person
    game)
  in a committee, 207
Goals, 5–12
  relative to objectives, 6
Goal programming, 93
Grémion, Catherine, 77
Group
  acting as a coalition, 197–200
  acting as a foundation, 197–200
  acting as a team, 181, 197–200

Group decisions, 4, 181–210
   condition of citizen's sovereignty
      in, 195
   condition of independence of
      irrelevant alternatives in, 195
   condition of non-dictatorship in,
      195
   quality of, 200–2
Groups, learning in, 202
Group utility function, 53, 192–97
Guaranteed improvement, 147–49

H

Hammond, John S., 125
Hatry, Harry P., 17, 31–34
Hayslowe, Rosemary, and Steiner,
      Ivan D., 229
Hertz, David, 97
Hillier, F.S., and Lieberman, G.J., 89,
      96, 101
Historic store of data, 227–29
Homeostatic processes, in
      organizations, 9
Howard, Nigel, 130, 137, 141–66
Howard, Ronald A., 91
Human brain, 5, 224
Human judgement, 2
Human system, 5
Hurwicz, Leonid, 74

I

Ideals, 5–12
   relative to objectives, 6
Imperfect information, value of,
      106–14
Inducement in a game situation,
      172–76
Inescapable improvement, 147–49
Infeasible scenarios, 151
Information, use in decision problems,
      2–3
   cost of, 3
   passage in a committee, 206

Information (*Contd.*)
   perfect, 100, 132–34
   related to satisficing, 217
   sharing in groups, 201
Information system, in support of
      decision making, 223–30
   broad specifications for, 225
   information retrieval system, as part
      of, 225–28
   management reporting system as
      part of, 225–28
Integer programming, 90
Interface, in a completely specified
      process, 213, 227
Interpersonal comparison of utilities,
      193–97
Interval scale of measurement, 42–51
   von Neumann-Morgenstern interval
      scale utility, 47–51

J

Jointly rational outcomes, 145
Joint utility evaluation of a risk,
      186–90

K

Kaufmann, Arnold, 69

L

Laplace criterion of decision, 76
Leavitt, H.J., 206
Lee, Alec, 102
Lee, Sang M., 93–96, 217
Lee, Wayne, 37, 53, 57, 67, 110, 130,
      137, 188–90
Likelihood, in Bayes' formula, 109–12
Linear programming, 58–59, 85–91,
      118
Little, John D.C., 16
Loasby, Brian J., 218–19
Logrolling, 207

Luce, R.D., and Raiffa, H., 37, 53, 57, 69, 75, 115–17, 129, 132–35, 189, 196
Luce, R.D., and Tukey, J.W., 52

M

Magee, John F., 103, 114, 125
Majority rule, 192, 196–97
Majumdar, Tapas, 45
Management
  aspects of, 12
  by objectives, 12
  decision making as part of, 12
Managers, involvement in complex decisions, 14
Management Science Centre, University of Pennsylvania, 149, 156
March, James G., 5, 11, 13, 77, 147–48, 216–19
Margolis, Julius, 220
Markowitz, H., 40–42
  utility function of, 41
Marschak, Jacob, 50
Marshall, A., 192
Maximax decision criterion, 74, 105
Maximin decision criterion, 72–76, 116, 188
Maximum expected value, 62–71
May, K.O., 52
McDonald, John, 115
Measures
  of benefits, 32–35
  of effectiveness, 31–32
  of efficiency, 31–32
Meta-equilibrium, 144–46
Metagame analysis (see Analysis of Options)
Metagames, theory of, 141–45
Meta-rational outcome, 144–45
Miller, D.W., and Starr, M.K., 35, 37, 57, 69
Minimax decision criterion, 72–78, 105, 116

Minimax regret decision criterion, 75–76, 105
Minimization of uncertainty, 3, 78–79, 218–20
Mixed strategies, 117–19, 129–33
Model of a decision process, 13
  construction of, 16–17
Monitor function, in a completely specified process, 213, 227
Mosteller, F., and Nogee, P., 50
Multiple objectives, 8, 19, 32, 62, 92–96, 214, 217

N

N-person game situations, 115, 120–21
Negotiation set, in bargaining, 188–90
Networks, application of linear programming to, 89–90
von Neumann, J., and Morgenstern, O., 37, 115, 129
  interval scale utility, 47–51, 189–90
Newell, A., 20
Newman, J.W., 103, 125
Non-completely specified decision processes, 23–24, 214–26, 222, 228–30
Non-linear programming, 90
Non-zero-sum games, 115, 134–40

O

Objectives, 5–12
  conflict between, 7–8
  covert, 7
  group, 198
  multiple, 8, 19, 32, 62, 92–96, 127, 214, 217
  need for review, 9
  of components of an organization, 9
  of staff members of organization, 6, 10
  organizational, 7
  overt, 7

Objectives (*Contd.*)
  priority between, 8, 20, 32, 51
  related to function of organization, 6
Objective function, 30–32, 86
Objective probability, 66–68
Objective rationality, 133–34, 140–42
Office of the Mayor, New York City, 33
Old, Bruce S., 205
Open systems, 5
Opportunity costs, 74–75
Optimism, criterion of, 74
Options, choice between, 3
  specification of available, 18
Ordinal ranking, 35, 44–47
Ordinal scale of measurement, 42–47,
    127, 131
Organization
  as a group, 191
  decision making in, 211–32
  stage of development of, 10
  seen as a system, 5
  types of group found in, 198–200
  utility function of, 42–43, 204
Organization entropy, 11

P

Pareto optimality, 186–88
Pareto optimal set, 187–91
Partial information, value of, 109–14
Penalty for being wrong, 43
Perception and formulation of a
    decision problem, 13, 16
Perfect information, 100, 132–34
  value of, 106–14
  relation to objective rationality,
    140
Personalistic involvement in decision
    making, 19–21
Pessimism, criterion of, 72–74
Peterson, R., and Silver, E.A., 91, 98
Planning, 12
Policy
  seen as a group decision rule, 200
  short term and long term, 219
Preferences for options, 3–4, 21, 127
  variation of, 4

Priorities between objectives, 8, 20, 32,
    51, 127, 214
Prisoners' dilemma, 136–45
Probabilistic models, 98–101
Probability
  posterior, 67, 109–14
  prior, 67, 109–14
Programmed decisions (*see*
    Completely specified decision
    processes)
Proxy measures of effectiveness,
    33–35
Pure strategy, 129
Purposefulness
  of an organization, 11
  of a system, 5–6

Q

Quantitative parameters, 3, 17–18,
    29–56
  decisions involving, 83–125

R

Radford, K.J., 9, 21, 23, 213, 224–28
Raiffa, Howard, 5, 37, 69, 125, 183–90,
    196
  and Schlaifer, R.O., 103
Rapoport, Anatol, 137
Rationality in decision making, 19–21
  breakdown of, 138
  objective and subjective, 133–34
  related to equilibria, 130
  relationship to information, 133
Ratio scale of measurement, 42–47
Regret, criterion of, 74–76
Rejection set, of risks, 183–86
Risk
  attitude towards, 19, 21, 24, 72
  decisions under condition of, 57,
    59–61, 99, 105, 182–83
  sharing, 182–90
Risky Shift Phenomenon, 202–4

Rosove, Perry E., 224
Rothenberg, Jerome, 193–96

S

Saddle point, 116
Sanction, 147–49
  credibility of, 155
Satisficing, 77, 147–48
  versus optimizing, 216–18
Savage, L.J., 37–40, 66, 74
Scales of measurement, 42–47
Scenario, 146, 151
  stability of, 146
Schlaifer, R.O., 103
Security level, 129–35, 188–89
Sensitivity analysis, 96–98
Shapley procedure, in bargaining,
  189–90
Shaw, Marvin E., 201–2
Shortest route problems, 90
Simon, Herbert A., 4, 20, 21, 77,
  147–48, 167, 201, 216–17, 221
Simulation, 97, 101–2
Single play situations, 131
Sisson, R.L., 24–25
Social welfare function, 53, 193–97
Solandt, Omond, 15
Special project team, 221–23
Spetzler, Carl S., 200, 204
Standard gamble method of
  determining utility, 47–51
Stochastic models, 98–101
Stochastic utility theory, 52
St. Petersburg paradox, 70–71
States of nature, 59, 171
Strictly competitive decision
  situations, 129–34
Subjective expected utility, 66–69
Subjective probability, 66–68
  use of, 102–14
Subjective rationality, 133–34
Subjective value of an outcome, 36–37
Sure-thing strategy, 174
Swalm, Ralph, 41–43, 50

System
  closed, 6
  human, 5
  open, 5
  purposefulness of, 5–6
  state-maintaining, 6, 9
Systems group, 221–23

T

Tannenbaum, Robert, 13, 16, 221
Team, 181, 197–200, 206–7, 215
Transitivity, 35–36
Transportation problem, 89–90
Two person game situations, 115–20
Tullock, Gordon, 207

U

Uncertainty
  application of analysis of options,
    168–72
  decisions under, 3, 57–61, 105, 214
  introduction into deterministic
    models, 96–98
  minimization of, 3, 78–79
Unilateral improvement, 146–66, 170
Utility, 36–53
  compound, 52–53
  function, 38–43
  function, descriptive or
    prescriptive, 41–42
  function, group, 53, 192–97
  function of an organization, 42–43,
    204
  interpersonal comparison of,
    193–97
  of money, 36–43

V

Value of a game, 117–19, 129
Value of information, 106–13

Voting paradox, 192
Vickrey, W., 39

W

Wagner, Harvey, 87–92, 96–98, 101
Wald, Abraham, 72

Weighting factors, between objectives,
    32
Wickens, J.D., 12
Wiener, Norbert, 224

Z

Zero-sum games, 115–20, 129–33, 134